Snaring The Other Tiger

By Ian Ward

MEDIA MASTERS
SINGAPORE

Acknowledgements

I would like to thank my longtime journalist friend, David Webb, who read this manuscript at various stages in its production and offered such constructive comment. I also extend my gratitude to Mr John Pepper and his colleagues at the Australian Archives, Canberra, the staff of the Australian Archives, Melbourne, the staff of the Mitchell Library, Sydney, Ms Pareen Reynolds at the Lionel Murphy Library, Canberra, and the many knowledgeable research experts who assisted me at the Australian War Memorial, Canberra, Imperial War Museum, London, Public Record Office, Kew, London, and the US National Archives, Washington DC.

The personal recollections of Mr Arthur "Chappie" Chapman, Mr Robert Tyson, Mr Harry Morris, Mr Arthur Weston, Mr Charles "Chick" Warden, Mr Stan Bryant-Smith, Mr Roly Dean, Mr Geoff O'Connor, Mr Frank Nankervis, and Mr Michael Crewdson were absolutely vital to establishing accuracy in various segments of this book. Gentlemen, I am greatly indebted to you all for your patience and interest.

Separate research was undertaken by my "Old Asia Hand" friend, Mike Caldwell and my Vietnam War colleague, Nguyen Ngoc Phach. I am also obliged to New Zealand author, Mr James MacKay, whose quite extraordinary book, *Betrayal in High Places,* provided me with a number of critical insights into the war crimes interrogation career of James Gowing Godwin.

Again I must acknowledge the excellence of research work and interviews undertaken on my behalf in Japan by Australian journalist, Mr Cameron Hay. His command of Japanese, tact and commitment to accuracy had been fundamental to work we jointly undertook for my previous book, *The killer they called a god.* So many aspects of this latest undertaking relied on Cameron repeating the process.

This he has done, and more so. I could not have asked for a more conscientious collaborator.

Makoto Nishimura and his wife, Ayako, became important to this publication in the very last stages of its preparation when the decision was taken to include an epilogue. I thank them both for their kindness and assistance.

As in the past, my wife, Norma Miraflor, has been with me on every step of this project. Her intuition as a researcher resulted in many of the high points of our hunt through files in different parts of the world. She has edited the book and written the epilogue. Once again I salute her.

Ian Ward

About the author

Ian Ward, an Australian by birth, was South East Asian correspondent for the Daily Telegraph, London, from 1962 to 1987. He spent the greater part of this quarter century as a war correspondent covering regional conflicts. He resides with his wife in Singapore.

By the same author

The killer they called a god
Media Masters Publishers (1992)

Photo credits

P. 10, Media Masters; p. 24, by courtesy of Mr Harry Morris; p. 27, (top) Media Masters, (lower) by courtesy of Mr Arthur Chapman; p. 28, by courtesy of Mr Makoto Nishimura; p. 32, by courtesy of Mr Harry Morris; p. 35, Media Masters; p. 39, Media Masters; p. 67, Australian Archives, Melbourne; p. 69, Imperial War Museum, London; p. 83, The New Straits Times; p. 86, (top) by courtesy of Mr Robert Tyson, (lower) The New Straits Times; p. 93, Fairfax Photo Library, Sydney; p. 96, National Archives, Washington DC; p. 106, Fairfax Photo Library, Sydney; p. 121, Australian Archives, Melbourne; p. 138, by courtesy of Mr James MacKay; p. 162, Courier Mail, Brisbane; p. 167, Fairfax Photo Library, Sydney; p. 178, Fairfax Photo Library, Sydney; p.200, Australian War Memorial, Canberra; p. 207, by courtesy of Mr Makoto Nishimura; p. 209, by courtesy of Mr Charles Warden; p. 243, Fairfax Photo Library; p. 252, Fairfax Photo Library; pp. 261, 262, 265, 267, 269 and 271 by courtesy of Mr Makoto Nishimura; p. 272, Media Masters.

Preface

———— ✦ ————

Four years of research have gone into *Snaring The Other Tiger*. With 25 years' experience as a war correspondent to call upon, it is not that I am particularly inept at delving into the background of military events. Rather, the project took so long because much of the original classified documentation that should have been readily available in official archives, war museums and libraries had either been stolen, purposely destroyed, intentionally misplaced or otherwise camouflaged.

As the months turned into years, I became acutely aware of the highly controversial nature of the information I was unearthing and collating. The concept of Australia's purposeful execution of a prominent but innocent Japanese general, condemned after a shamefully rigged trial, scarcely sat well with the nation's vociferous claims to Pacific War righteousness. It was quite obvious that both sides of the modern war crimes argument could seize on these events as ammunition for their respective positions. Furthermore, there was always the possibility that, on publication, I would be required to run the gauntlet of entrenched opinion in my native Australia preferring such matters remain concealed. More than once it has been suggested to me, by people whose views I have long valued, that no good could come from pursuing these enquiries. Far better, to leave the past where it is.

It is said the past is prologue. In Australia this appears certainly the case with so much of our folklore and national character steeped in military history. My question then is: have we the right to view the past selectively?

I have no position, one way or the other, on the war crimes trial issue. My motivation for telling this story is purely that the events portrayed, happened and were, in the main, deliberately hidden from public scrutiny. Whatever the lessons to be learned from this account, I am convinced Australia — and Britain as well — have moral obligations at least to set straight the records of miscarried war crimes justice. To continue supporting the principle of such trials and at the same time ignore obligations when terrible mistakes occur, is to make a mockery of principles. At the same time, the repeated protestations of our political and civic leaders, demanding Japan come to terms with her war-related activities, are hollow indeed as long as we refuse coming to terms with our own.

For the record I would like to make clear that I met the son of executed Lt. General Takuma Nishimura, divisional commander of the elite Japanese Imperial Guards, Emperor Hirohito's personal troops, only after completing all the research and writing for chapters 1 - 16 of this volume. In order to prepare the epilogue, my wife and I travelled to Tokyo to talk to 64-year-old Makoto Nishimura and his wife at their home in Machida. The condition under which the general's son agreed to meet us was that it should be emphasised he had made no contribution whatever to any part of this work outside the epilogue. "I ask this for the credibility of the book in Japan," he explained.

And for the credibility of the book outside Japan, it was an arrangement to which I was more than happy to accede.

Ian Ward
Singapore, October 1996

Contents

To my friend Charles "Chick" Warden and his surviving Muar Front comrades-in-arms who, for all their sufferings, would never have sanctioned or supported the gross miscarriage of justice revealed in the following pages.

Where it all began. The bridge at Parit Sulong.

Chapter 1

Exacting the final price

———————— ◆ ————————

O ut of the still, hot night, across the dark waters of
Seeadler Harbour, drifted the faint sound of dipping
paddles.

Lt. Commander Arthur "Chappie" Chapman (RAN)
followed the steady cadence and strained his eyes seawards.
Finally, the vague outline of a native *lakatoi* emerged from
the blackness.

By the time the native outrigger canoe had run aground in
the shallows opposite his beachside Quonset hut, Chapman
could just discern the silhouettes of two Manus islander
boatmen and their Caucasian passenger. The thick-set
European leaped nimbly from the craft and the two-man
crew, paddled back without ceremony into the oblivion of
the tropical night.

Chapman, commandant of the Lombrum Point War
Criminals' Compound on Los Negros island, glanced at his
watch. Seven o'clock. Saturday night. Right on time. Just as
Lt. Colonel Norman Quinton, officer in charge (OC) of 1
Australian War Crimes Section, had ordered.

Quinton's unit, indeed, the entire Australian Army
presence on the island was headquartered at Nutt Point, four
kilometres by road around a small bay to the south. It was
from Nutt Point that the *lakatoi* crew had just paddled.

Striding across the short stretch of crumbled coral sand to
greet the visitor, Chapman found himself thinking: what an

odd way for Australia's officially appointed hangman to appear for his grisly task.

Shrouded in secrecy, the almost surreal arrival arrangements had been Quinton's idea. The 49-year-old colonel from Melbourne had been among the original Australian war crimes' team sent to isolated Los Negros in the Admiralty Islands group, 120 nautical miles across the Bismarck Sea from New Guinea's northern coastline.

Quinton had flown in on April 25, 1950. Except for five-days cricketing leave in Townsville, he had been on the island the whole time — more than 13 months. Not many Australian servicemen assigned to Los Negros enjoyed their postings. Quinton did. What was more, he knew he would really be rather sorry when the time came for him to leave. In a despatch to Army Headquarters (AHQ) in Melbourne a few weeks earlier, the colonel had noted: ". . . twelve months up here is more than enough for most people. Fortunately, I am holding out very well myself and do not mind staying on for a while longer." The truth was that Quinton liked the place, liked the job and dreaded the idea of going back to his mundane former employment at the Melbourne Metropolitan Board of Works (MMBW). Privately, he had been busy lobbying Army friends and contacts for another military posting once his Los Negros functions wrapped up.

Charged with overseeing Australia's final batch of Japanese war criminal executions — along with a host of other command duties on the island — Quinton was not the man you argued with on Los Negros. He was the *old hand,* he called the shots and was widely recognised, rightly or wrongly, as having direct access to the highest military echelons in both Canberra and Melbourne.

So it was that nobody questioned Quinton's long held conviction that ugly demonstrations would erupt among the 247 Japanese prisoners in the Lombrum compound should news of the hangman's presence somehow leak before the unreprieved went to their deaths. When this became the rationale behind the melodramatic arrival arrangements for the executioner, the very few entrusted with execution day details saw little point in appealing for moderation.

Prison commandant and executioner withdrew to the naval officer's hibiscus and palm bordered patio for the obligatory welcoming gins and tonic. Conversation was stilted with both men avoiding direct reference to the task at hand. Chapman's guest was an affable man with receding dark hair and easy smile. Conscious of the security overkill under the ubiquitous Quinton, Chapman took it for granted that the man had introduced himself with a cover name. From the small-talk that followed, Chapman gleaned that the hangman, though now a civilian, had served in the Australian Army, had been a sergeant and seen action in the Pacific.

As the two men chatted beneath the patio's striped awning on the eastern edge of the prison complex, another stiflingly humid night, like so many others that had gone before, enveloped the condemned block 500 metres down the beach.

Here, the last twelve Japanese combatants, on whom Australia sought to inflict the maximum penalty for Pacific theatre war crimes, awaited word of their fates in their timber and corrugated iron solitary cells. In the event, this particular airless night would have special meaning for all death row inmates. It would be the last they would spend in agonized uncertainty. Within twenty-four hours, seven of them would learn that the powers in Canberra had spared their lives. The remaining five would be told otherwise. For them, there would be no escaping their appointments with the genial hangman.

The designated execution time: dawn, Monday, June 11, 1951. Barely 34 hours away.

With the Sabbath looming as a day of meticulous preparation for the hangman, the awkward Saturday night beach welcome — thankfully, as far as prison commandant Chapman was concerned — concluded early.

The following afternoon, a military aircraft flying the official Australian press party to the executions landed at Momote airfield on the eastern side of Los Negros. An army jeep was on hand to transport the three accredited newsmen across the island to special billeting arrangements at Nutt Point.

Public sentiment generally, and the nation's post-war military hierarchy, specifically, favoured continuing retribution for Japan's wartime atrocities. However, under strong international pressure, Canberra had by this time formally announced the nation's war trials were at an end. This, then, would be the last time the 14,000 or so former Australian prisoners of Imperial Japan, their families and the public at large could feel part of the process dispensing post-war military justice. It would be the last time they could read details of how the condemned enemy paid for their wartime barbarism.

The three reporters needed no convincing that their trip to Los Negros was an important assignment.

Quinton devised the euphemistic codename "Point Charlie" in a curious bid to keep under tight security wraps not only the location of the gallows, but the fact that a place of execution existed at all. It was a pointless exercise, doomed from the moment he employed a team of Australian engineers and labourers, all civilians assigned to Los Negros by the Department of Works and Housing. Quinton gave this team, normally tasked with accommodation, road and harbour construction work, the job of building a shed to house the gallows. From day one, every Australian on Los Negros, civilian and military alike — and probably most Japanese as well — knew exactly where the executions were to be held.

"Point Charlie" was approached down a narrow crushed-coral jungle track. This led off in a westerly direction from the stretch of road hugging the Seeadler Harbour shoreline between Lombrum Prison and Nutt Point. A kilometre in from the road, the track snaked past the makeshift, two-storeyed galvanized-iron shed built by the Works and Housing team on the side of a steep incline. The shed's upper floor had double doors opening directly onto the crest of a dirt ramp.

During America's wartime occupation of the Admiralties, the site had been the centre of a sizeable vehicle repair facility. This had spread in a semi-circle around two parallel concrete ramps that allowed jeeps and trucks to drive onto elevated positions which, in turn, enabled US Army mechanics to work on the exposed undersides of the vehicles.

The place of execution was Quinton's personal choice. He had designed the shed himself with the help of a Works and Housing engineer. Its configuration provided height enough at the second storey level for the extraordinarily cumbersome scaffold equipment shipped specially to Los Negros from Australia. At the same time it ensured ample room at the lower level for the required neck-breaking drops.

At the centre of the scaffold's platform on the upper floor was the trapdoor operated by a steel lever conveniently located to one side. A wooden railing a metre from the trapdoor separated the executioner's immediate working area from the designated press gallery.

Quinton was well aware that the whole subject of the scaffold and its intended operation had been allotted an extremely sensitive security priority. All relevant messages from AHQ in Melbourne's St Kilda Road Barracks came blanketed by *top-secret* classifications.

Original planning meetings held at AHQ in late February, 1950, saw the Adjutant General's (AG) department demanding scaffold arrangements for Los Negros be treated as matters of some urgency. Curiously, when the very first "provision for scaffold" orders were issued to the Quarter Master General (QMG) two weeks later on March 9, they were couched in somewhat diffident phrases.

It was proposed, said the orders, to construct special parts such as trapdoors, beam etc., back in Australia. This, they pointed out, was in anticipation of a scaffold being required. The various parts would be forwarded to the place of execution "when required as A Branch have indicated that it is inadvisable to erect prior to a conviction being made."

"A" Branch, which in this case dealt with the administration of legal affairs, sought to avoid accusations that the military was, in any way, pre-empting the court's findings. Equally, the Army was anxious to avoid public claims at home and internationally — particularly in Japan — that early erection of the gallows merely demonstrated how much executions were an integral part of Australia's vindictive final war trials' plan.

Within 24 hours of the first scaffold instructions being circulated, a senior officer on the AG's staff intercepted the order and added a series of terse hand-written observations in the margin. "I did not want the scaffold erected before a conviction," he noted, in an obvious attempt to correct the record. "The equipment should be crated and shipped to Manus well in advance. Delay between trial and execution due to legal requirements is usually about two and a half months."

The senior officer continued: "I suggest that it would be advisable to get this equipment on the water at the latest by the time trials commence. If we are too squeamish and wait for a conviction (which really includes confirmation of the executions) are we not being rather inhumane, and is there not some risk that condemned men will overflow the limited condemned cell accommodation?"

These comments left no doubt about the ultimate intentions of the influential clique headed by the AG himself, Major General Warren Melville Anderson. The scaffold would indeed be an integral part of the trials' paraphernalia to be shipped out of Australia. What was more, there would be no pussy-footing by the military about its ultimate operation. Or would there?

Contrasting sharply with the Army's determined preparations for the Los Negros hangings was its decided sheepishness on the matter of providing a hangman from military ranks. Initially, the AG's office proposed that the six Australian state governments each be approached. The hope was that one would surely be willing to despatch an experienced executioner to Los Negros. The approaches came to naught and political direction soon made it clear that the Army would have to provide its own man for the job.

Again the AG sought to avoid responsibility. On October 6, 1950, his office signalled Colonel Quinton:

REQUEST YOU ADVISE URGENTLY IF HANGMAN CAN BE PROVIDED FROM LOCAL RESOURCES.

Quinton immediately called in Mr Harry Morris, Manus Project Officer for the Commonwealth Works and Housing Department and, as such, head of the Australian civilian labour force on the island. The colonel bluntly asked Morris to organise a hangman from volunteers among his expatriate workers. Morris, now a septuagenarian living in retirement in Perth, recalls how he first protested it was the Army's duty to provide the official executioner. Under pressure from Quinton, Morris finally agreed to see what he could do but voiced serious doubts whether any of his men would look favourably at the opportunity of becoming a legal multiple killer.

The Project Officer would soon discover just how misplaced were his reservations. That evening no less than eight men from his 200-strong labour force — a 4 percent return rate — put their names forward. Morris, who had been captured by the Japanese at Rabaul and later escaped, was appalled by the enthusiastic response. He was also very glad that the final selection was not his. Of the eight names he submitted to the Army, only one was an ex-serviceman. This volunteer, an electrical foreman, was called in by Quinton and, according to Morris, "spoke nobly of honour and duty, God and the King, and avenging his fallen comrades." He got the job and was assured of absolute secrecy. On October 11, 1950, just five days after being tasked with finding a hangman, Quinton despatched a confidential signal to AHQ. It read:

PERSONAL FOR COLONEL MACDONALD FROM QUINTON. REFERENCE TO YOUR AG 5477 OF 9TH OCTOBER '50. PERSON REQUIRED CAN BE PROVIDED FROM LOCAL RESOURCES.

Ten weeks before the executions, Quinton reported in an official letter to Melbourne: "We are all set to carry out the hangings. I run trial drops and drill once a week on the scaffold. This, by the way, is a huge ungainly affair. Capt. Wheatley and I altered the design substantially but as the timbers and parts were shipped here, we could not do very much to lighten it."

On the eve of the hangings the visiting journalists were taken on an execution site tour. All three were unnerved to find their allotted positions on the scaffold platform itself. They would be required to stand just behind the railing, almost within touching distance of those destined to depart through the well-tested trapdoor. While explaining the hanging procedure, the escort officer gestured towards a corner of the shed's upper level.

The hangman had been busy. Five newly stretched rope nooses, each tagged with a number, lay there on the floor.

Close by slumped a large canvas sack filled with sand — the required implement for stretching the ropes. From a heavy wooden beam directly above the trapdoor dangled a sturdy steel chain. Along its length five individual links had been marked corresponding to the varying weights of the condemned men. It was explained to the newsmen how each execution would entail the hangman attaching an individual noose to the chain at the correct link, in order to ensure five separate fatal drops of varying heights. The heaviest man would hang first; the lightest last. Before the reporters left they were given a special demonstration of the lever mechanism's efficiency. A light tug and the trapdoor, at the centre of which was a painted white circle, dropped open with a sickening crash.

The understandably shaken journalists returned to Nutt Point and quickly repaired to the officers' mess for much needed nerve-numbing drinks.

❋ ❋ ❋ ❋

As far as Australian public opinion in 1951 was concerned, the Lombrum compound's death row was occupied by just another bunch of faceless Nip war criminals with improbable names; that is, with one exception. He was the occupant of cell A1: 62-year-old Lt. General Takuma Nishimura.

In the 12 months since his conviction on June 22, 1950, Nishimura had not only emerged the death row's star attraction but had become regarded as the most important Japanese ever to face charges before an Australian war crimes court. Widely publicised evidence had portrayed him as the person directly responsible for perhaps the most hideous single atrocity perpetrated against Australian forces throughout the entire Pacific conflict. The case against him had centred on the heart-stopping account of horror provided by a lone Australian survivor of mass slaughter at a place called Parit Sulong, a nondescript village in Malaya's southernmost state of Johore.

Some 110 Australians and 45 Indians, all of them severely wounded casualties from four days of ferocious battle on the Muar River front, were captured near the village's distinctive stone bridge. The bridge spanned the narrow, swift-flowing Simpang Kiri river at the southern entrance to the township. The wounded had been abandoned when the surrounded and battered Allied unit, comprising British, Australian and Indian troops, was ordered to cease fighting and escape ultimate annihilation by infiltrating from the battlefield in small groups.

The Japanese first herded their wretched prisoners in a wooden building near the main road running through the centre of Parit Sulong. Despite their appalling injuries, the wounded were ordered to strip naked. Their pleas for medical attention and even water were repeatedly refused. Ultimately the Japanese led the captives to an area of open ground near the river and there machine-gunned them, doused them with petrol and torched the bodies, some of them still alive. The lone Australian survivor had miraculously escaped by feigning death some metres short of the killing area. Amazingly, he was able to testify how he had witnessed a very senior Japanese officer actually issuing orders prior to the massacre. The implication was obvious.

It was impossible to forget the prosecution's dramatic summation of Nishimura as "an evil man who cared nothing for human life or suffering . . ." If ever an enemy soldier fitted the post-war Australian public's concept of a barbaric Jap, it was Lt. General Takuma Nishimura, the beast of Parit Sulong.

From the Australian military viewpoint, Nishimura's arraignment, trial, conviction and ultimate death by hanging seemed to meet a very special requirement. The immediate post-war British and Australian Army hierarchies were both incensed at the inability of either nation to place on trial

Imperial Japan's 25th Army commander, Lt. General Tomoyuki Yamashita.

Yamashita, awarded the glowing sobriquet "Tiger of Malaya" by an adoring Japanese wartime press, had been responsible for the shattering fall of the Malayan Peninsula and seizure of Singapore — collectively, the greatest ever defeat in British military history and, of course, in Australia's as well. The "Tiger of Malaya" tagline quickly stuck in British and Australian command throats. Allied wartime propaganda responded by portraying Yamashita, in reality unmatched by the Malayan theatre Allies in terms of leadership and sheer strategic brilliance, as a bloodthirsty conqueror. This became an easy theme to pursue into peacetime as teams of Allied investigators began uncovering evidence of Japan's brutality in occupied territories.

In the heady atmosphere of post-war victor's justice, Yamashita before an Australian or British court would certainly have helped assuage the perceived shame of the 1941-42 Malayan theatre debacle. In the event, the satisfaction of trying the "Tiger of Malaya" as a war criminal went to the Americans. The Japanese commander had surrendered to US General Douglas MacArthur's forces in the Philippines shortly after Tokyo's unconditional capitulation on August 15, 1945.

With Yamashita hanged outside Manila on February 23, 1946, Australian senior officers clearly saw Nishimura as the best alternative target for legal redress over the Malayan Campaign. After all, Nishimura had been commanding officer (CO) of no less than the god-incarnate Emperor Hirohito's personal troops, the elite Konoye Imperial Guards Division. Under Nishimura's direction, the Guards had defeated the Australian defenders in Johore's critical western sector and had then gone on to rout Australia's 27th Brigade from the vital Causeway segment of Singapore's northern defence line.

It was no co-incidence that Australian press reports, soon after Nishimura arrived in Los Negros to face trial, began referring to him as Yamashita's "chief aide" and his "chief side-kick." Both descriptions were wildly inaccurate. Yamashita and Nishimura had been arch rivals for years. They had held strongly opposing views on tactics for Malaya and disliked each other intensely. Furthermore, there had been little personal contact between them throughout the fighting. But the obviously inspired linkage of the two officers served a useful propaganda purpose, adding to the overall impression that, by moving against Nishimura, military investigators had obviously moved against a Malayan Campaign enemy figure of both substance and responsibility. Not surprisingly, the Australian press would soon be describing Nishimura as "the second Tiger of Malaya."

The day after the court sentenced Nishimura to death by hanging, the Melbourne Herald published an editorial closely reflecting Australian public sentiments. Under the headline, **DEATH SENTENCE IS A JUST ONE**, it read:

The death sentence passed on Japanese Lt. General Nishimura for the murder of 145 prisoners of war in Malaya is one which the civilised world must find fully justified.

The only criticism that can be made of this war trial is that it was not concluded earlier. It is almost five years since Japan surrendered. It must be remembered, however, that Nishimura was tried in 1947 for another war crime for which he was sentenced to life imprisonment.

The case against Nishimura was clear cut. The charge did not concern any generalised question of war guilt. It related to one particular horrifying massacre of helpless prisoners.

Nishimura might never have been brought to justice but for the amazing survival of one of the men whom he had ordered to be killed, Lt. Ben Charles Hackney, now of Bathurst, New South Wales. This witness, who lived only because the Japanese believed him to be dead, was able to describe what happened.

There could be no plea that Nishimura was acting on orders from his seniors. He gave the order to kill. His former personal aide, Captain Nonaka, who transmitted the order, though also found guilty of murder, has been sentenced to six months imprisonment only. The responsibility lay with Nishimura and, rightly, he is being punished for his crime.

❋ ❋ ❋ ❋

As prison commandant on Los Negros, Chapman, a former merchant navy deck officer, but by then building a career in the RAN, received his authority through a special warrant from the nation's Governor General in Canberra. Under Australia's War Crimes Regulations all convicted Japanese sentenced to death were technically held "in the custody of the court" while formal reviews of their cases were completed, petitions and appeals considered and sentences officially promulgated. On Los Negros, this meant they were interned in Lombrum Prison's condemned cells and came under Chapman's close care and responsibility.

The Nishimura case, the most celebrated of the so-called *Manus Trials* , had opened on June 19, 1950. His conviction, three days later, afforded the Japanese former divisional commander the dubious honour of becoming the first inmate on Lombrum's death row.

The condemned section consisted of three single-storeyed blocks comprising eight cells each. These three units, together with an ablutions block, were arranged in a rough square. This was surrounded by high security fencing topped with coiled barbed wire. Armed Papua New Guinea (PNG) police, manning two corner guard towers, provided 24-hour surveillance.

Nishimura's cell, like the 27 others, was windowless but

The Lombrum Point War Criminals' Compound showing vegetable gardens in the foreground and Seeadler Harbour to the rear.

The primary application of Japanese war criminal labour at Los Negros was on construction of the main Lombrum Wharf. Here an Australian Works and Housing Department foreman oversees a labour gang of convicted Japanese at the site.

had ventilation bars running around the tops of the surrounding four wooden walls. Compound regulations allowed condemned prisoners two hours exercise every morning and two additional hours every afternoon. But, for the remaining 20 hours of each day, they were restricted to solitary confinement. They ate alone in their cells. Medical inspections were conducted once a week.

Chapman's routine called for daily rounds of the condemned blocks which brought him into regular contact with the inmates there. While he worked at maintaining a professional aloofness from the prisoners in general, Chapman, who now lives with his wife in retirement at Bowral, New South Wales, can recall vividly how, over the months, he became personally impressed with the quiet conduct and bearing of the occupant of cell A1.

For all his reputation as a mass killer, Nishimura handled his prison torment with an outward calmness and gentle stoicism that won him widespread admiration. Quite obviously, prison staff and fellow inmates alike regarded him as the compound's senior inmate. Chapman unhesitatingly credits Nishimura with having personally instilled a high level of discipline and morale on Lombrum's death row during the long months he spent there. As a direct result, the commandant and his staff experienced no problems whatever running the condemned section or, for that matter, the adjacent general prison compound. Paradoxically, Nishimura ensured that Colonel Quinton's theatrical security measures were, in the final analysis, rendered pointless.

Chapman remembers Nishimura as an officer "from head to toe" who carried himself ramrod straight "as though somebody had strapped a beam along his back." With a height of 5 ft 5 ins (1.65 metres), the former Imperial Guards commander was already taller than the average Japanese of his day. Chapman recalls that Nishimura's constantly erect stance and his trim frame — he weighed 133 lbs (60 kgs) according to prison medical records —made him stand out as taller and fitter than the other prisoners, despite his advanced years.

Prison rounds on Sundays were more relaxed than other days so it was on these occasions that Chapman invariably found himself dallying in conversation with Nishimura. The condemned general spoke broken English. Sometimes this became the medium of communication. More often, though, they chatted through the Australian Army interpreter who always accompanied the commandant on his rounds.

Usually they sat on wooden stools in the cell: Australian Lt. Commander in crisp, white tropical shirt and shorts, long white cotton socks and shoes; Japanese Lt. General in vivid orange prison shirt and shorts and barefooted. Nishimura would speak sadly of his beloved Japan, and the havoc the war had wrought upon her. Sometimes he spoke of his war experiences. Once he explained how Japan's wartime Prime Minister, Hideki Tojo, had been deeply suspicious of Yamashita and personally envious of the Tiger of Malaya's almost cult-hero status at home.

From time to time the prisoner expounded on Japanese military history. He talked about Tokyo's strategy for China going back to the 1800's. On one occasion, and then only briefly, Nishimura mentioned how he had been the catalyst for an historical trend in Japanese politics As an appointed court martial judge, his deliberations on a major trial of rebellious officers had, he said, prevented Japan's entire military fabric from renting asunder. It was an obscure period of Japanese politics unknown to Chapman. The prison commandant made a mental note of the remarks at the time but tended to regard them as little more than the troubled musings of a condemned man.

On Sunday, June 10, 1951, Chapman, conducted his routine tour of the prison. Without revealing his knowledge that Nishimura was scheduled to die the following morning,

Arthur "Chappie" Chapman, now retired and living with his wife, Judy, in Bowral, New South Wales, was a Lieutenant Commander in the RAN in 1950-51 and the appointed commandant of Australia's Lombrum Point Japanese War Criminals' Compound. One of his charges was General Takuma Nishimura, the prisoner in cell A1 on the compound's death row. Chapman frequently spoke to Nishimura during prison rounds. In one of Nishimura's last letters to his family he wrote: "The Australian prison manager Chapman is a kind man."

Lt. Commander "Chappie" Chapman (centre of the seated row) poses with his staff at Australia's Lombrum Point War Criminals' Compound in early 1951.

This 1943 photograph shows retired Lt. General Takuma Nishimura shortly before being posted abroad as Japanese military governor, first in the Shan states of Burma and later in the occupied Dutch East Indies.

the commandant made a special point of chatting at some length with the prisoner in cell A1.

At 5 pm that afternoon the death row inmates received a second official visit, this time led by a sombre Colonel Quinton.

Accompanied by Chapman, two interpreters and the prison's resident Japanese Buddhist priest, Quinton began calling on the condemned cells, one by one, to deliver the 12 inmates the final official pronouncement on their death sentences. The relief on the faces of the reprieved seven was obvious. Otherwise there was little reaction from the doomed five to the formal orders read to them by Quinton and simultaneously translated into Japanese by the interpreter.

Nishimura was reserved when he learned his fate. The Japanese priest wanted to be alone with the general and asked the Australians to leave the cell. Quietly Nishimura rejected the idea. The holy man's ministrations, he said, were unnecessary. Instead, he asked for a pen and paper to write his last will and a final letter to his family. Before the official party departed his cell, Nishimura requested his compliments be relayed to his fellow prisoners. Alone in his cell once more, he began writing in neat and deliberate script: "Tomorrow morning I will be in heaven . . . . "

Darkness fell quickly that night, aided by looming black clouds that swept in from the north across Seeadler Harbour. The air was heavy with the suffocating humidity that invariably precedes a tropical storm. Not long after the Australians had departed the stockade, the singing began. The voices that rose from death row's desolation that night were faint at first. But as the hours passed they took on a fluid resonance, modulated and soothing. By midnight the communion in song was over and, except for the flashes of the gathering storm, all was quiet.

✳ ✳ ✳ ✳

When the night duty sergeant at Nutt Point roused the three journalists from their sleep at 3. 45 am the wrath of the storm god had reached its height. Screaming winds tore through the coconut palms outside, breaking waves pounded Seeadler Harbour's nearby shoreline and the heavens unleashed torrents of rain that swept by in blinding, horizontal curtains. A drowsy steward served tea and toast in the officers' mess. By 4.30 am, when a jeep called to take the journalists to Point Charlie, the winds and drenching rain persisted.

Over in the prison compound the Australian commander of the PNG police unit began issuing orders as laid down in the British *Manual on Military Executions*. Prison guards then entered the five condemned cells. Swiftly seizing each prisoner, they handcuffed them behind their backs, lashed their elbows together with rope, shackled their ankles and pulled numbered canvas hoods over their heads. The five men were then led barefooted and shuffling through the rain to a waiting five-ton army truck for the ten-minute drive to the gallows. Above the foam streaked surface of an angry Seeadler Harbour, the first tentative grey smudges of dawn were breaking the eastern darkness.

Meanwhile, all the carefully laid preparations at Point Charlie were falling apart. A furious Colonel Quinton was frantically issuing alternate orders to stem the chaos caused by the storm. The deluge had short-circuited the generating unit specially installed to illuminate the execution site. With the scaffold in darkness, the hangman pronounced it impossible to function at the top level. Similarly, the two Australian Navy doctors, positioned and ready to confirm deaths below, stipulated they, too, were unable to perform their allotted tasks.

Quinton ordered a jeep into position on the track outside the upper level of the execution shed, its headlights blazing onto the gallows through the rain and open double doors. Likewise, he had a second jeep driven to the lower level and positioned so its headlights shone on the drop area immediately beneath the trapdoor.

With his improvisations in place, the ever adaptable Quinton then led the pressmen to their rail-side positions and, standing beside them, ordered the hangings to begin.

The truck in which the condemned rode to Point Charlie had been halted some 50 metres down the track from the execution shed while the storm-forced alterations to plan were concluded. Finally the prison's Japanese Buddhist priest, a man roundly disliked by the Australian contingent on Los Negros, was positioned at the shed's entrance. There he was permitted to spend a few final moments with each of the condemned as they passed enroute to the scaffold.

The first Japanese to be lifted from the truck and placed in a jeep for the final short drive to the shed door bore No 1 on his hood. He was 41-year-old naval lieutenant Takahiko Tsuaki. Tsuaki had been convicted of beheading the first victim among 200 Australian soldiers slaughtered in the 1942 Ambon Massacre. Tsuaki briefly thanked the priest. He was then seized by the hangman's assistants and propelled to the point where his bare feet stood within the painted circle on the trapdoor. Instantly the noose was slipped over his head and tightened into position. It was precisely 5 am. Nimbly the executioner moved across to the lever, pulled it sharply, and the small, hooded figure, garbed in orange, dropped from sight.

It took ten minutes before Tsuaki died and was ordered taken down from the scaffold by the two RAN doctors who worked with stethoscopes from a ladder.

At 5.35 am Ipachi Miyamoto, a 46-year-old civilian convicted of beheading a number of Australian troops in 1942, stood poised within the trapdoor's circle, the noose in place. From beneath his hood marked No 2 he shouted in Japanese "Long friendship and prosperity to Australia and the Japanese Empire. Banzai! Banzai! Banzai! A thousand lives

The execution chamber on Los Negros Island was codenamed "Point Charlie" by the OC 1 Australian War Crimes Section in a vain effort to keep its existence secret. The Army began regular weekly hanging drills here as early as November 1950. It wasn't until June 11, 1951 that all the rehearsals were finally put to the test.

Preparations for the Shinto rights cremation ceremony that was to have followed the Los Negros executions. The cremation pit itself had originally been part of a US military vehicles repair and maintenance facility on this island. But the wood for the pyre, shown on the left of the pit,. became water-logged in a tropical storm and refused to burn.

to the Emperor. Goodbye." He was still shouting as the trapdoor slammed open.

General Nishimura was third in line and in position for execution at 5. 51 am. He was calm to the end. His final words to the priest were brief. "I go in good health," was all he said. On the scaffold he shouted a last: "Banzai! Banzai! Banzai!"

Forty-seven year-old naval captain, Tamao Shinahara, who murdered two Allied prisoners at Surabaya in 1945 and subsequently ordered a doctor to experiment on their bodies, died at 6. 35 am beneath hood No 4. The final hanging was that of 45 year-old naval ensign Yutaka Suzuki, convicted of murdering an RAAF flight-lieutenant in Dutch West New Guinea in 1944. He dropped to his death at 6. 44 am.

By 7 am, five bodies lay in a row beneath a tarpaulin at the foot of the scaffold, ready for the scheduled Shinto cremation ceremony. Planning for this part of the programme had taken weeks as neither Quinton, nor any of his staff, had knowledge of Shinto rites. Security prohibited reference to the one man on the island who did — the prison compound's resident Japanese priest. Now, all attempts to light the funeral pyre's rain-soaked logs were proving futile. The colonel ordered the pyre doused in fuel and ignited. Time and again the flaming gasoline burned away leaving the sodden wood unscathed.

An incensed Quinton finally cancelled the Shinto ceremony and instead ordered the five executed men immediately be given burials at sea. His instructions were that the bodies be enclosed in weighted canvas shrouds and placed aboard a naval workboat from the local RAN shorebase, *HMAS Tarangau.* Two navy sailmakers were given the task of sewing up the shrouds. The workboat crew, together with prison commandant Chapman, were then made responsible for sailing out to the 100 fathom mark and there consigning to the deep the last five Japanese war criminals executed by Australia.

Quinton, whose entire military career had been desk-bound, knew little of the conditions a tropical storm could create at sea. As the workboat motored across comparatively protected Seeadler Harbour, Chapman and the crew realized they were in for a terrible buffeting once they had cleared the harbour entrance and were in open waters.

As the first giant waves crashed over the vessel's bows, Chapman glanced at the chart and roughly estimated it would take at least an hour of relentless pounding through these seas to make the nearest 100 fathom point. Conditions were so bad that he began seriously wondering if the small craft could survive that long.

On the afterdeck, where the canvas-wrapped bodies lay wedged into position ready for burial, the crew struggled to maintain order as the boat heaved, lurched, shuddered and dived from mountainous crest to cavernous trough and back to looming crest once more. Then, as if the same storm gods who had decreed the weather suddenly granted the dead Japanese a final comment on the day's proceedings, all five canvas covered corpses broke loose in unison and went careering violently about the gyrating deck. In a macabre dance with death, deckhands desperately lunged at the rolling, tumbling, thrusting bodies. No sooner had one corpse been pinned in a restraining bearhug than another would crash into it, breaking the deckhand's embrace and threatening to propel crewman and cadaver into the raging Bismarck Sea.

Reviewing the mayhem, Chapman ordered the burial take place at the much closer 60 fathom line. As opportunities arose, shrouded corpses were secured, lifted into position and hurled unceremoniously overboard. With each departure, danger to the crew appreciably lessened. Finally, it was over and the workboat could turn and make course for the safety of Seeadler Harbour.

Back at Nutt Point, Harry Morris walked from his living quarters to the nearby Works and Housing mess hall for an

Harry Morris was Manus Project Officer for the Commonwealth Works and Housing Department in 1950. From his 200-strong Australian labour force came eight eager volunteers for the job of hangman at the Manus executions. Morris, now in his 70's lives in retirement in Perth,. Western Australia.

early morning cup of coffee. It was shortly after 8 am when he swung open the door of the converted Quonset hut and stepped inside. The scene that confronted him sent shivers of revulsion to the pit of his stomach.

Atop a breakfast table at the far end of the hall stood the hangman, fresh from his duties at Point Charlie. Above his head he clutched a pillow to which he had attached a length of rope. Morris recalls how the executioner's face was flushed and beaming as he revelled in his frightful moment of glory. Around the table surged an appreciative crowd of sneering workmates. The Australians roared their approval every time the hangman let the pillow drop and rope tauten in mocking recall of his deeds an hour or so earlier. A disgusted Morris turned and strode away, too sickened to intercede.

In the military section of Nutt Point, quite oblivious to the ghoulish pantomime being enacted a short distance away, the three journalists wrote their accounts of the executions and ultimately filed these through the military communications facilities made specially available. The following day, under Los Negros datelines, Australia's leading newspapers carried prominent stories on the hangings. The chosen headlines revealed much about a nation's basic feelings.

"Be Friends," then . . . **HE YELLED HIS LAST "BANZAI"** screamed one. **JAPS DUMPED IN SEA AFTER MANUS EXECUTIONS** crowed another.

They expressed precisely the sentiments a nation, still hungry for revenge six years after the end of hostilities, had been waiting to read.

❊ ❊ ❊ ❊

More than four decades have passed since the Manus executions. Can Australia today — still nurturing deep rooted anti-Japanese sentiments — bring herself to contemplate that the evidence presented by the prosecution at the Nishimura trial was wilfully concocted, slanted and falsified? Can she accept that a man, tried by an Australian Military Court was, by calculated manoeuvring, deprived his most basic rights of defence? Are Australians, who celebrate *fair dinkumness* as a valued national trait, who cling to the Pacific War's moral highground with a tenacity unparalled by any of the other combatant nations, prepared to acknowledge that their system knowingly and vindictively hanged an innocent man?

What follows is the true story behind the case of Lt. General Takuma Nishimura — "the other Tiger" — the most significant Japanese war criminal ever prosecuted by Australian authorities. In a letter written from cell A1 on Lombrum's death row, the Japanese general urged his wife and two small children, a son and a daughter, living in Akita, not to anguish over his plight. He would go to his death, he assured them, calmed by his innocence. He quoted the brief lines of a Japanese poem.

Time will solve everything.
I'm waiting for spring.

With all earthly hope gone, he was placing his trust in eternal justice.

Chapter 2

The survivor and the accused

———— ✦ ————

The nature and speed of Japan's military campaign against Malaya and Singapore ensured that the Parit Sulong Massacre, as far as the outside world was concerned, would remain a dark secret for three and a half years. It was not until both territories were finally liberated by British troops in September, 1945, that the first official reports on the incident were lodged with respective military headquarters in Australia and the United Kingdom.

For Australian survivors of the Muar fighting, however, rumours and speculation on the fate of their abandoned, wounded comrades began the moment units started their ordered withdrawal from the battlefield at 9.00 am on January 22, 1942. To have to leave behind physically broken, defenseless men to the mercy of an advancing Japanese force, itself so bloodied in four days of ferocious fighting from Bakri to Parit Sulong, was a nightmare decision that would haunt the Australian CO concerned, Lt. Colonel Charles G. W. Anderson, for the rest of his days. If anything, the rumours and speculation only gathered pace with the fall of Singapore and the incarceration of Britain's defeated Malaya Command Army, of which Australia's 8th Division was part.

Men of the captured Australian division along with their British comrades-in-arms had marched into their respective Changi prison compounds, on the north-eastern corner of

Singapore island, on February 17, 1942. Seven months later, 25 year-old Lt. Ben Hackney, apparently the only survivor of the Parit Sulong Massacre, rejoined his incredulous 2/29th Battalion companions at Changi. Overnight an eyewitness account of the mass slaughter of Australian, British and Indian wounded replaced rumour and speculation along the prison grapevine. Hackney recalled how he spent five harrowing weeks dragging his shattered leg and bayonet-skewered body through southern Johore jungles. He told of foraging for food, struggling to heal his gruesome wounds, of the friendly and not so friendly locals, and his fight to avoid recapture. Eventually his luck had run out. Seized for a second time by the Japanese, he was transported north to Kuala Lumpur's Pudu Jail and finally brought south to Singapore and Changi with a mixed batch of Australian and British fellow prisoners, all of them captured during the Muar fighting.

Severely traumatised, Hackney was seen by some to be suffering from anxiety, mood swings and deep depressions. Others who knew him at the time recall that the young farmer from Bathurst, normally quiet and reflective, was perhaps more withdrawn than normal but handled his psychological anguish with amazing self control. Despite these differing observations, the general consensus of fellow prisoners close to him was that Ben Hackney, whose bowed leg and extraordinary war experience gave him a certain prominence in Changi, nonetheless needed the special support and protection of his mates to come to terms with his ordeal.

As the months of imprisonment passed, Hackney found at first solace, then strength, in a burgeoning desire for retribution. One day he, sole survivor, would be uniquely placed to ensure those responsible for the Parit Sulong horror were severely punished.

Stan Bryant-Smith, an intelligence sergeant with the 2/29th, remembers one afternoon counting Hackney's bayonet wounds. He had been stabbed no less than 52 times, all over

Stan Bryant-Smith, an intelligence sergeant with the Australian 2/29th Battalion, fought the Japanese near Bakri. Captured after the fall of Singapore, he survived the infamous Thai-Burma railway and knew Parit Sulong survivor, Ben Hackney, throughout their incarceration as prisoners of war.

his body. Considering the rudimentary medical treatment available, Hackney's wounds had healed remarkably quickly. Indeed, by the end of 1942 he was sufficiently recovered, physically and mentally, to be contemplating writing a detailed account of everything he could remember about the massacre. What was more, he had joined a special intelligence unit operating from within the Changi prison compound. The unit's members included Colonel S. A. F. Pond, the 2/29th battalion commander, and prominent 8th Division staff officers, Lt. Colonel Wilfred Kent-Hughes and Captain Adrian "Curly" Curlewis.

In addition to his other camp duties, "Curly" Curlewis, a Sydney barrister before his Army enlistment, had become the Australian prisoners' self-appointed authority on war criminal matters. He was ambitious, intelligent and strong willed. He would be a New South Wales district court judge by 1948 and a knight of the realm by 1967. Curly Curlewis took the young Hackney under his wing, encouraging him to get his thoughts down on paper and tutoring him on the legal requirements of evidence for a military court. As far as Curlewis was concerned, Hackney's recollections were unquestionably the stuff of a war criminal conviction.

Ben Hackney left Singapore on April 18, 1943, bound for the Thai-Burma railroad as a member of the 3,662-strong

Australian grouping within the ill-fated F-Force prisoner of war labour contingent. In his luggage was a large, unused British Army ledger book in which he proposed to write his story. He had found this and a similar book abandoned in a Selarang Barracks office. Stan Bryant-Smith, agreed to carry the second book so Hackney would be sure of sufficient writing material during his time up north.

Like all other members of F-Force, Hackney and Bryant-Smith departed Singapore with Japanese promises ringing in their ears of vastly improved conditions awaiting them. F-Force was not to be a working party. There would be better food, superior medical facilities, blankets, clothing and mosquito nets all available in the far more conducive hill country along the Thai-Burma frontier. The prisoners could even take a military band with them.

It all seemed too good to be true. And was. Hackney and Bryant-Smith soon jettisoned their respective ledgers and any immediate plans for penning the definitive report on the Parit Sulong massacre. Survival had suddenly become the major priority. By May, 1944, 1,060 F-Force Australians had died as a direct result of the outrageous treatment and conditions they suffered labouring for the Japanese on the Thai-Burma railroad. In contrast, of the 3,334 British F-Force prisoners who went north with the Australians, 2,036 were dead within twelve months. Once again Ben Hackney came through. Back in Changi in December, 1944, Hackney's resolve to set down for history the Parit Sulong affair, as only he could tell it, now became an obsession.

Whenever the opportunity arose, the young lieutenant sought the legal expertise of "Curly" Curlewis. Fellow prisoners noted the two men, huddled together for hours at a time, preparing the document they hoped would one day be fundamental to a major prosecution of Japanese war criminals. By the first weeks of 1945 the task was completed. Hackney showed his written account to several senior

Australian staff officers then buried it for safe keeping in a used artillery shell casing within the perimeter of the Changi prison compound.

While Curlewis became the focal point for Australian prisoners anxious to prepare war criminal cases against the Japanese, a highly influential British officer, Major Cyril Wild, was undertaking similar duties for the British in their section of Changi. The charismatic Wild, completely fluent in the Japanese language, had been the official British interpreter at Malaya Command's February 15, 1942, surrender to General Yamashita. More specifically, though, the gangling, Oxford-educated Englishman was widely recognised among British and Australian prisoners alike as having personally saved many lives along the Thai-Burma railroad. At great personal risk he had repeatedly used his linguistic skills and related influence to intervene on behalf of suffering prisoners. In the course of this activity Wild had himself been the target of severe beatings at the hands of his captors. The Japanese referred to Wild as "the tall man who never sleeps," a reflection of their grudging admiration.

Although Wild and Hackney toiled together in F-Force and spent identical periods incarcerated in Changi, the two men did not actually meet until shortly before Japan's unconditional capitulation on August 15, 1945. Wild took extensive notes and was clearly shocked by what the Australian had to say. Hackney let Wild read the lengthy report he and Curlewis had prepared. From this Wild extracted a short synopsis for his official records.

Hackney signed this truncated document on September 4, 1945, a day before troops of the 5th Indian Division landed to re-occupy Singapore on behalf of Britain and begin imprisoning all Japanese on the island. Eight days later the Supreme Allied Commander South East Asia (SACSEA), Admiral Lord Louis Mountbatten, formally accepted the surrender of the region's Japanese forces at an emotionally charged ceremony in Singapore's City Hall.

Emerging from the surrender hall, Lord Louis read out the text of his order of the day from the top of the City Hall steps. Across the *padang* below, a victory parade of former Allied prisoners of war, together with a huge crowd of locals heard Lord Louis say: "The defeat of Japan in the last month is the first in history. For hundreds of years the Japanese have been ruled by a small set of imperialists, and they have been told to look upon themselves as a superior race of divine origin. They have been taught to be arrogant to foreigners and to believe that the treachery they practised at Pearl Harbour is a virtue so long as it ends in Japanese victory. They are finding it very hard to accept the defeat or try to wriggle out of the terms of surrender."

Lord Louis made it clear he was fully expecting enemy deviousness as the terms of the capitulation went into force but reassured he would tolerate "no evasion on the part of the Japanese."

He went on: "I am telling you this because I wish to warn you of the situation you may find when you proceed to liberate other territories in this command. In the new territories you will be occupying, the Japanese have not been beaten in battle. You may well find, therefore, that these Japanese, who have not been beaten, may still fanatically believe in the divine superiority of their race. They may try to behave arrogantly. You will have my support in taking the firmest measures against any Japanese obstinacy, impudence, or non-cooperation."

Lord Louis' order graphically encapsulated the mood of those most dramatic days. But behind the elation, the relief, and rejoicing lay a logistical nightmare for South East Asia Command senior officers. The Command's number one priority was clearly the return of Allied servicemen, particularly those who had been prisoners of war, to their homelands.

Personally singled out by Lord Louis to head the British military's investigation of Japanese war crimes throughout South East Asia, Major Cyril Wild quickly discovered just how difficult his task was going to be. In a letter home, he described the problems he was encountering during the "really critical stage" when the military was "evacuating everyone as fast as they could, and the evidence *had* to be collected and collated before they went."

Wild wrote: "To help me I had no officers and about one-third interest in a rather unwilling clerk. However, I got it and did it so far as the 50 or so really major atrocities were concerned, and the rest can wait, for every single individual who has been a prisoner or internee of the Japs has at least one perfectly genuine atrocity story to tell, either at first or second hand. By major atrocities I mean episodes such as the burning alive with petrol of a hundred Australian and fifty Indian wounded in Johore; the marching into the sea, machine-gunning and bayoneting of 30 Australian nurses; and the cold-blooded murder of 200 Medical officers, orderlies and wounded at Alexandra Hospital, including our friend Dr Allardyce, who was our doctor in Kobe; and others, worse than these, which I prefer not to repeat.

"It has been worth 12/15 hours work a day since release. For if I had not done it, there was no-one to take my place. Besides, I have a wider knowledge of these matters, probably, than anyone. I have handled a lot of these cases at the time: I have been the recipient of countless stories in captivity from victims of ill-treatment: I can identify a large number of the criminals, and when I interrogate them they dare not lie because I know the facts."

Wild went on: "I have, in fact, made many of the arrests myself, and done most of the interrogation, in addition to grappling with the enormous documentary side. For this I am some sort of a GSO2(I), and at least I have the satisfaction of emerging from captivity into the same style of job which I had before; and I shall go home as a soldier from a campaign, and not as an ex-POW."

It is interesting to note the obvious importance Wild placed on the Parit Sulong Massacre case from the very outset of his war crimes work. In this letter to his family he put it top of the list of cases on which he was directly involved. It also occupied the No 1 position in a very early document prepared by Wild and headed **"Atrocities Committed in Malaya and on Singapore Island During Action — 1942."**

As his investigations continued through September into early October 1945, Wild sought Lord Louis Mountbatten's personal intervention with the Americans in order to secure an interview with General Yamashita, then under detention and awaiting trial in Manila. With his war crime dossiers expanding rapidly, Wild felt it imperative at this early stage to pin down the former Japanese 25th Army Commander on links he may have had to the various Japanese atrocities of the Malayan Campaign. At the same time Wild wanted to interrogate Yamashita on the separate roles played by his three divisional commanders.

A signal from Lord Louis to American military supremo, General Douglas MacArthur, immediately opened all doors. Wild flew to Manila from Singapore on October 23 and, five days later, was speaking to Yamashita in the detained commander's heavily guarded prison cell. Prominent among the files Wild took with him to this meeting was his dossier on the Parit Sulong Massacre including Ben Hackney's signed synopsis.

Immediately after his meeting with Yamashita, Wild prepared a lengthy official report. This listed the Japanese commander's reaction to all allegations being made against him personally and against the general conduct of his troops throughout the 70-day Malayan Campaign. Top item on the atrocities list with which Wild challenged Yamashita was the Parit Sulong Massacre.

Wild's report noted:

"Ref. No. 1. (Two massacres of Australian and Indian wounded and prisoners after the battle of Muar.) Yamashita stated that the 5th Division under Lt General Takuro Matsui was attacking down the central Johore road. The outflanking movement on the right, including the landings near Muar, was performed by the Konoye Division ('a very good division'). This division fought the battle of Muar and conducted the pursuit. He agreed that troops of this Division must be considered responsible for both massacres. The Division Commander was Lt General Takuma Nishimura, now in Japan. Yamashita agreed that Nishimura should be interrogated and wrote out his name in Japanese characters."

Initial difficulties locating remains of dead Allied troops on Muar Front battlefields led investigators first to believe there had been two massacres at or near Parit Sulong. Hence the reference to *two massacres* in this section of Wild's report. It took several months to clear up the confusion and limit the investigations to a single atrocity.

Wild's report went on to describe Yamashita's separate reactions to four other atrocity reports — the shooting of an Australian sergeant at Yong Peng, the Alexandra Hospital Massacre, the shooting of 14 Australian prisoners in Singapore and the massacre of Chinese civilians in Singapore. In the body of his account Wild noted Yamashita had expressed "his past ignorance and present disapproval of such things, and in proof of the latter he agreed to assist by naming those responsible."

Wild continued:

"He also disclaimed all previous knowledge of each of these atrocities, as I recounted them in detail. He took notes, including the names of some witnesses. He

did not question any of the evidence. On several occasions he condemned the perpetrators in fairly strong terms."

Clearly impressed by what Yamashita had to say and the manner in which he had said it, Wild drafted a personal letter to Mountbatten to accompany a copy of his official report. In this letter dated November 7, 1945, he noted that "Yamashita had given the impression of speaking the truth when he disclaimed previous knowledge of these Malayan atrocities."

Wild went on to recommend that Lt. General Nishimura together with 18th Division commander, Lt. General Renya Mutaguchi, prime suspect in the Alexandra Hospital Massacre, be brought in for interrogation. He advised:

"The threat of putting the pair of them on trial as war criminals will probably be enough to make them talk. Also news that Yamashita has himself nominated them for interrogation and has condemned these acts will be a further strong inducement."

Wild then proceeded to make a most revealing observation:

"It is, in any case, a notable and helpful feature of interrogation of the Japanese since the surrender that senior officers are generally willing to give away their subordinates, while junior officers and other ranks are ready to incriminate their seniors. This abject reversal of the long tradition of personal loyalty is one of the most striking proofs of their awareness of defeat."

Here Britain's most experienced Japanese war crimes authority was acknowledging the ace card of his department's developing interrogation techniques. For all the many problems posed by the machinations of a devious enemy eluding blame for war crimes, senior Japanese officers, properly handled, could be persuaded to incriminate their subordinates and vice versa.

The day after he wrote to Mountbatten, Wild, back in Singapore, started gathering his thoughts on how investigations might best proceed in view of Yamashita's reactions. He needed to articulate guidelines and advice for those conducting interrogations of senior Japanese military officers. Wild was anxious to speak personally to the three 25th Army divisional commanders: Lt. General Nishimura (Imperial Guards), Lt. General Mutaguchi (18th Division) and Lt. General Takuro Matsui (5th Division). He also wanted to confront Major General Arimura, the Japanese officer directly responsible for Allied prisoners of war in Malaya from December, 1942 until January, 1944.

Wild prepared a document which he headed: **Notes on Proposed Interrogation of Japanese General Officers in Japan.** Again reflecting the importance he attached to the Parit Sulong Massacre, Wild began by dealing with his proposed interrogation of Lt. General Nishimura. In fact two thirds of his report dwelt on the Nishimura situation as he saw it. He wrote:

There is good reason to suppose that the Parit Sulong massacre of 110 Australian and 35/40 Indian wounded, by machine-gunning and burning alive with petrol of 22 January 1942, was personally ordered by Lt-Gen. Nishimura. The sole surviving witness is Lt B. Hackney, 2/29 Bn, AIF, whose evidence has recently been confirmed by discovery of the victims' remains. The following information was given to me verbally by Hackney shortly before the Japanese surrender. It is also contained in a lengthy written report which he took back to Australia, but is omitted from the short

synopsis of which SACSEA hold a copy.

(a) These surviving wounded, from an ambulance-column which the Australians had been trying to extricate for three days, were confined on capture in two small rooms of a block of coolie-quarters adjacent to the Muar-Parit Sulong road. Along this road troops in MT, tanks and artillery of the Konoye Division were pouring past for many hours in pursuit.

(b) Then a special convoy halted on the road. It consisted of two groups of medium tanks, in front and rear, with a number of staff-cars between them. From these a very senior officer and his staff emerged, and were paid full compliments by the troops on the spot.

(c) This officer inspected the wounded from the doorway. They were in great distress, lying piled on one another's bodies on the floor. Many of them had fresh wounds, in addition to those which they had received three days or more before. They had been refused water by the Japanese, who had amused themselves by bringing it to them and pouring it on the ground outside.

(d) After his inspection, this officer was seen to give orders to the Japanese outside before re-entering his staff-car. Full compliments were again paid him and the convoy moved off.

(e) The remaining Japanese immediately proceeded with the preparations for the massacre. The prisoners were fastened into small groups with ropes and signal-wire. There was not enough of this, and Hackney and a few others were not so fastened, but their hands were trussed up behind their backs. On being moved off at the point of the bayonet, Hackney's broken leg gave way and he was clubbed and bayoneted several times on the ground. He still bears the scars on his head and body.

(f) After the firing had stopped, a number of

Japanese walked past him to the road and returned carrying tins of petrol. The cries and screams broke out afresh and shortly ceased.

(g) Hackney was joined that night by Sgt Croft, 2/29 Bn, and one other Australian. These two had rolled away from the pile of bodies before it was set alight. Their clothing still reeked of petrol. Neither of them survived.

(h) The Konoye Division was the only formation in the Parit Sulong area. It is highly probable that only the Divisional Commander would have travelled in such a strongly protected convoy. Lieutenant Hackney, an intelligent and reliable witness, might still be able to identify a full-length photograph of Lt General Nishimura, in uniform and cap.

(i) In August or September 1942 a party of British prisoners were taken to the Muar area from Kuala Lumpur gaol to take part in a film of the battle. A British officer, who had heard Hackney's story in the gaol, asked a Japanese officer why they had killed our wounded. The answer was that a Regimental Commander (Colonel) had been killed in action and that the troops were told to take no prisoners, in revenge.

(j) Regarding the separate executions by beheading of 200 Australians and Indians, the only evidence consists of the statements of two surviving Sepoys and some local natives, and the discovery of the victims' skulls and bones.

1. (ii) It is suggested that the interrogating officer, after referring to Yamashita's statement, should assume as a fact that Nishimura was the senior officer in question. In face of the evidence, it is likely that he will admit guilt by offering the defence of a 'mercy-killing'. Failing this, he will be in such a position that he must

disclose the names of subordinate formations and commanders, from whom the necessary evidence should be obtainable.

Coming, as it did, from the pen of the authoritative Major Wild, this was a particularly damning document for Nishimura. Viewed in the light of Wild's earlier written remarks on the ease of getting incriminating evidence by playing senior officers against junior officers and other ranks, his final paragraph's suggestions for interrogators held special meaning. Certainly, the official finger of suspicion now pointed resolutely at Nishimura.

Who, then, *was* this man portrayed as the prime suspect in the crime topping Britain's Pacific War atrocity list?

Takuma Nishimura was born in Kokura city, Fukuoka prefecture, in 1889, the oldest son of a large family. His father, from a *samurai* background, had been "adopted" by his mother's family which had no sons to ensure the continuation of the Nishimura name.

During the Meiji restoration the *samurai* class, along with all other classes, was stripped of its feudal rights and privileges. To compensate for this loss of income, former *samurai* were given a one-time cash payment. While many *samurai,* who had no experience of business matters, soon lost all their money and became destitute, Nishimura's father built up a successful construction company.

Following family tradition, the young Takuma was educated at the Army Junior School in Kumamoto in central Kyushu, after which he went on to the Military Academy and finally the Military Staff College. Strong in mathematics and science, he chose to specialise in artillery, at that time the most modern and prestigious section of the Army.

After graduating from the Staff College in 1920, he was stationed at Yura on Awaji Island, just south of Osaka, where the garrison guarded the entrance to the Inland Sea. In 1933, as a Lt. Colonel, he was appointed President of a court martial of ten cadets from the Military Academy who had participated in a revolt the previous year. Dubbed the *5.15 incident*, because it had taken place on May 15, the revolt — and in particular the trial and its aftermath — were destined to become critical events in the passage of modern Japanese military history.

On May 15, 1932, a group of young navy officers and some civilian fanatics assassinated Prime Minister Takeshi Inukai as part of an effort to purge government corruption. The cadets, although they had not participated in the attack, were involved in the plot and their trial preceded those of other conspirators. Nishimura, as court president, was deluged with letters pleading with him to show leniency towards the accused who were seen by many as merely idealistic youths. This he did — sentencing them to penal servitude for four years. In his public judgment Nishimura said: "We can understand, to some degree, your pure motive, but the crime you have committed is a severe breach of military discipline."

His judgment was criticised by many as encouraging the military's growing incursions into civilian politics. His accompanying remarks would ultimately be judged as incitement to the infamous *February 26 Incident* three years later which, in turn, led to the the military's eventual domination of Japanese life and the inevitability of the Pacific War.

The *February 26 Incident* in 1936 was an attempted coup against the civilian government by troops stationed in Tokyo. By this stage, Nishimura had been promoted to Chief of the Bureau of Military Affairs. In a parallel career, Tomoyuki Yamashita, four years older than Nishimura, occupied a slightly more senior position, that of Chief of the Bureau of Army Affairs.

During the 1936 Tokyo stand-off between rebel soldiers and troops loyal to the government, Yamashita planted a banner in front of rebel positions stating: "His Imperial Highness has read your demands and understands them." In Japanese, as in English, this message was ambiguous and could be taken to mean that the Emperor sympathised with the rebels. The Emperor was reportedly furious when he discovered Yamashita had boosted the rebel position by alluding to royal support of both the coup and the various political assassinations that had taken place.

The controversy initiated a serious rift between Nishimura, on the one hand, and Yamashita, on the other. Nishimura maintained the older officer had no right to demonstrate tacit support of the rebel side. It was a curious position to adopt in view of his remarks to the military court three years earlier. Albeit, the rift soon became recognised within Japan's military hierarchy as a significant power struggle between two prominent officers destined for high positions. As the months passed, both gathered support from different officer factions until a level of antipathy consolidated between them. It would persist for the rest of their military careers.

Like numerous controversial senior officers, including Yamashita, Nishimura was transferred to Manchuria following the February 26 Incident. There he served until 1940 when he was assigned to Saigon as commander of Japanese troops in French Indo-China. In 1941 he was appointed commander of the Konoye Imperial Guards. He led this division, within the overall command of his long standing rival, now 25th Army Chief Yamashita, throughout the Malayan Campaign and in the final assault on Singapore. Battlefield records and entries in Yamashita's private diary all confirm that relations between the two men were severely strained throughout the fighting.

From the moment Singapore fell on February 15, 1942, Nishimura was under urgent direct orders from Tokyo to re-organise, reinforce and move his entire division to Sumatra by the following month. It was a huge task and one which,

By the time he was 49, Takuma Nishimura had been promoted to major general. This picture taken in Manchuria in 1938 shows Major General Nishimura (left) with a fellow officer shortly before leaving for battlefields in China.

The year is 1940. Takuma Nishimura is 51 years old and the commander of Japanese forces in French Indo-China. The picture was taken in Saigon and probably shows him walking from the Continental Hotel in the centre of the city. Later that same year he was promoted to lieutenant general and was appointed commander of the elite Imperial Guards.

Lt. General Tomoyuki Yamashita, Tiger of Malaya*, photographed in Singapore some time after the British surrender. Yamashita and Nishimura were long standing rivals by this stage and there existed a high level of animosity between the two senior Japanese generals.*

remarkably, he accomplished within the given deadline. From March to May, 1942, he served with the Imperial Guards in West Sumatra, returning then to Japan where, at the age of 53, he retired from his country's regular army register.

In April, the following year, Nishimura was despatched to Burma as governor of the occupied Shan States. Early in 1944 he transferred to the occupied Dutch East Indies, now Indonesia, and served in the Madura region in a similar administrative capacity to his Burma posting until the Pacific war concluded.

Chapter 3

Australia's case falls apart

───── ◆ ─────

In order to retain the services of the invaluable Major Wild in South East Asia over the critical immediate post war period, the British Army promoted him to the rank of full colonel. The Army also allowed Wild's young wife, Celia, to accompany her husband on his Singapore posting and moved the couple into substantial accommodation at Raffles Hotel.

With 1945 drawing to a close, the War Office's hopes for bringing Japanese war criminals to justice rested on a plan for establishing a separate War Crimes Section within its South East Asia Command (SEAC). This would be located in Singapore's Goodwood Park Hotel on Scotts Road. It would operate as a central registry into which all information and intelligence on suspected crimes and criminals would be fed. The War Crimes Section would be responsible for collating all in-coming data and keeping files on suspect identities.

Colonel Wild's official title was War Crimes Liaison Officer, Malaya and Singapore. This gave him direct control over three British investigating teams operating in the immediate area and the Goodwood Park central office itself. Wild's title, together with his new rank and reputation ensured him immense influence over the Australian war crimes office functioning within SEAC. Attached to the Goodwood Park registry was what was known as 1 Australian War Crimes Section (SEAC). This was the unit charged specifically with directing investigations into Japanese war crimes where Australian nationals had been victims. Although within SEAC's command structure, it answered directly to AHQ in Melbourne.

If the British were chronically short of experienced investigators, linguists in Japanese, Chinese and Malay, and legal experts, 1 Australian War Crimes Section was even more so. As a result, investigations into the Parit Sulong Massacre, despite the original fillip given to the case by Wild's personal meeting with Ben Hackney and his subsequent interrogation of Yamashita, went into sudden decline in early 1946.

Still, there wasn't an officer in the Australian section at the Goodwood Park then who hadn't poured over the 11 single-spaced typed pages that comprised Lt. Ben Charles Hackney's detailed evidence sworn before Mr. Justice Mansfield in Sydney on November 12, 1945. Hackney's chilling recollections of the tortures inflicted on the wounded at Parit Sulong (See Appendix A, page 281) were almost too graphic to read. But what made his affidavit so compelling was his apparent identification of the culprit. This began on page 5 at paragraph 25 after Hackney had described the brutal measures employed by Japanese troops transferring the Parit Sulong prisoners from trucks in which they were captured to nearby coolie quarters:

Later, many staff cars came along, two of which were preceeded by tanks and motor cyclists and followed similarly. They halted in front of the place where the prisoners were and many Japs came over. They were met by the Jap in charge of the prisoners amidst much shouting, saluting, and bowing of this Jap and the personnel of the guard. Other Jap soldiers in the area also gave their attention to the party which consisted of officers and some very senior ones.

Paragraph 26 went on:

One of these new arrivals was outstanding and presumably the commander of the Japanese forces in the area — a short, stocky fellow. A bodyguard kept close with him always. He was well dressed, his sword hanging low and with a great amount of brown cord at the hilt, knee high boots and spurs all glistening. The attitude of the Japs to this officer was as though he was something far and above any of them, as though to them he was as a god.

And paragraph 27:

He looked at the officer prisoners who were made to move off the steps and stand then mounted the steps, the bodyguard keeping very close, and looked through the window at the mass inside one of the rooms.

And paragraph 28:

Upon leaving the building he spoke to one of the officers accompanying him who, in turn, passed on what were apparently orders to the Jap in charge of the prisoners.

And finally paragraph 29:

Leaving a couple behind, this party then departed. Again came the yelling, bowing, and saluting. At first the tanks, then the cycles and then the cars moved off, and after them were more cycles and tanks. Along the road wherever Japanese were to be seen, they paid their compliments to those two cars very reverently.

Wild regarded Hackney's account as positively identifying one man: Konoye Imperial Guards Divisional Commander, Lt. General Takuma Nishimura. To the decidedly less experienced Australian investigators at the Goodwood Park, the evidence was similarly conclusive. Back in Australia, Ben Hackney became consumed by the idea of securing the conviction of the "short, stocky" man he'd seen inspecting the wounded. He could never forget the image of the nattily dressed officer strutting about that frightful place. He could visualise him as clearly as he had seen him that stifling January afternoon four years earlier. He was Nishimura, all right. Hackney was positive of it. The bastard had to be punished.

The problem was that by March, 1946, seven months after the war had ceased, Ben Hackney's sworn statement remained as the only piece of evidence in the investigation master file. This was held by 1 Australian War Crimes Section at the Goodwood Park. The only other papers in the file were copies of routine administrative signals sent back and forth between Australia and Singapore, and between the Australian investigators and related British military departments on the island. Pointedly, none of the mounting paperwork had advanced the case one iota. Frustratingly, no one knew Nishimura's whereabouts and there the case stuck.

If the truth were known, the same master file served to underline the stunning inefficiency of the Australian war crimes investigation effort. It demonstrated just how much this detachment from the antipodes quaked in the shadow of the towering Colonel Wild. No one moved without the British say-so. And if the British weren't saying, nothing got done.

On January 23, 1946, for instance, the AG in Melbourne, signalled 1 Australian War Crimes Section requesting information on progress in the Parit Sulong Massacre case. Specifically, the AG wanted an estimate on when some arrests might be forthcoming.

When the AG's request landed in Singapore the Australian OC, bereft of a reply, communicated with Wild's department seeking the requested information "as urgently as possible." It took more than a month for the Australian detachment to inform Melbourne:

AS REQUESTED IN PARAGRAPH 5 OF YOUR MEMO, IT IS ADVISED THAT THE BRITISH WAR CRIMES AUTHORITIES HAVE ARRANGEMENTS IN HAND FOR THE INTERROGATION OF LT-GEN NISHIMURA TAKUMA GOC KONOYE DIV AT THE BATTLE OF MUAR JAN 42, WHO APPEARS LIKELY TO BE IMPLICATED.

Over the following weeks the Australian section was able to signal the AG that the British had requested the Americans in Tokyo to locate and detain the three Japanese 25th Army Divisional Commanders (Nishimura, Mutaguchi and Matsui). All three, according to the signals, were believed to be in Japan. Once detained, the British intended flying them back to Singapore on the pretext they were wanted for historical research. The trio would then be asked by the British to write full accounts of their respective divisions' activitites throughout the Malaya Campaign. Only when they had completed these assignments, AHQ was informed, would Colonel Wild begin interrogating them on specific atrocities — like the Parit Sulong Massacre — and any other matter considered relevant to investigations.

For all the information on British activity, there was still no indication of meaningful investigative work on the case by the Australians. And for a very good reason. Except for two brief visits to Muar Front battlefields the previous October, the Australian team had done nothing. It had all been left to the British. Still, Melbourne pressed for tangible results.

Now caught embarrassingly flatfooted, the OC 1 Australian War Crimes Section, Lt. Colonel, R. C. Smith, scrambled to explain his department's woeful lack of results. In a message dated March 18, 1946, he told AHQ:

NO DEFINITE INFORMATION HAS YET BEEN RECEIVED REGARDING THE TRANSFER OF LT GENS NISHIMURA, MUTAGUCHI AND MATSUI TO SINGAPORE.

THE MATTER HAS BEEN FULLY DISCUSSED WITH COL. C. H. D. WILD OF THE BRITISH ARMY, WHO IS TO CARRY OUT THE INTERROGATIONS AS OUTLINED IN REF (B) (II).

IMMEDIATELY UPON THEIR ARRIVAL THE SUSPECTS WILL BE PHOTOGRAPHED AT FULL LENGTH FOR IDENTIFICATION BY LIEUT. HACKNEY. IN THIS CONNECTION, SHOULD IT BE DEEMED DESIRABLE, COULD LIEUT. HACKNEY BE MADE AVAILABLE IN SINGAPORE TO GIVE EVIDENCE? IN VIEW OF THE IMPORTANCE OF THIS TRIAL AND OF THE SHOCKING NATURE OF THE ATROCITY IT IS STRONGLY RECOMMENDED THAT LIEUT. HACKNEY BE MADE SO AVAILABLE IF REQUIRED.

SUCH ENQUIRIES AS ARE POSSIBLE IN THE ABSENCE OF THE SUSPECTS ARE BEING PURSUED.

A confused head of the Australian detachment seems, at this point, to have been under the impression that Mutaguchi and Matsui were as much suspects in the Parit Sulong affair as Nishimura. This, clearly, was not the case. The same message illustrates the indolent approach to the case adopted by Australian investigators. As far as they were concerned Nishimura was guilty. It was just a matter of locating the former general, having Hackney identify him and then give evidence at his trial. It was an open and shut case. No further investigations were necessary.

Getting Hackney to identify photographs of Nishimura as the officer he saw giving orders at Parit Sulong was an obvious move. It had been ordered by Wild and became regarded as the final act required for tying up the prosecution case. Australian investigators in Singapore, for their part, became transfixed by the requirement. In the weeks that followed, scarcely a message went back to Melbourne without some reference to the expected photographs. There were discussions on the size of the prints, the required photographic angles, whether or not Nishimura should be taken in full general's uniform and, of course, repeated assurances that the photographs themselves would be forthcoming just as soon as the suspect was located.

In mid-March, 1946, Colonel Wild, under intense workload pressure, delivered a thoroughly unnerving pronouncement to the Australian investigators. He had little alternative, he said, but to hand over full responsibility for the Parit Sulong investigations to 1 Australian War Crimes Section. Accordingly, he instructed his various teams to forward to the Australian detachment "any documents which you have relating to this case with any useful information regarding investigation to date, contacts etc."

A mood of decided unease rippled through Australia's investigating ranks where the realisation was that without British assistance, and specifically the input of Colonel Wild, there simply wasn't the capacity to handle such complicated enquiries. On April 2, 1946, Lt. Colonel Smith called on Wild at his Fort Canning office. His aim was to dissuade the Englishman from his intended course of action.

It was a most successful meeting for Smith who, on his return to the the Goodwood Park later that day, wrote Wild a letter confirming their conversation. "It is agreed," he said, "that the best results can probably be achieved by joint investigation of the various Johore atrocities coupled with your own interrogation of the Japanese generals who are being brought to Singapore."

Wild, for all his accommodation of the Australians on this occasion, at least achieved one concession. Smith confirmed in his letter that he was immediately detailing a Major Denniston to head the Parit Sulong investigations on the Australian side. It had taken seven months for the Australians to put some semblance of order into the case.

A flurry of activity followed in the Australian camp. Suspected Japanese war criminals under detention in Changi Jail were interrogated and reports prepared. None of these, as it happened, threw any light on the events that had taken place at Parit Sulong.

Copies of Hackney's sworn affidavit were despatched in all directions. British investigating teams received them. So did their Australian equivalents. One even landed in the Goodwood Park War Crimes Registry. Under operational procedures the Australians, located just along a Goodwood Park corridor, were required to feed war crimes' information into the important central bureau immediately it was gathered. But the Australians had neglected to provide the one piece of evidence they held. They realised their omission only when a formal request for the statement was lodged by the Registry. Acting on the request, Lt. Colonel Smith penned instructions to Major Denniston: *Please have copy made Hackney's statement to Commission and forward saying we hold original — also that further evidence re exact location etc has been asked for already and copy will be supplied etc.* By the time the Hackney statement landed in the Registry it was more than four months overdue.

Around the same period the Australians despatched an all-points message to Allied investigation teams seeking *"the fullest possible information"* on the Parit Sulong matter. *"In particular,"* the message informed, *"it is desired to obtain statements from local inhabitants who either witnessed the atrocities or who had received any reliable and relevant information. Detailed sketch maps of the areas, together with references to the ordnance maps, would be appreciated."* Considering the case had, from the outset, been given top priority on every command investigation list and that AHQ had repeatedly signalled its pressing interest, these were deplorable requests to be making at this late stage.

Urgent appeals also went out for experienced investigators to be sent from Australia. One of those who was to fly north to join the ranks was Major Norman Frederick Quinton, the same Norman Frederick Quinton who, almost five years later, would be on hand at Los Negros Island to build the gallows, carry out hanging drills and ultimately supervise the execution and burial at sea of General Nishimura and four other convicted war criminals.

On April 17, 1946, Quinton was appointed OC 3 Australian Prisoner of War Contact Enquiry Unit (SEAC). He served in this capacity until August 1 when he joined 1 Australian War Crimes Section (SEAC) at the Goodwood Park. Thus began what can only be judged as a bizarre association between Quinton and the Nishimura case. Given the workings of the two SEAC units and the prominence of the Parit Sulong incident, it is simply impossible for Quinton to have missed some form of involvement with related investigations. Certainly he must have acquired a good knowledge of Nishimura's suspected connection to the killings, if only because of the continuing flow of messages on the subject from headquarters in Australia.

Quinton, born on April 10, 1902, was living in Davis Street in the Melbourne suburb of South Yarra when the Pacific War broke out. He was approaching his 40th year when he filled out his initial enrolment form for military service, noting his previous employment as a "clerk" in the Melbourne Metropolitan Board of Works (MMBW). Beneath the column seeking special qualifications, he wrote the word "nil." On February 2, 1942, Quinton found himself appointed as a lieutenant in the Australian Army's Provost Corps and attached to the Special Investigations Branch (SIB) at Melbourne's St Kilda Road Barracks. The following year he was raised to the rank of temporary captain and transferred to Land Headquarters (LHQ), Brisbane, where he became OC of the SIB detachment there. He remained with this office until war's end. It was with the rank of temporary major that Quinton became OC of the SEAC enquiry unit and then on attachment to 1 Australian War Crimes Section where he ultimately sat as a member of British and Australian military courts in Singapore. In this capacity he deliberated and helped pass judgement on several Japanese war criminals during five separate trials.

Major Quinton was still serving with the Singapore section when, in late July, 1946, word came through that prime suspect Nishimura had finally been located in, of all places, Changi Jail. The long awaited photographs were quickly taken by a British military cameraman within the prison precincts. They depicted the general in four separate poses.

On August 2, 1946, the photographs were despatched to Melbourne. The Australian OC in Singapore obviously felt under some pressure to explain to AHQ how the suspect they had been supposedly hunting relentlessly in Japan for nearly a year suddenly turned up under their noses, a long time resident of a Changi cell. Accompanying the photographs went the following letter:

1 AUST WAR CRIMES SEC (SEAC)
2 AUGUST 1946
A.H.Q.
MELBOURNE

SUBJECT: PARIT SULONG MASSACRE

1. FORWARDED HEREWITH ARE 4 PHOTOS OF LT. GEN. NISHIMURA TAKUMA. IT IS REQUESTED THAT THEY BE SHOWN TO LT. B. C. HACKNEY TO SEE WHETHER HE CAN IDENTIFY NISHIMURA AS THE HIGH RANKING OFFICER WHO VISITED PARIT SULON (sic) IMMEDIATELY BEFORE THE MASSACE TOOK PLACE

2. LT GEN NISHIMURA HAS BEEN LOCATED AT CHANGI GAOL WHERE HE APPARENTLY ARRIVED ABOUT A MONTH AGO. OWING TO THE GAOL RECORDS NOT BEING CORRECT HIS PRESENCE WAS

ASCERTAINED BY ACCIDENT A FEW DAYS AGO BY NO 7 WAR CRIMES INVESTIGATION TEAM (BRITISH).

3. AT PRESENT LT. GEN. NISHIMURA HAS BEEN GIVEN THE TASK OF WRITING A COMPLETE RECORD OF HIS MALAYA CAMPAIGN. WHEN THIS HAS BEEN DONE IT WILL BE CHECKED AGAINST ALL INFORMATION HELD AND THE GENERAL THEN INTERROGATED AS TO SPECIFIC CRIMES IN AN ENDEAVOUR TO ASCERTAIN THE RESPONSIBLE OFFICERS FOR EACH OFFENCE.

SIGNED   LT COLONEL R. C. SMITH
O.C. 1 AUST WAR CRIMES SEC (SEAC)

Nishimura had indeed been located in Changi Jail a month earlier. It was also true to say that Britain's No 7 War Crimes Investigation Team had stumbled across him after clarifying faulty jail records. These had resulted from an administrative error on the part of the prison authorities. What Lt. Colonel Smith omitted telling AHQ was that Nishimura had been in Changi since shortly after the formal Japanese surrender in Singapore in September, 1945. At the cessation of hostilities he had been arrested as the senior Japanese administrator at Madura and transferred to Changi as a precautionary measure. And there he had languished. It was just that the Australians had never bothered to look for him in the obvious place.

On August 19, 1946, Melbourne forwarded the Nishimura photographs to Eastern Command Headquarters at Victoria Barracks, Sydney, with orders to show them to Ben Hackney. If Hackney could recognise the photographs as the high ranking officer referred to in his affidavit, Eastern Command was to enquire whether the Bathurst farmer would be prepared to travel to Singapore. The proposal was that he then be given a short attachment to 1 Australian War Crimes Section to facilitate his appearance as a witness at Nishimura's trial.

Over a month went by before Hackney drove his sports car into the Paddington Barracks to view the photographs. On September 24 Eastern Command sent the following signal to AHQ, Melbourne:

WAR CRIMES – MASSACRE AT PARIT SULONG, MALAYA
NX71148 LT B. C. HACKNEY
REF: AHQ 62065 OF 19 AUG 46

THE ATTACHED PHOTOGRAPHS WERE SHOWN TO EX-NX71148 LT B. C. HACKNEY, WHO WAS HOWEVER, UNABLE TO IDENTIFY THEM AS THE HIGH RANKING OFFICER REFERRED TO IN PARAS 26, 27 AND 28 OF HIS AFFIDAVIT OF 12 NOV 45.

Despite all the intricate detail in Hackney's recollections, when it came to identifying Nishimura as the culprit, as the "short stocky" officer he had seen giving orders, he simply couldn't recognise the man. As far as Hackney knew, he had never before laid eyes on the figure in the photographs.

Before this shattering news could reach Singapore, calamity struck the British war crimes effort in South East Asia. Colonel Cyril Wild had flown to Tokyo in late August, 1946, to give evidence before the International Military Tribunal for the Far East (IMTFE) which was conducting the Major War Crimes Trials, the Pacific conflict's Nuremburg.

While waiting to enter the IMTFE witness box in the converted auditorium of Tokyo's War Ministry, Wild busied himself researching ministry files. He also carried out a series of interrogations of Japanese war criminal suspects detained in nearby Sugamo Prison. He began his formal evidence on Tuesday, September 10 and concluded it nine days later. Anxious to return to Singapore as soon as possible, Wild flew on the first available military aircraft to Hong Kong where he

Full face.

Right profile.

Left profile.

These are three of the four photographs taken of General Nishimura in the precincts of Changi Jail to assist Parit Sulong survivor Ben Hackney in identifying the "short, stocky" officer described so fully in his sworn statement. In the event, Hackney failed to recognise Nishimura.

67

was forced to wait as all onward flights to Singapore were fully booked.

At 9. 30 am on September 25 he was among 14 passengers and five crew who boarded a Royal Airforce Transport Command Dakota at Hong Kong's Kai Tak airport for a flight to Singapore via Saigon. Two minutes into the ascent across bustling Kowloon, the aircraft lurched and its wings wobbled violently. Moments later it slammed into Kowloon Tong hillside between Lion Rock and Beacon Hill, exploding into a huge fireball on impact. All aboard died instantly. It was Hong Kong's worst air disaster.

Word of the 38-year-old Wild's death reached a stunned military community in Singapore shortly after midday. Wild's wife, Celia, learned of the tragedy when she read the evening newspaper. The sudden obliteration of this larger than life personality who had provided such inspiration, direction and knowledge to British war crimes work in the Far East, delivered an incalculable blow to the on-going investigations effort. For the British, Wild would prove truly irreplaceable. From the day of his death onwards, the calibre of their detection work would nosedive. So, too, would the standard of their prosecutions as incompetently researched cases were pushed through the courts. This, in turn, resulted in several truly serious miscarriages of justice.

Wild's demise was equally disastrous for Australian interests. Gone was 1 Australian War Crimes Section's omnipotent counselor. As far as the Parit Sulong Massacre was concerned, enquiries ground to a halt. For months the AG's office in Melbourne had been poised, waiting for the promised Wild—Nishimura meeting. Singapore had repeatedly explained its inability to push investigations further until this essential interrogation had taken place. Now it would never happen.

Six days after Wild's death, a one-line signal from Melbourne landed on the desk of OC 1 Australian War

Colonel Cyril Wild, the mainstay of British war crimes investigations in the Far East is shown during his nine days of testimony to the IMTFE hearing in Tokyo in September, 1946. On September 25 he perished in an air crash at Hong Kong while enroute back to Singapore. The quality of both British and Australian war crimes investigations plummeted following his death.

Crimes Section. It read:

LT HACKNEY UNABLE TO IDENTIFY NISHIMURA.

Perhaps fortuitously, the OC was on leave at the time. On the bottom of the in-coming message the acting OC noted:

"N.F.A. till we receive Nishimura's a/c of Malaya Campaign when he will be interrogated."

News of Hackney's failure to recognise Nishimura dropped like a bombshell in the Australian camp at the Goodwood Park Hotel. Within 24 hours every member of the detachment had learned of the developments and considered their sobering implications. The case against the former Imperial Guards commander, considered so watertight, had disintegrated.

Apart from the Hackney statement, there was nothing else to link Nishimura to the crime. Australia's desultory detection work over the months had assured there was no other suspect.

Back from his break, Lt. Colonel Smith was once again in contact with the British. On October 14 he wrote them asking, somewhat lamely, about the progress being made on interrogating Nishimura. *"This Section is particularly interested in evidence concerning the massacre on the Muar-Parit Sulong Road in January 42,"* Smith said. He then went ahead to inform the British about Hackney's failure with the photographs. Some three weeks later, on November 6, a newly appointed OC of 1 Australian War Crimes Section sent the following signal to AHQ, Melbourne:

SUBJECT: PARIT SULONG MASSACRE

1. REF OUR 792 OF 2 AUG 46 AND YOUR 7026/AG OF 301445K

2. LT-GEN NISHIMURA HAS NOW COMPLETED HIS RECORD OF THE MALAYAN CAMPAIGN AND A COPY HAS BEEN FORWARDED FOR INFORMATION PER LT-COL SMITH.

3. A PRELIMINARY INTERROGATION SUGGESTS THAT NISHIMURA WAS NOT RESPONSIBLE FOR THIS MASSACRE BUT THAT THE HIGH RANKING OFFICER CONCERNED MAY HAVE BEEN MAJ GEN KOBAYASHI TAKASHI WHO AT THAT TIME WAS ON INF. BDE. COMD OF THE 2ND JAP IMPERIAL GUARDS DIVISION.

4. KOBAYASHI IS STATED TO BE IN TOKIO AND A REQUEST HAS BEEN MADE THAT HE BE LOCATED AND ARRESTED.

5. YOU WILL BE KEPT INFORMED OF FUTURE DEVELOPMENTS.

From this point onwards Australia's finger of suspicion moved right away from Nishimura. So much so, that by June 26, 1947, the Australians had actually closed the Nishimura file. On that date they sent a formal communication to the British War Crimes Section. It read:

SUBJECT: LT. GEN. NISHIMURA TAKUMA.

THE ABOVE NAMED SUSPECT IS NO LONGER REQUIRED BY THIS SECTION.

By now 1 Australian War Crimes Section should have stepped back and re-examined its whole approach to handling the Parit Sulong massacre enquiries — enquiries that were obviously getting nowhere. Rather than pursuing investigations to a pattern dictated by the Hackney statement, the Australians should have endeavoured to identify first those who physically carried out the atrocity. From there they could have worked back to establishing whether or not the Hackney statement with all its innuendos, inconsistencies, and emotions provided an accurate indication of who had been responsible. But this was not to be.

Instead, as the November 6 communication (quoted above) clearly demonstrates, the Australians chose to seek alternative senior Japanese to fit the Hackney description. One of the early alternatives was Colonel Takeo Iwakuro, former CO of the Imperial Guards' 5th Regiment. Investigations into this officer fizzled when it somehow proved impossible to trace his whereabouts despite the fact he was living in Tokyo quite openly under his own name. Australian Army sleuths, mesmerised as they were by Hackney's statement, plodded ahead with their quest to locate an appropriate suspect on whom they could pin the massacre.

It was an illogical, incompetent approach. It resulted in investigations that were either directionless or misleading. On July 7, 1947, yet another OC 1 Australian War Crimes Section was informing Melbourne that a Major Kikuo Nakamura, of the 4th Imperial Guards Division was the latest suspect on their list. He had just been located and was incarcerated in the Johore Bahru Prison. Nakamura had probably been in the Parit Sulong area at the time of the killing, the OC told headquarters, and would be interrogated in the near future. His message concluded:

ALL OTHER SOURCES OF INFORMATION HAVE BEEN INVESTIGATED AND NO PROGRESS IN LOCATING SUSPECTS HAS BEEN MADE TO DATE.

The wording of this signal indicates enquiries were fast running into yet another dead end. For Major Kikuo Nakamura, the misfortune of being the last of the chosen Nishimura alternatives before Australian enquiries once again spluttered to a standstill, would have extremely unpleasant consequences. He first went from prime suspect to forgotten suspect, shunted between prisons in Malaya and Singapore.

Eventually the British released Nakamura so he could be repatriated back to Japan by ship leaving Singapore on October 30, 1947. As soon as the Australians discovered their forgotten prime suspect was missing, they sent immediate instructions to Tokyo demanding his re-arrest. By mid-November Nakamura was imprisoned once more, this time at Sugamo. As it happened the Major had not even the remotest connection to the massacre. His problem was that he had passed through Parit Sulong sometime after the action there and was short and stocky.

In a wrap-up gesture to the Nishimura side of investigations, Captain Alwyn Sherlock from Australia's Goodwood Park office sought one final interrogation of the former Imperial Guards Commander. This took place in Changi Jail on August 27, 1947.

It is not difficult to imagine Captain Sherlock's unease at being the first Australian to confront the man for so long held responsible for the Parit Sulong slaughter. It is not difficult, either, to imagine the captain's surprise when he first sighted Nishimura. For the Japanese general quite obviously bore no physical resemblance to the officer described in Hackney's affidavit. Nishimura was certainly not short by Japanese standards of those days. In fact, he was somewhat taller than the average Japanese; indeed, taller than some of the British military guards entrusted with security at the jail. Furthermore, Nishimura could never be described as stocky. He was trim and fit with scarcely an ounce of fat on him. And he had been that way all his military career.

During this meeting, Nishimura readily made a sworn statement about Parit Sulong. In this he admitted passing through the town on January 22, 1942, accompanied by "a few tanks."

He recalled that while there he had noticed on the north side of the bridge several trucks of prisoners of war. He stated he had previously issued instructions that all prisoners were to be sent back to headquarters and that these were located some distance to the rear.

"I do not know of any prisoners being shot, and if such things did happen, they were without my knowledge as I had given definite instructions that all prisoners of war were to be sent back to Headquarters," Nishimura reiterated.

In the light of these remarks he was asked to provide names of junior officers who might have been involved in the killings. In particular, he was probed for details about the new suspect, Nakamura.

He responded: **"It was a long time ago that this battle was fought, and I have forgotten the names of any of the junior officers. I do not know Captain Nakamura, but he may possibly have been one of the company commanders."**

Prior to signing the document, Nishimura reviewed what he was about to swear on oath. Among other alterations, he requested a full-stop be inserted after the word "Nakamura." He also deleted the remainder of that sentence, thus removing any suggestion that he could have been alluding to Nakamura's blame. (See Nishimura's original statement: Appendix A, page 316.)

Nishimura's statement on this occasion amounted to seven brief paragraphs occupying less than half a typed page. Delivered off the cuff without the benefit of preparation, the document represents his first reaction to Australian allegations of his involvement in Parit Sulong. Significantly, he would go to his death without wavering one jot from his initial claim that the only order he ever gave for prisoners was that they should be transferred to rear headquarters. Nor did he on this, or any subsequent occasion, try to fudge the issue by offering excuses. Nor did he attempt to switch the responsibility to others. By this stage he had been subjected to at least two and possibly three interviews at Changi.

Nishimura's reactions under interrogation are significant in the light of Wild's earlier predictions. The guilty Nishimura would likely offer the defence of a "mercy killing," Wild had advised. Failing this he would readily divulge the names of subordinate commanders. The Englishman had been quite wrong. Nishimura did neither of these things. His whole style and demeanour were entirely different.

In forwarding the latest interrogation report, together with the Japanese general's sworn statement, Captain Sherlock made the cursory observation that Nishimura's recollections agreed, in part, with Hackney's original statement. Of more immediate concern to the captain, it seemed, was the fact that he was forwarding two photographs of the latest Parit Sulong suspect, Major Kikuo Nakamura — the man Nishimura had been unable to recall. Did Hackney know the man in the photographs?

This time it took Eastern Command, in Sydney, more than four months to get the Bathurst farmer's reaction. On February 12, 1948, came the reply:

EX NX71148 LT B. C. HACKNEY STATES THAT HE IS UNABLE TO IDENTIFY PHOTOGRAPHS S6 AND S6A OF MAJ NAKAMURA KIKUO. ALTHOUGH THERE IS SOME LIKENESS, HE IS NOT PREPARED TO SWEAR THAT THIS JAPANESE OFFICER WAS ONE OF THOSE PRESENT AT ANY ATROCITIES WITNESSED BY HIM

The "some likeness" line was enough to retain the detention order on prime suspect Nakamura. But shortly thereafter he was forgotten once more. Australian investigators came and went on overseas postings. Enquiries into the case languished. The office of 1 Australian War Crimes Section, closed down in Singapore, re-opened in Hong Kong, and eventually moved back to Australia. Nakamura remained in his Sugamo cell.

Almost certainly prompted by the Americans, 2 Australian War Crimes Section in Tokyo on April 1, 1949, despatched the following signal to AHQ:

FROM 2 AUST WAR CRIMES SEC SCAP 0016201
TO   ARMY MELBOURNE

A98 UNCLASS. PARIT SULONG MASSACRE SUSPECT MAJ NAKAMUREA (sic) KIKUO. INSUFFICIENT EVIDENCE TO WARRANT HOLDING THIS SUSPECT ANY LONGER AND STRONGLY RECOMMEND RELEASE. PLEASE ADVISE.

Three days later authority came through for Nakamura's release. By then the Japanese major had been wrongfully imprisoned under Australian military orders for a year and nine months. With Nakamura's departure from Sugamo, Australia's enquiries into the now seven-year-old Parit Sulong Massacre were back to square one.

Even had Nishimura known how far Australian suspicions had now swung away from his possible involvement, he would have scarcely been relieved. Other crises had flooded in to fill the void. While the Australian investigations were stumbling along, Nishimura had been indicted and convicted by a British military court for complicity in the massacre of Chinese civilians in Singapore. His punishment: life imprisonment.

Chapter 4

Politics and British colonial justice

———————— ◆ ————————

Of all the war criminal hearings in Singapore to suffer from Colonel Cyril Wild's untimely demise, no judicial process was undermined more thoroughly than the island colony's infamous Chinese Massacre trial. For Takuma Nishimura, the trial began an unscrupulously manipulated legal process that would lead him inexorably to the gallows on Los Negros island.

During Wild's research into files at Tokyo's War Ministry in late August and early September, 1946, he uncovered a series of 26 highly incriminating Japanese military reports previously overlooked by American investigators. One of these was titled *"A proces-verbal concerning the punishment of Chinese residents in Singapore."* The document had been prepared immediately after the Japanese surrender by a Ministry sub-committee known as the 4th Unit. The authors had given their document a "secret" classification. With good reason. Its aim was to whitewash the military's involvement in the Singapore Massacre which accounted for the deaths of some 15,000 to 20,000 Chinese males between 16 - 45 years of age. Their slaughter occurred during a bloody four week period following Britain's capitulation to General Yamashita on February 15, 1942.

The massacre was essentially a demented exercise in population control through terror. Its aim was to ensure the unquestioning obedience of local Chinese to the newly installed Japanese military regime and thereby avoid the type of security quagmires into which the Imperial Army had frequently fallen on mainland China. The Singapore killings were devised, organised and ordered by 25th Army Intelligence Staff Officer, Lt. Colonel Masanobu Tsuji. Despite his rank, Tsuji enjoyed an untouchable position within the 25th Army's hierarchy through the extraordinary influence he wielded in Tokyo's top corridors of power. He had, for instance, the ability to report directly from the field to Premier Hideki Tojo thus circumventing the authority of General Yamashita. What was more, he regularly exercised this power.

Prepared in the full expectation of Allied war crimes investigations, the 26 War Ministry reports discovered by Wild had a common theme. All provided recognisable guidelines for defence presentations and rebuttals to anticipated charges. Wild was astounded to find that the sub-committee responsible for the document on the Singapore Chinese Massacre had been headed by none other than the 25th Army High Command's Intelligence Chief, Lt. Colonel Ichiji Sugita. This was the very man who, since September 1945, had been No 2 on Wild's "Most Wanted Japanese War Criminals" list.

Sugita, ostensibly Tsuji's immediate superior, had headed the department from which the mass killing of civilians in Singapore had been directed. Wild could personally attest to Sugita's involvement. Shortly after the British surrender he had confronted Sugita during a meeting in Changi and demanded that the killing of civilians be stopped. Sugita had been adamant it would continue.

The discovery of the 4th Unit's document was added evidence to the ever growing Sugita file kept by Wild in Singapore. In the final week of August, 1946, Wild drove to Sugamo Prison and formally arrested Sugita for his part in the killing of the civilian Chinese. At the same time he had the former intelligence chief despatched in handcuffs on a military flight to the island colony. Sugita, in fact, was transferred to a Changi cell to await trial even before Wild entered the IMTFE witness box in Tokyo.

It is a measure of the chaos created within Britain's Far Eastern War Crimes Section by Wild's death that Sugita would somehow emerge cleansed of suspicion before the Chinese Massacre trial got underway. Instead of fighting for his life as a defendant, Britain's No 2 most wanted Japanese, the man whose department had issued the vital hit lists on which the civilian slaughter was based, inexplicably became a key prosecution witness.

Two further factors impacted on the confusion, each creating its own special ingredient of judicial distortion. Firstly, from within Singapore's majority Chinese population came serious signs of dissatisfaction over Britain's preference for trying war criminals charged with atrocities against white troops or white civilians. Pressure groups on the island demanded justice be done, and done quickly, on behalf of the thousands of Chinese civilian victims of Japanese brutality. Political advisors warned that the delicate process of reimposing British colonial rule in Singapore, after Japan's military occupation, was now in danger of being severely undermined by political dissent. The immediate fear was, of course, that communist-leaning Chinese, both in Singapore and Malaya, would quickly exploit this obvious racial issue. Britain's answer was to appease local sentiments by advancing the Chinese Massacre hearing schedule and turning the trial itself into an orchestrated political exercise.

The second factor with serious ramifications for post-war British military justice in the Far East concerned London's growing disillusionment with the continuing process of war crimes trials. By September, 1946, Wild's department had brought nearly 300 cases to court. Over 100 of these had resulted in death sentences. In addition, British military courts had handed down some 150 terms of imprisonment.

Another 50 Japanese defendants had been acquitted and set free. Significantly, a further 100 cases waited in the pipeline.

Washington, too, began exhibiting war trials weariness. Political strategists were calling for a far more concerted effort among Pacific War Allies to encourage the rebirth of a democratic, non-communist Japan. Japan, it was hoped, would emerge North East Asia's strong buffer-state against communism should China fall to the red menace. Indeed, behind scenes, the word was being passed along Allied political corridors that all Japanese war criminal trials should be terminated by mid-1947. From the War Crimes Section's viewpoint in Singapore this created ever mounting pressures for speedier handling of cases yet to be brought before military tribunals.

So, it was against this politically charged backdrop that the highly publicised Chinese Massacre trial opened in Singapore on March 10, 1947. The centrally located Victoria Theatre, with its substantial seating capacity, had been specially converted for the occasion.

Lt. General Takuma Nishimura was the highest ranking of the seven Japanese officers who appeared jointly charged with responsibility for the massacre of civilians in Singapore. Beside him in the dock was Lt. General Saburo Kawamura, occupied Singapore's first garrison commander. The other five defendants were *kempeitai* (military police) officers — a captain, two majors and two lieutenant colonels.

Tsuji, the man who had meticulously planned the mass killing programme and ultimately ordered it, was not in the dock. Neither was Sugita, the Japanese officer who knew all the details and had very obviously been involved. Wild had understood the importance of both these men to the real killing plot.

An ominous question mark has long hung over the roles undertaken by British investigators and prosecutors left to scrape together the case in the wake of Wild's death. There can only be two explanations for their actions. Either, they had no grasp whatever of the true story behind the massacre and the identities of the real plotters and went ahead with the case, willy nilly. Or, in the interest of facilitating a politically appropriate judgement, they simply pursued a prosecution, fully realising it to be based on utterly false premises. A recently discovered document (See Appendix B, page 334.) indicates the second explanation almost certainly provides the answer.

The Chinese Massacre Trial centred around the prosecution's claim that Nishimura and his six fellow accused were all involved in *a common plan or conspiracy* to slaughter the civilians. The prosecution argued that, as co-conspirators, those involved were individually responsible for all acts performed by any persons in execution of the overall plan. In other words, evidence against one must be considered as evidence against all.

With this as the dynamic of the case against the seven men, the prosecution went ahead to claim that a package of orders for the killing — the very nucleus of the so-called plot or conspiracy — simply came from Army Chief Yamashita, passed through generals Kawamura and Nishimura, and thence through various sector commanders down the line where action was finally taken. Those through whom the order passed were, by the prosecution's definition, co-conspirators.

Even had the massacre plot been as straight forward as this — and it certainly wasn't — it was an outrageously dangerous legal argument on which to base a complex case where the lives of seven men rested in the balance. Indeed, historical research has now established, beyond all doubt, that the massacre of Chinese civilians in Singapore had nothing whatever to do with orders issued by Yamashita. Orders issued surreptitiously by Lt. Colonel Tsuji — without the knowledge or consent of Yamashita — were what triggered the slaughter. In short, the real story of the

Singapore killings was vastly different to that offered in court as the foundation of the British case against Nishimura and his six co-defendants.

Pointedly, the sadistic, megalomaniacal Tsuji flew on to the Philippines after the Singapore killings. In Manila, the then officially appointed trouble shooter for the Tokyo High Command proceeded to instigate the Bataan Death March. He applied almost identical tactics for disseminating killing orders in the Philippines to those he had employed previously in Singapore. Over ten thousand American and Filipino troops would ultimately perish as the result of Tsuji's manipulations.

Extraordinarily, both Britain and the United States later ensured Tsuji would never be brought to trial for his crimes in Singapore, the Philippines or any other part of the Pacific theatre, for that matter. Protected by American military intelligence, he went on to become a celebrated best selling post-war author, the most popularly elected Japanese politician of his day and one of four co-founders of his country's all-powerful Liberal Democratic Party.

Nishimura, like his fellow accused in Singapore, pleaded not guilty. From the witness box, he repeatedly attempted to describe for the court Tsuji's real role and responsibility as far as the Chinese Massacre was concerned.

He explained how, in the immediate aftermath of the fall of Singapore, men from his command had been seconded by and moved under the direct control of a 25th Army Headquarters' department headed by Tsuji. This department had been charged with "mopping-up" operations around the island.

The nub of Nishimura's defence was that any Imperial Guardsmen involved in the killings were under the control of and acting within another command structure at the time. His claims were entirely accurate. What was more, no evidence was ever produced by the prosecution to challenge them.

As the senior Japanese officer among seven to be tried for the Chinese Massacre in Singapore, General Nishimura leads his fellow defendants into the island's Victoria Memorial Hall under British Military guard.

General Nishimura wears an identification number before entering the Singapore court. Both pictures on this page clearly demonstrate Nishimura's height in relation to his British military guards.

Reinforcing his claim of non-involvement, Nishimura recounted how, two days after the British surrender on February 15, he had received instructions for his division to move to Sumatra by March 6. As a result, his time in Singapore had been completely dominated by the need to prepare for the foreward movement of his troops.

That the Guards had met their tight departure deadline was a matter of historical record. At no point did the prosecution make any attempt to challenge Nishimura's insistence that throughout the massacre time frame he had been fully occupied with other matters. Nor did they suggest he had ever been even remotely involved with the killings.

In the course of research for my previous book, *The killer they called a god"*, former 25th Army Intelligence Chief Sugita, then living in retirement in Tokyo, confirmed during a recorded interview details of Tsuji's activities in Singapore. He also revealed how Tsuji, on one occasion, had come to his home to apologise personally for the trouble he had caused over the Chinese Massacre. Sugita, who in the early 1960's went on to become Chief of Staff of Japan's Ground Self Defence Force, has since died. But the historically important tape recording of his remarks remains in my possession.

Nishimura and his six co-defendants were all found guilty by the disgracefully misdirected British court. General Kawamura and the *kempeitai* commanding officer, Lt. Colonel Masayuki Oishi, were sentenced to death. Nishimura, for his part, was ordered life imprisonment as were the remaining four *kempeitai* officers.

Given the conditions under which the trial was held, the tenuous legal arguments and sheer falsehoods of the prosecution's case, Nishimura's Singapore conviction and life sentence can only be viewed as major miscarriages of justice. That the former Imperial Guards commander went within a whisker of also being hanged in Changi Jail on this occasion remains a further indictment of the British trial procedure.

It required a unanimous vote among the five British officers hearing the case before a death penalty could be imposed on any of the defendants. The five fully concurred that General Kawamura and Colonel Oishi should hang. But when it came to deciding on the appropriate punishment for Nishimura, one of those sitting in judgement refused to go along with his four colleagues' insistence on a third death sentence.

The recalcitrant was Captain Robert H. Tyson, then a 22-year-old Japanese-speaking officer from the Intelligence Corps. He is, today, the only surviving member of the Chinese Massacre Trial bench and lives with his wife in retirement in Surrey, England. Tyson recalls that, from the evidence presented in court, he became deeply concerned over the extent of Nishimura's guilt. During the presiding tribunal's private deliberations he expressed strong preferences that Nishimura be given a life sentence rather than death. Tyson, the only Japanese-speaking officer on the bench, had been impressed, in part, by the straightforwardness of the evidence given by Nishimura while under oath in the witness box. Furthermore, the youthful British court member had been persuaded by Nishimura's "good bearing" throughout the trial and the "impressive responses" he had made under cross examination.

According to Tyson there was one other "vital point" in Nishimura's favour. Quite obviously the Imperial Guards commander had been under orders to plan "an imminent move to Sumatra and could not have had the time or inclination to get personally involved in the detail of the massacre."

Largely, these were the responses provided by Tyson when, some days after the conclusion of the hearing, he was summoned before the Judge Advocate General in Singapore and ordered to explain why he had been the odd man out when it came to sentencing Nishimura. After all, death had been the punishment recommended for Nishimura by the

Robert Tyson is the only surviving member of the five-man British Military Tribunal that tried General Nishimura at Singapore in early 1947. The lone dissenting vote of the then 22-year-old Tyson, a Japanese-speaking intelligence officer, saved Nishimura from the gallows on this occasion.

The Britsh Military Tribunal, convened in Singapore to try General Nishimura and six other Japanese officers for the Singapore Chinese Massacre, are shown taking their oath before commencement of the hearing. The youthful Tyson is on the extreme right.

prosecution and agreed to by his four decidedly more senior and experienced bench colleagues.

Tyson held firm. He knew very well the Judge Advocate General's enquiry had been prompted by the sudden threat of a political crisis in re-occupied Singapore. Within hours of the trial's conclusion on April 2, 1947, a group of prominent ethnic leaders had begun organising the Singapore Chinese Appeal Committee. There was widespread dismay among the island's dominant Chinese community that, of all people, Nishimura, the most senior officer in the defendant line-up and the "second tiger" to Yamashita, was escaping the gallows. The committee issued statements complaining of the "inappropriately lenient" sentences, demanding these be reviewed and agitating for all seven convicted Japanese to be put to death at a public execution.

The British quickly countered by announcing that the constitution of the War Crimes Courts simply prevented retrials and the imposing of heavier sentences. Behind scenes they worked feverishly to find a compromise acceptable to the local Chinese. This ultimately came in the form of manipulative execution theatrics.

It was discovered that a *kempeitai* officer, widely recognised as having been implicated in the Chinese Massacre affair had, prior to the Singapore trial, actually been convicted and sentenced to death in Kuala Lumpur. The crime for which he was due to die was unconnected to the Chinese Massacre. Seizing the opportunity, the British delayed his execution in Kuala Lumpur and quietly transferred him to Singapore. There they arranged to hang him — a substitute for Nishimura — at the same Changi Jail execution rites organised for General Kawamura and Lt. Colonel Oishi.

This extraordinary "three for the price of two" deal came accompanied by a British offer to allow eight representatives of the Chinese community — including two women — to witness the hangings. Placated but far from fully satisfied, the Chinese went along with these arrangements and the three Japanese jointly dropped to their deaths from the Changi scaffold at 8. 45 am on June 26, 1947.

As for Nishimura, he was driven back to Changi immediately following his sentencing and admitted as a "long sentence prisoner" with the number 1647/M312. On August 27, barely four months into his term, he was taken from his cell to a prison interview room where Captain Alwyn Sherlock, the investigator with 1 Australian War Crimes Section, was waiting to question him on Parit Sulong.

His meeting with Captain Sherlock would be the last Nishimura would hear about Parit Sulong for almost three years. On August 29, 1947, he was transferred from Changi to Singapore's Outram Road Jail where his prison record showed his life sentence was due to expire on April 1, 1967, and that he could expect 1,826 days remission of sentence for good behaviour. At very worst, he would be released on April 1, 1962. Chances were, the Allies and the Japanese would arrive at a political accommodation on war criminals long before this. As it happened, they did.

As the months of detention folded into years Nishimura regularly wrote to his wife, young son and daughter back in Japan. Eagerly he awaited their return correspondence. In the meantime, he took care to keep his prison record clear, determined that nothing should stand in the way of the ultimate reunion with his loved ones. It was the expectation of that reunion that alone kept him determined to survive his prison ordeal. By early 1950 just one slight blemish marked this otherwise model prisoner's slate. On October 15 the previous year, he refused a body search while warded at the Outram Road prison hospital. Guards eventually found him in possession of a single illegal cigarette. Prison authorities were to prove reasonable. After an enquiry, Nishimura was let off with a warning.

Chapter 5

The American Supremo's ultimatum

———— ✦ ————

ollowing the cessation of hostilities in the Pacific on August 15, 1945, the Allied powers involved undertook to prosecute suspected Japanese war criminals under two confusingly titled categories: "major" war criminals and "minor" war criminals.

"Major" war criminals were defined as Heads of State and responsible government officials, leaders, organisers, instigators and accomplices participating in the planning, preparation and initiation of warfare in violation of international treaties, agreements or assurances.

"Minor" war criminals were seen as those persons who, during the conduct of the war, had committed violations of the accepted laws and customs of warfare, such as murders, ill-treatment of prisoners etc., and who did not come under the "major" definition.

The IMTFE or "major" war crimes trial, began its deliberations in Tokyo on April 29, 1946 and lasted more than two and a half agonizing years. It was to give evidence before this tribunal that Colonel Cyril Wild flew to Tokyo on the assignment from which he would never return. He was one of 419 witnesses to appear before the international bench headed by Australia's celebrated jurist, Sir William Webb, Tribunal president. There were 818 court sessions covering 417 days during which 779 affidavits and depositions were presented. The recorded trial transcript ran to more than

50,000 pages and ten million words. It took seven months for the Tribunal to prepare its opinion which, on publication, was 1,218 pages long.

Seven of the 28 accused, including Japan's wartime leader, General Tojo, were sentenced to death. Sixteen were given life sentences. One received twenty years and another, seven years imprisonment. Two died during the hearing and one was deemed unfit to stand trial because of insanity.

"Minor" war criminals, for their part, were generally brought to trial by military courts of the countries whose nationals had been victims in the investigated incidents. Between 1946 and 1948 Australian military courts sitting at various times in Labuan, Wewak, Morotai, Rabaul, Darwin, Singapore and Hong Kong, dealt with a total of 270 separate trials involving 811 accused. From these deliberations resulted 143 death sentences of which 109 culminated in executions by hanging. The remaining 34 went before firing squads. In addition, another 432 Japanese appearing before Australian military courts received prison sentences ranging from a few months to life.

On March 17, 1947, the Allied Far Eastern Commission, reflecting growing political unease among victor nations over the whole issue of continuing war crimes trials, reiterated two earlier recommendations made to member governments. The first called for investigations, if possible, to be completed before June 30 that year — a cut-off date with just three months' leeway. Secondly, the commission urged that all trials should finish by September 30, 1949. In effect, this called for the entire Japanese war crimes issue to be wrapped-up within 18 months.

Through diplomatic and military channels the Americans, British and Dutch made clear to Canberra their concurrence with the commission's proposals. All aimed to phase-out their respective war crimes courts by late 1949. Australia, however, stood strongly opposed to such ideas.

Ignoring the commission, Canberra remained committed to investigating Japanese atrocities, searching for the perpetrators, carrying out arrests, detaining suspects and conducting trials. In April, 1948, Britain bluntly moved to undermine Australia's obvious enthusiasm for the post-war legal process. She served notice on the Australians to vacate the Hong Kong military court premises they had been occupying. Providing the decidedly flimsy excuse that accommodation was short in the colony, the British told the Australians to be out within four months. Undeterred, the Labour government of the day, headed by Prime Minister Benjamin Chifley, sought US approval for Australia's Hong Kong military court to transfer to Tokyo and there continue its functions.

Equally disenchanted by what they interpreted as Australia's apparent commitment to a never-ending war trials programme, the Americans, too, moved to curb Canberra. General Douglas MacArthur, Supreme Commander Allied Powers (SCAP) in occupied Japan, made sure that the entreaties of all senior Australian military and diplomatic officers sent to argue their country's case were firmly rebuffed.

By August, 1948, Washington moved to cap Australia's repeated approaches and flatly told the External Affairs department that SCAP could never entertain the idea of an Australian court opening in Japan more than three years after the war had ceased. The overriding inference was that Australia, by this time, should be setting vengeance to rest and concentrating on the infinitely more important post-war strategic problems associated with making peace in the Pacific work.

Unwilling to take *no* for an answer, Canberra immediately went back to the British who grudgingly stretched their Hong Kong quit order an extra three months. Instead of August, the Australians now had be be out by end November, 1948.

Having gained the briefest of breathing spaces the Australians inexplicably began knocking on American doors once again with new requests for Tokyo court facilities.

On November 18 that year, a draft Cabinet Agendum was submitted in Canberra recommending that war crimes' trials cease on the withdrawal of the military court from Hong Kong, an event only days away. Cabinet met on November 19. Instead of approving the recommendation, they directed that further consideration be given to "alternatives to ceasing the trials."

The Australian military court in Hong Kong duly shut down operations in December, 1948. No further trials were scheduled but investigations continued and 87 suspected Japanese war criminals that the Australians were hoping to put on trial remained locked in their cells in Tokyo's Sugamo prison, without any charges laid, without due process of the law and without any forseeable hope of release.

The next nine months saw an Australian Labour government transfixed by the prospect of an approaching election. Prime Minister Chifley and his Cabinet were unwilling to take any firm decision on the war trials issue — particularly one calling a halt to the programme — for fear it might trigger a detrimental reaction in the ballot boxes. Time and again, during this period, expert submissions were made at the highest levels for the trials to be dropped.

Repeatedly, the Government ignored the experts, both local and foreign, ultimately bowing to political pressures from the nation's influential post-war military establishment and her powerful returned services lobby which in those days centred on the Returned Sailors' Soldiers' and Airmen's Imperial League of Australia. (RSSAILA). (See glossary of abbreviations, page 277).

Paradoxically, it was a concluding American war crimes trial in Tokyo that brought matters to a head for Canberra. On September 6, 1949, after a marathon hearing lasting

*Prime Minister Benjamin Chifley failed to articulate a firm war
crimes policy for Australia from mid-1948 to late 1949. Throughout
this time the Labour leader ignored mounting international pressure
urging Canberra to abandon her seemingly endless plans to bring
suspected Japanese war criminals to trial by military courts. Chifley
feared a halt to the trials would trigger an adverse reaction in the
ballot boxes come the next elections. As it happened Labour was
voted out of office in December, 1949.*

nearly 11 months, Admiral Soemu Toyoda, formerly Commander-in-Chief of the Japanese Navy, walked from the dock a free man. All charges against him had been dismissed by a seven-man military tribunal headed by Australian Brigadier John O'Brien. The Admiral had been arrested by the Americans on December 12, 1945, and held in custody in Sugamo prison until his trial commenced on October 29, 1948, and thence until his ultimate release — a total of three years and nine months incarceration. He was the last high-ranking Japanese officer to be tried by the US and, as such, drew considerable attention from the international press. At a post-trial press interview Admiral Toyoda demanded: "What is Australia going to do about the 90 Japanese prisoners held in Sugamo Prison?"

Suddenly it became public knowledge that Australia, having failed to convene a war crimes court for almost a year, had been detaining in prison nearly 100 suspected Japanese through a special arrangement with the Americans. More embarrassing still, the Australians were continuing to press the Americans for additional arrests and were pushing ahead with further investigations of pending cases. These revelations came as the US was on the verge of announcing a formal end of its war trials. Britain, for her part, had ceased hers.

At AHQ, Melbourne, Lt. Colonel John W. Flannagan, had been Director of the Prisoners of War and Internees (DPW&I) section since 1946. As such, the 48-year-old trained barrister was responsible to the AG for all war crimes investigations. He was also the AG's top advisor on every related issue. When Flannagan read the cables from Tokyo in early September, 1949, he immediately saw the writing on the wall. By September 12 he had prepared a Minute Paper predicting serious consequences for the military should the government continue failing to formulate a war trials policy. He drew attention to various "soldier organisations" that were pressing for news of trials in which their units had specific interests.

"If further delay is incurred there may be serious repercussions and grave embarrassment may be caused to ourselves in the event of further enquiries of a similar nature," observed Flannagan. "Questions may well be asked in Parliament and the press may start a programme of adverse criticism. One press report on the delay in bringing suspects, who are in custody, to trial has already appeared," Flannagan added. This was, of course, a reference to Admiral Toyoda's outburst the previous week.

In the final paragraph of his Minute Paper, Flannagan sought permission to fly to Canberra for face-to-face discussions with the Prime Minister's Department and the Department of External Affairs. He wanted to present both with a full appreciation of the nature of the cases ready for trial and the problems the military were facing in the light of the latest US pressures. His final sentence summed up his frustrations: "It might also have the advantage of accelerating a decision."

Flannagan had only a day or two to wait for his predictions to materialise. Military cables from Tokyo reported that press representatives from AAP-Reuters were endeavouring to obtain information on Japanese war crimes suspects being held at Sugamo Prison by the Americans on behalf of the Australians. Right on the heels of these came other signals from the Japanese capital indicating the Americans now flatly refused to sanction the apprehension of any more Japanese on behalf of Canberra "until such time as we give them a definite understanding that suspects will be moved from Japan for trial by Australian courts."

US impatience with Canberra finally snapped on September 16, 1949. That afternoon the Australian Mission in Tokyo received a special communique from SCAP's Diplomatic Section. Sent on the personal directive of MacArthur, the message began by extending compliments to the Mission and expressing honour at being able to draw

American Supremo, General MacArthur, was deeply involved in a whole range of strategic problems at the time he was pressuring the Australians to release war crimes suspects in Tokyo. Here MacArthur (second from right) listens to Nationalist Chinese leader, Chiang Kai-shek (standing) briefing on the state of his war with the communists. Seated at the far left is MacArthur's controversial intelligence chief, General Willoughby.

Australia's attention to the plight of the 87 Japanese war criminal suspects confined in Japan under Canberra's orders. Diplomatic niceties stopped there. The remainder of the communique tore strips off the Australians.

"Of the 87 individuals," it pointed out, "eight have been confined for over 2 years, 18 from $1\frac{1}{2}$ to 2 years, 28 from 1 to $1\frac{1}{2}$ years, 22 from six months to a year and 11 under 6 months. One of the group has been imprisoned since April 8, 1947."

There had been no indication, the communique noted, of Australian authorities being prepared to accept delivery of the suspects for transfer to Sydney for trial. Prolonged detention of the accused without trial was "contrary to the fundamental concepts of justice," MacArthur informed the Australians. Under these circumstances, he said, "it would appear both just and appropriate to take positive action to remedy the situation."

It could, of course, be argued that MacArthur was the last

person qualified to champion fundamental concepts of military justice. His authority to do so had been so thoroughly undermined when, three years earlier, he personally choreographed the Manila show-trial and subsequent execution of General Yamashita.

Notwithstanding his blotted copy book, MacArthur's arguments still remained valid and, what was more, he wielded the power to make them sting. As the kicker to the communique, the American Supremo served notice he intended releasing all the detainees being held on behalf of the Australians in 45 days. The release, he maintained, would be without prejudice to their re-apprehension should the Australian government be ready and able to accept their deliverance for trial.

Not satisfied with the sizzling written word, MacArthur instructed several of his aides to drive home the same points in private conversations with senior members of 2 Australian War Crimes Section whose offices were conveniently located on the 7th floor of the Meiji Building. A section of the SCAP headquarters was housed in the same building which overlooked Tokyo's Imperial Palace.

Colonel Alva C. Carpenter, head of SCAP's legal section, wasted no time buttonholing Lt. Colonel D. Beresford Goslett, OC of the Australian office, soon after the US communique was delivered. The American made it plain that should Canberra fail to deliver a definite statement of policy before November 1, the Japanese suspects would certainly be released. Furthermore, US authorities in Tokyo would be forced to make a public statement explaining their action.

In reporting this conversation back to AHQ, Goslett wrote: "Just what that statement will contain I do not know, but I strongly suspect that it will not reflect any credit to Australia, and that it may probably be used to further capitalise the US Occupation Forces with the Japanese public to the possible detriment of our country."

With the ruling Labour party by this stage nursing a complete mental block on the war crimes issue, the Army hierarchy at Melbourne's St. Kilda Road Barracks began preparing worst-scenario contingency plans. What steps could the Army take if the Americans made good their threat? What were the legal rights and ramifications of such an American move? The mantle of responsibility at AHQ fell firmly on the legal expertise of the highly regarded Lt. Colonel Flannagan.

He began by advising that should the release take place, it would be virtually impossible, subsequently, to re-arrest the suspects as the Americans were suggesting. In a special paper, important for its insight into Australian Army thinking at the time, Flannagan set out to establish the legal foundations on which the nation's war crimes trials programme could continue.

One legal side-step to the American threat, actively under consideration by the Army at that time, was to have the Sugamo suspects technically transferred from US to British Commonwealth custody in Japan. But there was official unease over whether this might require an Act or Regulation before the Commonwealth Commanding Officer concerned could lawfully step into the breach. Flannagan advised he saw no need for any regulation of this nature. He was also able to set official minds at rest on the obviously delicate issue of *habeas corpus* and how this might apply to the Japanese under continuing detention. According to Flannagan's interpretation, the Commonwealth would not be liable to *habeas corpus* proceedings compelling the release of the suspects.

Flannagan's advice to the Army top brass continued:

A victorious belligerent is entitled under International Law to exercise authority as a victor over the vanquished to require any member or members of the Armed Forces of the defeated Power to answer for any proved breach of International Law.

After discussing the legal authority of the Japan-based British Commonwealth Occupation Force (BCOF) to hold prisoners and convene courts, Flannagan concluded his opinion:

The subject of an enemy State has no rights at all. He is liable to be seized and imprisoned and the action of the Executive Government in so seizing and imprisoning him is not open to review by the courts of law by habeas corpus. Accordingly, suspect war criminals may be continued to be held in custody until their trial by Australian Military Forces Courts is effected.

Tough advice, indeed. But it was all quite meaningless if the Americans went ahead and unlocked the Sugamo cells. Flannagan knew it. So did the Army's top brass. Meanwhile the country's Labour leaders continued to procrastinate, by now well aware that elections would be called sometime in December.

It was not until October 8, just 24 days to the US November 1 deadline, that the Australian Government finally got around to replying to MacArthur's "try them or we'll release them" ultimatum. The American General was informed that Canberra was considering establishing a military court at Manus Island. In view of this, would he kindly defer the release pending a final decision?

A now angry SCAP fired back a response leaving no doubt whatever he intended carrying through his threat.

"In as much as that Government has not however so far desired to take delivery of these suspects and since it now appears that no final decision has yet been taken as to whether they will actually be brought to trial, GHQ is unable to discover adequate grounds on which to justify their detention for a further indefinite period.

"More than four years after the termination of hostilities and from one to two years after the original apprehension of the majority of the suspects their continued incarceration without specific charges and without even a certain prospect of eventual trial can scarcely be reconciled with fundamental concepts of justice."

MacArthur went on to address the Far Eastern Commission's directive calling for investigations to be completed before June 30, 1949 and for all trials to be concluded, if possible, before September 30, 1949. His response continued:

"In view of the foregoing considerations GHQ finds itself constrained to adhere to its intention as set forth in the Diplomatic Section's communication of 16th September, 1949, which contemplated release of the suspects 45 days from the date of that note, that is on 31st October, 1949. If custody of these prisoners is not effected by the Australian Authorities by 1st November, 1949, they will accordingly be released from custody by the United States authorities who do not have, and never have had, charges against the Japanese concerned."

There was now the grave prospect of the whole war trials crisis exploding publicly into a humiliating Australian election issue, exposing chronic ineptitude on the part of the nation's Labour leaders. Internationally, the implications were equally serious. Here Australia faced the danger of being portrayed as so vindictive towards the Japanese that the US, her major Pacific War ally, was prepared to censure her publicly for being hopelessly out of step with the political realities of the day.

Prime Minister Chifley took one final uncharacteristic gamble to save the situation. He sought the personal intervention of the commander of the BCOF, Lt. General

Horace C. Robertson. While General Robertson was the top Commonwealth officer in Japan, he also happened to be an Australian. Chifley reasoned that if Australia's chips had run out at SCAP headquarters, perhaps the combined Commonwealth had influence on which he could call. Even should this plan fail, there was always the legal side-step — transferring custody of the suspects to the BCOF.

On October 26, five days to the American deadline, Canberra sent a personal brief to General Robertson requesting him to arrange an immediate interview with MacArthur. The idea was for the two military men to hold wide ranging discussions on the Australian problem. During these, Robertson was to inform MacArthur that Australia was finally prepared to commit to a time frame for the long awaited decision on the Japanese detainees. This decision would be forthcoming before January 1, 1950, Canberra promised. Would MacArthur assist by extending his deadline accordingly? Should MacArthur prove intractable, however, Robertson, as Commonwealth military chief, was instructed to take custody of the Japanese suspects on behalf of Australia before November 1 and await further instructions.

The gamble paid off. In the report of his meeting with MacArthur, Robertson was able to inform the Australian Government that the deadline would be extended to year's end. The understanding was that the Australian government's decision would be communicated confidentially and in time for an appropriate plan of action to be in place before the new January 1 deadline.

Interestingly enough, while the Australian Government had been floundering on the issue, MacArthur had ordered his command's legal experts to do their homework on the pending Australian cases. They had examined all evidence, the Supremo told Robertson, and considered that only eight of the remaining cases merited trial. The rest were considered doubtful of conviction or would only receive prison sentences, a substantial proportion of which, in each case, would have already been served in Sugamo during the long wait. In fact, MacArthur and his legal staff would subsequently revise upwards their advised prosecution list from eight cases to nine.

Robertson concluded his report: ***"I recommend that decision be taken to try the few serious cases in some place outside Japan and that authority be given to me to release as opportunity offers those against whom proceedings are not to be taken."***

The cases to which MacArthur referred, and on which Robertson was ultimately urging the Australians to proceed, involved a total of 36 suspects. Pointedly, among the many case files rejected by SCAP's legal experts was the one marked "Parit Sulong Massacre." The file had seen a flurry of renewed activity only days earlier as Australian investigators in Tokyo once more scrambled to have Nishimura implicated before the US boom finally lowered, halting their activities for all time. The Americans were convinced the Parit Sulong evidence gathered by the Australians thus far would never result in a conviction. As we will later discover, they also had strong reservations about the officer leading the investigations and the methods he was employing to build the prosecution case.

When the gist of Robertson's report reached Melbourne it triggered immediate dismay at AHQ. Records showed a total of 42 cases, involving 117 suspects, ready for trial. Of the then 92 suspects under detention at Sugamo Prison, 78 could be immediately charged with complicity in the 42 prepared cases. The remaining 14 were subject to on-going investigations. Another 25 suspects were available for arrest. If the Americans got their way, 81 suspected Japanese war criminals wanted for atrocities against Australian servicemen would escape judgement.

Once again Lt. Colonel Flannagan's persuasive PW&I

department swung into action. This time it made a study of the 34 cases rejected by the Americans. It urged nine of those cast aside be resurrected. At the top of the resurrected list was Serial Number 42, the Parit Sulong Case.

The study noted:

This case is one of the most bestial in war crimes records. Approximately 110 Australian and 40 Indian prisoners were machine gunned, then covered with petrol and set alight while many were still conscious.

Lt Gen Nishimura who gave the order on the spot for the massacre, and Lt Nonaka who passed on the order are available for trial. Nishimura is at present serving a life sentence in Singapore, but it is suggested that owing to the particular heinousness of the crime and the number of Australians involved, he be tried by an Australian court. Nonaka is available for arrest in Japan.

In connection with this crime, it is anticipated that a Lt Fujita, in charge of the executioners, and some members of an artillery unit who carried out the executions will soon be arrested.

Politicians, too, manoeuvred to add cases to MacArthur's list but, by mid-November, Prime Minister Chifley had announced elections would take place on Saturday, December 10. Campaigning was quickly underway in a critical election where socialism and the communist menace would become the turning issues. These would largely absorb Australia's attention while the still unresolved war crimes crisis rumbled awkwardly on, held in abeyance by Canberra's 11th hour commitment to a policy decision before January 1.

Early in the campaign, Labour's Minister for the Army, Mr Cyril Chambers, was forced to defend publicly his government's handling of the war trials issue. Less than truthfully, he claimed arrangements for holding the trials on

Manus Island had been concluded with General MacArthur "many weeks ago." Furthermore, he said, the trials would take place just as soon as suitable accommodation had been erected on the island. Certainly SCAP in Tokyo knew none of this. Neither did 2 Australian War Crimes Section operating within the Supremo's headquarters; nor, for that matter, did General Robertson, or the AHQ in Melbourne.

Alerted by Admiral Toyoda's remarks, the press had begun delving into the story. Although Australian military investigators in Tokyo had been gagged by order of Canberra, SCAP public relations men in late November were quietly disseminating snippets of telling information to chosen journalists. The aim was to maintain pressure on Canberra throughout the election campaign period. Whoever won at the polls — socialists or conservatives — there would be no mistaking MacArthur's determination to wrap-up war trials and hold Australia to her word.

On December 5, five days before election day, *The Sydney Morning Herald* ran an editorial headed: **Australian Bungling Of War Trials.** The newspaper took Army Minister Chambers and the government to task for "inexcusable tardiness" that might have remained unchallenged but for the threatened American prisoner release.

"The Minister denies that there has been 'apathy.' Perhaps most Australians could think of a better word — 'bungling,' for instance," said the editorial. It recalled that regulations under which special military courts were constituted to deal with war crimes had been first gazetted in October, 1945. The first Japanese tried by an Australian Court had been found guilty at Morotai over four years previously. *"It could, therefore, be said that we made an expeditious enough beginning with this grim business. But today every other nation that had charges to pursue against the Japanese has finished its proceedings."*

The editorial concluded with a reflective observation. *"It is clear, from comments widely made, that no one resents the Government's fumbling in this matter more than the Australians who fought the Japanese on land and sea and in the air. The 'Nips' were dirty fighters, and justice demanded that the crimes they committed should be sheeted home. But the average ex-Serviceman feels that if they were to get what was coming to them they should have got it quick, not least because that might have made some beneficial impression on Japanese public opinion. Now, when others have wiped the slate, our belated proceedings will be regarded as mere vindictiveness. It is not enough to do justice. We should also appear to do it."*

If these sentiments mirrored the average ex-serviceman's viewpoint, he and the paper's editorial writer would have been shattered by the truth of what was happening behind scenes. For the custody crisis in Tokyo was just the tip of the iceberg. An obsession to justify the Pacific conflict's final round of war crimes trials had seized certain members of the Australian military both in Tokyo and Melbourne. International opinion be damned. For them, the Parit Sulong affair encapsulated everything they wanted to say in court, one last time, about the Japanese. What was more, the high ranking Nishimura, former commander of the Japanese Emperor's personal troops, the other Tiger of Malaya, represented an irresistible target for public retribution. His conviction was a must.

Prime Minister Robert Menzies inherited a languishing, directionless war crimes programme when his Liberal-Country Party Coalition came to power in December, 1949. In a speech to Parliament two months later he described the lead up to the Manus Trials as a "wretched state of affairs in which justice is denied because it is delayed." He promised prompt trials at Manus "consistent with the processes of justice." After a prompt enough trial, General Nishimura spent almost a year in solitary confinement while a bumbling Army bureaucracy seemed incapable of acting on his appeal.

Chapter 6

Reconsidering
a judicial lynching

———— ✦ ————

I n late 1949, Australia's ruling Labour Party was not alone
in its assessment of the combined political clout of the
country's military establishment and the RSSAILA. Three
days before the December 10 polls, the opposition Liberal
Party, headed by Mr Robert Menzies, took out prominent
advertisements in Sydney newspapers. These displayed
head-and-shoulder photographs of the party's candidates in
electorates throughout New South Wales. Under the heading
"A Splendid Team" the copy read: "A team that will pull
together. Eighty-four percent of these Liberal Party
Candidates are ex-servicemen. You can find no finer or more
able men anywhere to watch over your interests in
Parliament."

Quite clearly, both sides of the nation's political divide
recognised the vigour of the military vote and the surges of
national pride, gratitude and sympathy that accompanied it.
The country's moral debt to her fighting man was enormous.
Her victorious servicemen could do little wrong. Even if they
did, no leading politician of the day, protective of his public
destiny, would ever consider seriously grappling with them
on points of Pacific War morality or legal rectitude.
Particularly so, if it meant appearing in any way to champion
a Japanese cause.

The climate could not have been better for well placed,
like-minded Army officers considering a judicial lynching of

the highest ranking Japanese military figure reasonably available. Those conversant with the provisions of the Australian War Crimes Act of October, 1945, knew exactly how these could be manipulated to maximum advantage. The press could be controlled, moulded and diverted. Most important of all, official tracks could be concealed and secrets preserved.

The December 10, 1949 election was a resounding victory for the Liberal-Country Party coalition led by Mr Menzies. The new government's first working Cabinet meeting took place on December 19. Top item on the agenda called for a major decision on a war trials policy. The next day, General Robertson in Tokyo was ordered to inform MacArthur that Australia intended proceeding with "utmost expedition," on the nine serious cases the Supremo had originally recommended. In addition, the government favoured the proposal of releasing unwanted prisoners at Sugamo in small groups to avoid unnecessary embarrassment. Robertson would soon be reporting to Prime Minister Menzies how a "helpful and friendly" MacArthur had welcomed the Australian decision and had offered "all the co-operation he could give."

Privately, MacArthur was relieved at the news from Canberra. Unbeknown to the Australians, he had been agonizing for several weeks over intelligence reports suggesting the Soviet Union was on the verge of pressing for the extradition of Emperor Hirohito. Indications were that the Russians wanted to place Hirohito and four Japanese generals on war criminal charges before a Soviet military court. Should the request be forthcoming — and eventually it was — MacArthur had firmly resolved to rebuff it. He intended emphasising to the Russians that the US was committed to phasing out war crimes trials and on the point of doing so. But the Japanese suspects he held on behalf of Australia threatened to torpedo his stand.

Back in Canberra it was taking the government three weeks to tie up loose ends. There was a requirement to digest input from interest groups. Adjustments had to be made. At a Cabinet meeting on January 10, 1950, the Menzies government reiterated its intention of proceeding with MacArthur's nine cases. But there would need to be some last minute additions to the trial list.

Cabinet decided these could also be heard at Manus as long as they met certain criteria. They must come within the same "serious crimes" category as the MacArthur nine. Each additional case had to be specifically recommended for trial by the AG and approved by the Army Minister. Only suspected war criminals whose cases were ready for trial could be prosecuted. Finally, the complete list must be determined by the minister within a month.

In the meantime the Department of Works and Housing was ordered to provide temporary accommodation on Manus for the suspects, the Japanese Defence Team and 1 Australian War Crimes Section. This would entail renovation and building work estimated to cost about A£7,000. Additionally, the Army was instructed to make arrangements for the movement by sea of all suspects required for trials and to ready the Military Court and attendant administrative personnel.

Following the January 10 meeting, the newly installed Army Minister, Mr Josiah Francis, prepared a press release. Issued the following day, it gave a run-down of the Cabinet's decisions. It concluded: "The Government considers there has been an inordinate delay bringing Japanese suspects now held in Sugamo Prison to justice. It is determined that there shall be no further time lag in bringing the accused to trial."

The Menzies Government then launched a number of damage control measures. Some of these were aimed at restoring Australia's credibility among her wartime allies via diplomatic channels. Others were geared to the homefront where there was a perceived requirement to restrict and manage all information on the evolving trial process and related issues. On January 13, a secret order was despatched from AHQ to 2 Australian War Crimes Section in Tokyo.

It read:

ALL INVESTIGATIONS TO CEASE FORTHWITH. INSTRUCTIONS REGARDING REDUCTION STRENGTH YOUR SECTION FOLLOW.

On the same day another signal from AHQ ordered Australia's Tokyo-based investigating staff to refrain from any public statements on the remaining trials. Almost identical orders were repeated to the same Tokyo office on January 18. Then, driving home the point even further, a signal to Tokyo on February 24 ordered:

ALL MEMBERS YOUR SECTION TO BE INSTRUCTED THAT THEY WILL NOT DISCLOSE ANY INFO CONCERNING WAR CRIMES SUSPECTS OR TRIALS OR ANY ASSOCIATED MATTER EXCEPT IN COURSE OF MILITARY DUTIES.

The fact that Australia's war crimes team was operating in occupied Japan largely unhindered by the repercussions of publicity is an important aspect of this story.   Orders forbidding staff members to comment on their work and avoid all contact with the press had been initiated as early as August, 1949, by the previous Labour government. Significantly, the outset of the press blackout coincided exactly with the beginning of the Army's rejuvenated drive to indict Nishimura.   The Menzies government's follow-up measures ensured that the information clamp-down in Tokyo would remain for the duration of the Army's war crimes duties.

Related press stories from the Japanese capital invariably referred to the lack of cooperation on the part of Australian investigators. On December 3, 1949, for instance, an AAP-Reuter correspondent lamented in the middle of his report: *"Lt. Colonel D. Goslett, commanding officer of the Australian war crimes detachment in Tokyo has consistently declined in recent months to give any information regarding the number of prisoners at Sugamo, or any other details."*

If it was easy to impose information controls on the Australian Army office in Tokyo, it was easier still repeating the process for associated departments in Australia. So it was that the entire business of preparing the nation's final war crimes cases for trial was afforded the highest possible protection from public scrutiny. In addition, those involved gained further comfort from the knowledge that the trials, ostensibly in open courts, were still to be held on isolated Manus Island. Herein lay very special advantages when it came to the management of information.

No less a military figure than the AG himself, Major General Anderson, was acutely aware of these. Indeed, he took the trouble of drawing them to the Army Minister's attention in a special report dated January 6, 1950. Opting for Manus as the trial venue in preference to Port Moresby, the AG advised: ***"Because of the predominantly service population at Manus, it is hoped to avoid publicity by holding trials at that location."***

His report went on to become Appendix "C" to the Army Minister's submission to Cabinet for the all-important January 10 meeting. As such it became part of the basic document from which arrangements for Australia's final war trials were formulated.

It is difficult to determine at what moment the decision was taken within the Army to re-address the possibility of charging Nishimura. A likely date is sometime in April, 1949, when Major H. F. Dick, a legal officer within the PW & I department, was involved reviewing files. On re-examining the Parit Sulong Massacre folder, which had been virtually dormant for two years, the major prepared a special legal advisory on the case. In it he referred to Hackney's evidence of the high-ranking officer appearing to issue orders. But he also underlined the problems posed by Hackney's subsequent failure to identify Nishimura as that officer. There was insufficient information, he said, to charge anyone with personal participation.

Major Dick's report went on to suggest that sufficient evidence did exist, however, to support a charge of "command responsibility" against Nishimura. He also felt a similar charge could be sustained against Colonel Takeo Iwakuro, 5th Regiment commander, who had been identified by Nishimura as the officer responsible for holding the north side of the Parit Sulong bridge.

The Dick report is important for two reasons. Firstly, it articulated quite clearly the PW&I department's recognition of the critical stumbling block posed by the failed identification. Secondly, the Army hierarchy's lack of enthusiasm for the "command responsibility" route suggested by Dick would have served clear notice on investigators about the type of charges required before this case could proceed.

International legal opinion was by then demanding war crimes charges against Japanese suspects be more specific. The broad parameters offered by "command responsibility" — used so successfully for convictions during early war trials — had become largely unacceptable. So, any investigating officer anxious to nail Nishimura in mid-1949 had to find an alternate route around the fundamental flaw to the credibility of Hackney's evidence. There could be no falling back on "command responsibility."

Major Dick's recommendations probably revived lagging interest in the case. Yet it would take another four months before Army sleuths finally came close to learning the truth about Parit Sulong.

Chapter 7

Letting the killer walk free

———————— ✦ ————————

C aptain James Gowing Godwin arrived in Tokyo in early July 1947 with glowing recommendations from military authorities in Wellington. As far as Australia's office in the Meiji building was concerned, the 24-year-old New Zealander's background seemed tailor-made to his secondment as a war crimes investigator.

On completing training as a pilot at Woodborne Airport near his hometown of Blenheim on the northern reaches of New Zealand's south island, Godwin was posted briefly to Wigram Airbase near Canterbury in 1942. Eventually he moved to Canada for advanced training. In 1943, at the age of 20, he joined the Fleet Air-Arm with a lieutenant's commission and saw service in the Indian Ocean region aboard the aircraft carrier, *HMS Illustrious.*

Following home leave, Godwin was returning to Colombo to rejoin *Illustrious* on March 9, 1944, when the 8,000-ton merchantman on which he was a passenger was sunk by shell fire from a Japanese cruiser some 340 miles north-west of the Cocos Islands. Captured by the cruiser's crew, the young pilot was first interned in a prison camp near Batavia (now Jakarta) and eventually transported to Japan where he arrived on June 28, 1944. During 18 months as a POW, the 6 ft. 2 in.-tall Godwin suffered fearful ill-treatment at the hands of his captors. He was repeatedly beaten and tortured, deprived of medical aid, and subjected to a near-starvation diet. When captured, Godwin had weighed 214 pounds. When liberated at war's end, he weighed 85 pounds.

While in captivity, Godwin had picked up a smattering of Japanese and had also gathered first-hand insight into the enemy nation's wartime psyche. Together with his general background, it was thought the 15 months he had spent incarcerated in Japan would stand him in good stead when it came to deciphering the outpourings of devious Japanese war crimes suspects under interrogation.

Quite unnoticed, it seems, was the enormous amount of emotional baggage accompanying Godwin when he clocked-on with Australian investigators. Months of convalescence in New Zealand might have restored the handsome pilot, sporting an Errol Flynn moustache, to his old physical self. But his traumatic wartime experiences had left him in psychological torment. Secretly he believed fate had allotted him a special post-war mission. On June 30, 1947, a fortnight before joining 2 Australian War Crimes Section, Godwin, now in Army Intelligence, confided to his diary:

"I declare my determination to bring as many of these cowardly bastards who beat up old men and women, to justice. I witnessed all the horrors of captivity, and endured them to a point and on many occasions, exhaustion. I was beaten and clubbed almost senseless many times over. I saw brave Allied servicemen beheaded and a very sick old man clubbed to death. At POW Camp 15D in Japan, I was almost starved to death and saw many fellow prisoners who simply died from forced labour, medical neglect and appalling malnutrition. To all those who suffered and perished I am resolved to do my best to atone their miseries and deaths, unlamented as seemingly they are. Fate has given me the opportunity to represent the victims of Japanese barbarity in a most privileged and sacred task. I will speak for all those who perished at the hands of the Japanese. I can do no less."

In the months that followed, Godwin immersed himself in

his personal mission and made extensive notations in his diary as he did so. Colleagues in the Australian section came to regard him as brash and opinionated, but decidedly dedicated to the task at hand. They dismissed his sometimes overly zealous approach to work as the exuberance and idealism of youth.

The Americans in SCAP's legal section with whom the Australian office was required to maintain close liaison took a decidedly different view of the New Zealander. At first they expressed their criticisms of his activities verbally and mildly. But as the months passed they resolved that more formal complaints about Godwin had to be lodged with the Australian office. Before this occurred, however, Godwin had been placed in charge of the revived Parit Sulong Massacre investigations

By August 1949, Godwin held a master list of 376 names of Imperial Guards officers, culled from SCAP's extensive research and archive facilities. From this basic document, he had compiled two sub-lists: 5th Regiment officers and Command staff officers. His plan was first to establish who travelled in the Nishimura motorcade on January 22, 1942. From there he intended producing evidence to incriminate the divisional commander. Once again it was an investigation geared to the contents of the Hackney statement.

But a programme requiring such extensive tracing activities was, in the second half of 1949, a most optimistic pursuit. It was well recognised throughout SCAP military circles that prospects for continuing war crimes trials were indeed bleak. Inter-office scuttlebutt was even predicting 2 Australian War Crimes Section might well be closed down and withdrawn home by early new year. Godwin was undeterred. His mission now was to secure as many arrests and convictions as he could in the time remaining.

Australian investigators followed an effective, if laborious, system of rounding up Japanese officers considered likely sources of information on active cases. They filled in appropriate forms giving details of the men they required for interrogation. The forms were lodged with the US legal section on the 8th floor of the Meiji Building. Barring hitches, these requests set in motion commands to Japanese civilian authorities culminating in various district police stations being directed to locate the wanted men. The system ensured that the US Legal Section could monitor Australian enquiries at all times and keep close tabs on cases as they developed. SCAP was the dominant authority and its overseeing role the source of much irritation within the Australian camp. There was no greater critic of US interference than the brash New Zealander.

On August 23, 1949, Godwin selected the name "Tozaburo Fujita" from his main list of Imperial Guards officers. Enquiries led the investigator to suspect that Tozaburo Fujita might well be a mis-representation of the name Seizaburo Fujita. The latter was identified in SCAP files as once being a "general duties" officer attached to the 2nd Battalion of the Imperial Guards' 5th Regiment. As the 2nd Battalion had, by this time, been verified involved in the Parit Sulong action, perhaps Seizaburo Fujita could help investigations. As luck would have it, the archives could even provide a home address for the 39-year-old Fujita: Kanagawa-kan, Yokosuka-Zushi, Sakurayama, 2,260 banchi. In the closing days of August, Godwin filled out the *Request for Interrogation* form, submitted it to the US Legal Section and prepared to wait.

By September 4, an officer from the Zushi police station was calling on Fujita, demanding he present himself at the Meiji Building. Dutifully, Fujita informed his employer, the Asahi Chemical and Synthetic Industry Co., that he would be absent the following day. But when Fujita arrived at the Meiji Building on September 5, he discovered every office closed. It was a US holiday and the Australians had taken it as well.

A lone duty officer requested Fujita return 24 hours hence.

Fujita did as he was told. It wasn't long into the interrogation before Godwin realised that the former second lieutenant sitting opposite him was far more than just a "possible witness." Seizaburo Fujita had not only been in Parit Sulong with the 2nd Battalion of the 5th Regiment. He had, in fact, been the officer directly in charge of all captured wounded there. More than that, he had been their executioner. Seizaburo Fujita was the Parit Sulong killer!

Godwin interrogated with the assistance of US Army Sgt. Dix Asai, a nisei-American interpreter. The interview ran slowly, dragging into a second session the next day. It concluded about midday on September 7. An utterly inexplicable turn of events then followed.

After reviewing the notes he had taken throughout the two-part interrogation, Godwin decided the statement he wanted Fujita to swear could not be prepared and typed before the following day. The investigator told Fujita to go home and return the next morning for the required oath and signing. Not surprisingly Fujita departed the Meiji Building that afternoon never to return.

An unsigned Fujita statement, purportedly prepared by Godwin from his notes, would later be submitted by Australian prosecutors as damning evidence against Nishimura. They would claim it a true record of remarks made by the former second lieutenant in response to questions put by Godwin over the two-day period.

Both statement and interrogation should have become targets for highly critical challenges long before the Nishimura trial ever got underway. Neither did.

As it stood, the unsigned document (See Appendix A page 309) ran for 1,143 words. The first 235 words comprised a brief summary of Fujita's military history from December, 1941, until February 1, 1942. The remainder amounted to an account of his experiences for the two-day period leading up to the massacre. It was the precision of these details, considering they were being recalled seven years, seven months and 16 days after the event, that should have given rise to immediate suspicions. In turn, these suspicions should have magnified had comparisons been made between the statement prepared in Fujita's name and evidence provided three and a half years earlier by Hackney. The correlation between them was simply too close.

The Fujita document revealed how he had remained behind at the township of Bakri on the morning of January 21 while his battalion continued its advance down the road to Parit Sulong in pursuit of the Australians. He had been appointed OC of a burial party and ordered to stay back and clear the battlefield of Japanese dead. They were to be buried where they had died, a task that took Fujita and his men all day to complete. That evening, together with his burial party, he advanced towards Parit Sulong, stopping overnight in the jungle near a deserted village.

The narrative dealt with Fujita arriving at his unit's headquarters at 0700 hours on January 22 and discovering the enemy were about 1,500 to 2,000 metres further down the road. The battle for the Parit Sulong bridge still raged. When the sound of fighting ceased, he moved with his headquarters in the direction of the township.

Fujita then reportedly walked 1,000 to 1,500 metres to a point where he saw units of his battalion resting "about 30 to 40 metres in and to the right of the road." At this place he encountered "a large number of naked Indian and Caucasian prisoners of war." They were "grouped in a circle in front of two buildings located about 20 metres in from the right-hand side of the road and about 80 metres away from where we turned off to join up with the battalion." The document recorded Fujita as claiming he only "glanced" at this group of prisoners for "about a minute." Some of the prisoners were standing. Others were sitting down.

In one particular three-minute interval, Fujita counted "about 30 Australian prisoners of war in various postures." At the same time he noted the continuous movement of Australian prisoners in and out of a building. As he had not looked inside the building he was unable to state "how many prisoners of war were confined therein at that particular time." In the same three-minute time frame, Fujita had noticed one Indian officer but no other Indian prisoners of war.

The document went on to record that Fujita received verbal orders from his battalion adjutant, Lt. Sugihara, at 1630 hours. These tasked him to remain behind as the officer in charge of Australian and Indian prisoners. In addition, members of the battalion's artillery platoon were to remain behind at Parit Sulong and relieve 7 Company guarding the captives. Lt. Sugihara also instructed Fujita to contact Division headquarters "and make necessary arrangements for the removal of the prisoners of war to echelons in the rear."

In its penultimate paragraph the document noted Fujita had been unable to contact divisional headquarters before Lt. General Nishimura and a group of staff officers arrived on the scene. It described Nishimura conducting an inspection of prisoners and afterwards turning and speaking to the personal aide accompanying him.

By this point, four lines of the statement — a total of 51 words — remained.

They read:

"The aide then came over to me and said, 'It is the General's order that you execute all the prisoners of war, or words to that effect.

"After the General and his staff officers had left I caused the prisoners of war to be executed by machine-gun and rifle fire."

There the unsigned Fujita statement abruptly ended.

None of the Australian Army authorities associated with the case — senior investigators, PW & I department, AG's office, prosecutors, or members of the Military Court — ever felt compelled to question this preposterous document. Neither did they enquire as to its highly irregular preparation. Nor did the Army ever hold an official probe into the affair. It was as though there was nothing unusual about the Parit Sulong killer, the man for whom the Army had been searching for over four years, strolling into the Tokyo office, openly admitting he'd slaughtered more than 150 wounded prisoners, then being allowed — if not encouraged — to walk away.

Nobody apparently thought it worth asking Godwin why, after two intense interrogating sessions, Fugita's statement had been so short and his all-important confession confined to an almost throw-away last sentence, 24 words in length.

Had those 24 words really been Fujita's final answer to Godwin's concluding question? After the suspect had so succinctly confessed to one of the most beastial crimes in Pacific War history, had Godwin then said something to the effect: "Well, thank you very much Fujita-san. You can go home now. Please drop by tomorrow to sign your statement"? Had Godwin not thought it relevant, under the circumstances, to check aspects of the killing? Had the victims been roped and wired together in groups of 20 or 25? Was it true the bodies had been torched after the shooting with many of the victims still alive? If so, who had given the cremation order?

Had the interrogator not thought it worthwhile establishing with Fujita the time lapse between Nishimura departing Parit Sulong and the outset of the killing? Given Fujita's claim to have spent the previous day burying bodies of battalion comrades killed by the Australians, had the pertinence of determining his emotional attitude when appointed OC enemy prisoners somehow slipped by Godwin? Had Fujita felt compassion towards the wounded captives? Was he indifferent? Or had he, perhaps, been desperate to revenge the deaths of those whose graves he

The self confessed mass killer who was allowed to walk away. This picture of Lt. Seizaburo Fujita was taken from the investigation file of Captain Godwin.

had dug the previous day? Bearing in mind that the man had subsequently murdered all those in his charge, were these areas really unworthy of exploration?

Looking at the interrogation more generally, surely Fujita's verbal answers to Godwin's questions must have been couched in substantially different phraseology to remarks claimed as his in the unsworn statement?

Hadn't Godwin, in fact, put words into Fujita's mouth during the interrogation and again during the preparation of the statement? If so, what exactly had he done to massage the interrogation process?

If not, how did Godwin account for the overall tenor of the document he had prepared? It was purportedly the responses of a Japanese educated junior officer. Yet throughout, it exhibited distinctly English-educated overtones in terms of both organisation and approach to narrative. In fact, its choice of vocabulary was demonstrably un-Japanese. (See Appendix A, page 309.)

Australian files in Tokyo were packed with translated

121

interrogation statements reflecting the Japanese backgrounds, thought processes and phraseology of suspects under interrogation. None of them read like the Fujita document. None of them would read like any of the other affidavits to be prepared by Godwin for submission at the Nishimura trial.

From the purely investigative viewpoint, Fujita's unsigned statement neatly dissolved all legal hurdles that had long stood in the way of the Army bringing the case to conclusion. It replaced Hackney's failure to recognise Nishimura with a firm identification. Just as telling, it provided a much needed response to Nishimura's insistence that the only order he ever gave for prisoners was to have them moved to the rear. Here was Fujita confirming this had indeed been the original order but that the general himself had countermanded it on the spot.

At this point it is worth considering what the Army's reaction to Godwin's machinations might have been had an account of Fujita's sudden disappearance, together with an exposé of his known involvement at Parit Sulong, become matters of public record. However, with the information black-out firmly in place, both Godwin and the Army were quite safe.

Knowingly concealing a massive investigative blunder — if it was indeed a blunder — 2 Australian War Crimes Section allowed Godwin to pursue his line of detection unimpeded. All that really remained for the New Zealander now was to provide verification of the events as supposedly recalled by Fujita and the case against Nishimura was complete. Whatever the real cause of Fujita's disappearance, there were distinct advantages having him out of the picture. If he had been arrested and charged as the killer, his story would have undoubtedly changed drastically. This, in turn, would have seriously undermined the case against Nishimura.

Clearly, it was far more advantageous to have the required verification come from less involved sources. In this context it is fair to say that Colonel Cyril Wild was not the only military investigator of the era to have been aware that Japanese junior officers and other ranks under interrogation for war crimes were frequently ready to incriminate their seniors, and vice versa.

Two days later, on September 9, Lt. Colonel Goslett, OC 2 Australian War Crimes Section, filled out a *Request for Apprehension* form. (See Appendix B, page 318.) Addressed to the Criminal Registry Division, Apprehension Branch, it asked that Lt. Seizaburo Fujita be apprehended and interned in prison for trial as a suspect war criminal. The charge: *Murder of about 150 Australian and Indian prisoners of war in January, 1942.*

Under the section of the form requesting a synopsis of evidence to support charges, Goslett had typed the intriguing response: *Sworn statements held by this Division.* There were only two sworn statements of substance in the Parit Sulong file at this point — Hackney's and Nishimura's — and neither made any reference whatever to Fujita. Goslett's *sworn statements* line could only have been referring to the Fujita document prepared by Godwin. This was most definitely unsworn. Could this have been merely a clerical error by the Australian team? Or were there other explanations for the false entry?

Goslett submitted his form to SCAP's Legal Section on the day he wrote it. Exactly a week later, he was informing Melbourne that the Americans were refusing to apprehend any further Japanese suspects on behalf of the Australians until Canberra confirmed a policy for holding trials. Mass-murderer-on-the-run Fujita simply couldn't have asked for a better break — or made better use of it.

By this stage, Captain Godwin was determined American intransigence would not bring his new found momentum to a standstill. So the Fujita disappearance presented complications. So what! Fortunes could change — and change quickly — especially within the protected world the politicians and Army top brass had ensured for their Tokyo sleuths.

In the space of seven days, Godwin would be awash with good fortune. Two former Imperial Guardsmen he had summoned to the Australian office were able, between them, to provide an accurate run-down of the junior officers formerly working on Nishimura's staff. Both supplied direct leads to three particular staff officers known to have accompanied the Guards' divisional commander in Parit Sulong. Furthermore, the identified trio conveniently resided in Tokyo.

Godwin quickly traced and interrogated the three staff officers. The workload was such that he now required two interpreters — his old companion, US Sgt. Dix Asai, and another nisei American, US Sgt. Fred Oshima. From voluminous notes he had taken during lengthy interrogation sessions, Godwin prepared three tightly worded personal statements. The three interviewees were each asked to swear and sign their respective affidavits on different days. From the Australian standpoint, the affidavits represented the recollections of three individuals, speaking quite independently, each recalling events that had occurred seven years and eight months previously. There had been no collusion between the three signatories and, of course, no manipulation of their statements in any way by Godwin. It is most revealing, then, to compare the three documents against this supposed background of strict adherence to the pro-prieties of gathering evidence. (See Appendix A, pp. 294 – 307.)

All three accounts were in the English language only and their formats were identical. Each began with the same preamble stating the name, address and occupation of the signatory. This was followed by recognitions that they were under oath to tell the truth according to the dictates of their consciences. They would conceal nothing nor would they add to the facts.

The three former officers were Tadahiro Inagaki, who signed his affidavit on October 3, Harumitsu Sono, on October 14, and Fukashi Hinokuma on October 18.

The first paragraph of each statement comprised a brief summary of the signatory's military history over the period December, 1941, to February, 1942. This was followed by a paragraph detailing their respective positions within the Guards' headquarters, other officers with whom they worked and confirmation that Lt. General Nishimura and Colonel Kamejiro Imai had been, respectively, the divisional CO and chief of staff during the Malayan Campaign.

Inagaki, who had been a second lieutenant, said he was a liaison and administrative officer. Sono had been a captain and second senior adjutant to Nishimura. Hinokuma was also a captain and had been Staff Officer Intelligence.

The third paragraph of each affidavit began identically: "The following is briefly what I recall of my movement and events pertaining thereto from the Bakri area to Batu Pahat: . . . ."

The common introduction itself, displayed most unlikely Japanese phraseology.

All three statements then went on to provide disturbingly matching recollections of the convoy which had transported Nishimura and his immediate staff along the Parit Sulong road. Again, they gave almost word-for-word accounts of the convoy's arrival in the township.

When it came to the critical chronicling of the scene in the vicinity of the prisoners, there was further uncanny similarity in, not only the physical factors being recalled, but also the descriptive words and phrases used in the separate accounts. Equally disturbing were the extraordinary parallels between, on the one side, the former three staff officers' recollections and, on the other, the evidence provided by Hackney.

The accounts of Nishimura issuing the vital killing orders bore the same numbing resemblances one to another.

Inagaki: "After Lt. General Nishimura had stepped down off the porch and rejoined us other officers, he turned to Lt. Nonaka who was standing beside him and gave him, as far as I can now recall, the following oral order:

"'Instruct the officer in charge of the prisoners of war' (rank and name was stated but I now cannot remember same) 'to execute all the prisoners of war by firing squad, and then cremate their dead bodies.'"

Sono: "Almost immediately after Lt. General Nishimura and others had descended the steps and rejoined us other officers, he turned to his personal aide, Lt. Nonaka Shoichi, who was standing near him, and in the hearing of all those officers present, including myself, gave him, as far as I can now recall, the following oral order:

"'Instruct the officer in charge of the prisoners of war' (rank and name was stated but I now cannot remember same) 'to execute all the prisoners of war by firing squad.'"

Hinokuma: "After Lt. General Nishimura and others had stepped down from the porch and rejoined the other officers, he turned to his personal aide, Lt. Nonaka, and in the hearing of all those officers present, including myself, gave him, as far as I can now recall, the following oral order:

"'Instruct the officer in charge of the prisoners of war' (rank and name was stated, but I now cannot remember same) 'to execute all prisoners of war in a suitable manner.'"

It was almost as though a single source had dictated the three separate accounts, purposely inserting slight variations as transparently empty gestures to authenticity. Digressions from the set line were, more often than not, rationalised later in the affidavits.

Sono in his statement, for instance, went on to suggest that the command to cremate had actually not come from Nishimura, but from Chief of Staff Imai:

Sono noted: "Before Lt. Nonaka could turn to relay Lt. General Nishimura's order to the officer concerned, Colonel

Imai Kamejiro gave him the following additional order:

"'The bodies of the prisoners of war will be cremated on completion of the execution.'"

The fourth paragraphs in the statements by Sono and Hinokuma neatly addressed the cremation confusion. Once again these supposedly independent accounts exhibited a quite unnatural kinship.

Sono's read: "Before and during the Malayan Campaign it was obvious to me and all other headquarters officers that Lt. General Nishimura Takuma and Colonel Imai Kamejiro were not on friendly terms with one another. On most occasions Colonel Imai added to or varied Lt. General Nishimura's orders. His action, therefore, to Lt. General Nishimura's order in regard to the disposal of the prisoners of war at Parit Sulong was not unusual."

Hinokuma's ostensibly independent statement explained it this way: "Before and during the Malayan Campaign it was obvious to me and all other headquarters officers that Lt. General Nishimura Takuma and Colonel Imai Kamejiro were not on friendly terms with one another. On most occasions Colonel Imai's opinions differed from those of Lt. General Nishimura, and because of this he invariably added to or varied the latter's orders. Because of this unusual situation, I believe that Lt. General Nishimura did not discuss the matter of the disposition of the prisoners of war at Parit Sulong with Colonel Imai before or after his arrival there, and that the order for their execution was given arbitrarily by him."

Godwin's last interrogation in the case was of Shoichi Nonaka, now well identified as the aide to whom Nishimura had supposedly passed the killing order. Nonaka, aged 37, had been a lieutenant at the time of the Parit Sulong Massacre and had been promoted to Captain before his discharge from the Japanese Army. His recollections and descriptions bore all the familiar hallmarks of the Inagaki, Sono and Hinokuma documents. This was not surprising. Throughout Nonaka's interrogation frequent reference was made by Godwin to the earlier evidence supplied by the staff officers.

When it came to remembering that fateful moment all those years ago in Parit Sulong, Nonaka produced the inspired if familiar response:

"On joining those other officers Lt. General Nishimura turned to me and in the hearing of all those officers present, gave me the following oral order:

"'Instruct the said junior officer' (rank and name was stated but I now cannot remember same) 'to execute (shobun seyo) all the prisoners of war by firing squad'

"No sooner had I acknowledged Lt. General Nishimura's order by saying 'Yes, I will repeat' than the Chief of Staff, Colonel Imai Kamejiro, gave me the following additional order:

"'The bodies of the prisoners of war are to be cremated on completion of the execution.'" Nonaka signed his statement on October 28.

On November 2, 1949, with the diplomatic row over war trials between Canberra and SCAP at its height, Lt. Colonel D. Beresford Goslett forwarded the completed Parit Sulong file to Melbourne. In a covering letter he pronounced the "command phase" of the investigation complete with charge and abstract of evidence fully prepared.

It was now all up to AHQ.

Chapter 8

The outrageous document heist

————◆————

Long before he regurgitated the Parit Sulong Massacre
file, Captain James Godwin had been convinced a
shameful conspiracy among senior American military
figures in Tokyo was protecting large numbers of Japanese
war criminals from prosecution. An entry in his diary in April
1949 reveals how the young intelligence officer had been
astonished to learn more than 600 war crimes suspects were,
according to official estimates, successfully evading arrest.

"With the help of yakuza (criminal) *gangs and the
underground, they remain hidden,"* he wrote. *"I am
gaining the distinct impression that the worse the crime, the
greater is the chance of the mongrel responsible to be aided
and abetted as a fugitive from justice. Clearly, there is no
contrition or repentance from the Japanese population at
large. We are still the enemy. The simple expedient of
changing names and identities and moving to other parts of
Japan is the evasiveness and deception most often resorted to
by these bastards with guilty consciences."*

Two months later, Godwin noted bitterly: *"Words fail me.
I've recently learned that some of the top Japanese scientists
involved in experimenting upon and murdering thousands of
prisoners of war are not only immune from prosecution
(MacArthur's orders) but the mongrels have been given top
jobs in Japanese universities. I refer to the Biological and
Germ Warfare Centres in Manchuria and elsewhere that*

operated under the umbrella of Unit 731. My colleagues in the American section of war crimes investigations consider this the worst war crime uncovered of either the former Axis powers."

Godwin's diary entry went on to name General Macarthur, General Charles Willoughby, SCAP's intelligence chief, and Mr Joseph B. Keenan, the US Chief Prosecutor, as the key conspirators protecting the germ warfare criminals. *"I'm bloody astonished at the suppression of this major war atrocity, but worse, I'm angry at the fact that all those victims of these evil Japanese scientists, are victims twice over from a coterie of heartless Allied tin-gods who have ordered these mass murders and their perpetrators to go unpunished."*

Accompanying Godwin's all-consuming rage over what he saw as American military subterfuge went burning frustration over clear signals that continuing war trials were fast becoming politically unacceptable. The British had closed their Tokyo investigating office the previous year and were leaning hard on Canberra to follow suit.

On August 26, Godwin was called into his superior's office. The American Legal Department upstairs had lodged a formal complaint with the Australian section about the captain's handling of the Parit Sulong Massacre case, specifically files 151G, 168, and 151H. His superior, a Major Williams, indicated the Americans were particularly concerned with the way personal comment had been injected into his reports. They had singled out various remarks the New Zealander had made about Lt. General Nishimura. These sort of personal observations in reports were to cease forthwith.

That night Godwin reached for his diary. *"It seems I've upset some Yanks for calling a spade a spade,"* he wrote. *"At least Major Williams agrees that General Nishimura is a bloody evil bastard and should have been hanged. I made the mistake of opinioning the same fate for this mongrel, but in* writing as a well-intentioned comment. I feel that not only the British but the Yanks are going soft on the Japs. Time is becoming the healer so far as war crimes and their accountability is concerned. Besides, as Major Williams avers, there's a hell of a lot of wheeling and dealing going on between the Yanks and the Japs. Let bygones be bygones seems to be the name of the game."

Godwin rounded off his entry with the observation: "The way things are going I forsee a sell-out of principles and everything we fought for in crushing these vermin. I hold strong views about my own imprisonment by the Japs and have the growing feeling Japan will be given a peace document excluding any claim for compensation from them. It's early days, but I may yet be proved right."

For all his obsessive desire to see Nishimura hang, Godwin was reading the evolving politics quite accurately. Indeed, his fears on US military subterfuge were also well-founded. His problem was that the Allied camp — with the notable exception of Australia — believed important strategic returns would accrue from the broader concept of making Pacific peace work. War crimes investigations and trials simply couldn't continue until the last enemy criminal had been brought to victor's justice. A line had to be drawn somewhere.

By mid-September, the Americans had signalled their acute displeasure with Australia's lack of policy on charging and trying detained suspects. Godwin seethed. What had been the point of his past suffering? All his efforts were being wickedly thwarted. His "most privileged and sacred" mission was inexorably running out of time.

At this point, however, Godwin was well into reviving the case against Nishimura. On September 21, with all interrogations completed but with affidavits still to be prepared and signed, he submitted his Weekly Investigation Report (Appendix B, page 331) which duly found its way to the US Legal Section. In it Godwin set down details of his just finalised interrogation of Nonaka, the divisional commander's aide through whom, it would be alleged, all orders for the Parit Sulong Massacre had been channelled.

The document quoted Nonaka as claiming Nishimura issued the killing orders with the words: *"Instruct the officer-in-charge of the prisoners to execute (Shobun Seyo) all the prisoners by firing squad. Kill them all."*

Godwin's Weekly Report continued: *"No sooner had Nonaka acknowledged this order than the Chief of Staff, Colonel Imai, gave him the following additional order: 'The bodies of the prisoners are to be cremated on completion of the execution and all traces of their disposal obliterated.'"*

If this account of the vital killing commands, as supposedly recalled by Nonaka and recorded by Godwin, is compared with the final affidavit produced by Godwin in Nonaka's name, two significant discrepancies become very obvious. In the Weekly Report Nishimura is quoted as adding the verbal flourish *"Kill them all."* These words are noticeably absent from Nonaka's affidavit.

When it comes to recalling Colonel Imai's additional orders for cremating the massacred corpses, Godwin's Weekly Report has the Chief of Staff insisting all traces of the disposal be *obliterated.* Once again, this aspect of the order is conspicuously absent from Nonaka's affidavit.

Both discrepancies lead to the inescapable conclusion that, one way or another, Godwin manipulated the record of verbal responses during interrogations to suit his requirements. In fact he openly admitted to such practices in diary entries. In one he wrote: *"As a consequence this bloody testimony had to be damn well paraphrased, so confusing were the discrepancies in interpretation that even ATIS (Allied Translation and Interrogation Service) were at times hard put to determine phraseology in context. To make matters more*

difficult was the Jap alphabet, a bloody hurdle all by itself."
The importance of these discrepancies together with Godwin's admitted habit of "paraphrasing" interrogation responses will soon be apparent.

The captain concluded the September 21 Weekly Report by once again giving vent to his anger and frustrations through caustic comment. *"At most times and whenever a Class A war criminal is finally identified, particularly if formerly a powerful and influential senior officer, we invariably encounter subtle obstruction to their apprehension by means of deviousness and duplicity."*

He continued: *"For a variety of dubious circumstances too numerous to mention, the coincidences of major war criminals effectively disappearing is no accident, but when such vanishing acts are unaccountably but officially confirmed without investigation by Japanese authorities, one is tempted to suggest the word, collusion. It is hard to avoid being cynical. This charade happens too often with regard to officially sanctioned Japanese fabrications. The second part of this priority investigation should shortly be concluded and entered into Official Weekly Reports as quickly as possible.*

Godwin wound up his remarks on this occasion with a direct attack on SCAP's operations. *"I have only to add my disappointment that the powers that be (Legal and Prosecution Division) do not propose to proceed with a fresh prosecution against Lt-Gen Nishimura, a most evil man. Perhaps the sheer horror of what he ordered against defenceless and wounded Australian prisoners, particularly the large number, would shock the world."*

The New Zealander was now singlehandedly taking on the US military establishment in Tokyo. His outburst, not surprisingly, triggered another formal complaint from the Americans. This time they took the unusual step of issuing a round-robin directive to all Australian investigators warning them against including private opinions in their reports. Reports were for the compilation and dissemination of facts, the investigators were reminded, and should henceforth be restricted to same.

Some days later Godwin wrote in his diary: *"I've got a feeling I might be in hot water again. This time for criticising the Legal Division. I have no difficulty in accepting that the courts have reasonably full case-loads but most of the mongrels who are appearing for trial are the lesser vermin. Of course, disillusionment does erode zeal. The most powerful gods of war and who were responsible for bloody awful deeds such as Parit Sulong's General Nishimura, seem to bear unbelievable charmed lives. The higher up the ladder of influence and responsibility, most especially nowadays, the less likely the chance they will be nailed."*

By this stage Godwin's obsession with "nailing" Nishimura had begun to dominate his life. He was all but ignoring American requests to keep private opinions on the general out of his work. At the same time, personal viewpoints on war crimes policy were still regularly appearing in his reports.

In late November, with the Parit Sulong file passed on to Melbourne for action, Godwin became the target of further American denunciation. He described it in his diary this way: *"Well, it's happened. I rather guessed it would. I've received an official letter from the Prosecutor's Office. This will definitely be added to my private collection of papers. Here's the gist of the admonition received.*

"Quote: **'Captain Godwin, you are no doubt aware as per the recent circular FF/442, that personal opinions of investigating officers must be confined to the bare facts of cases under investigation or review. It is noted that you criticise the parole system of war crimes suspects in advancing your submission of custodial**

confinement. It is accepted that your comments are well-intended and offered with respect, but it is also recognised that your criticism covers a wider spectrum of concerns more properly within the jurisdiction of the Legal Dept. Please be advised that a reconciliation of common objectives between the Occupying Powers and Japan embraces higher considerations precluding agendas or criteria applicable to the years 1945-46-47-48. With 1950 almost upon us, it is important to view world events in perspective and to realise the desire of the Allied Powers to contain, not exacerbate the process of investigating Japan's wartime excesses. Your adherence to the advice herewith contained is expected. Yours etc.'"

Reacting to the sharp reprimand, Godwin wrote in his diary. *"Well, all I can say is that none of the drongos in the Legal Dept experienced the trauma of being a prisoner of the Japanese. Judging from the gist of the letter, I get the distinct impression that both Captain Scott and Major Williams* (colleagues in the Australian section) *are right. The writing's on the wall quite obviously. It is just a matter of time when all war crimes investigations and prosecutions cease in Japan."*

For all the flippancy and implied resignation in these remarks, the formal US complaint would have a devastating effect on the deeply troubled Godwin who was clearly finding it impossible to exorcise the prison camp demons crowding his mind. Almost overnight he resolved to embark on a one-man crusade to expose the American conspiracy headed by Generals MacArthur and Willoughby. He would achieve this, he reasoned, by ignoring the Official Secrets Act, under whose restraints he supposedly operated. He would steal large quantities of highly classified, sensitive files from the Australian office in which he worked. One day, he would unveil his secret stash of documents and a stunned world would finally learn the truth about America's duplicity over Japanese war criminals. By any yardstick, it was an outrageous plan.

He intended hiding his loot, he told his diary, in a *"secure repository somewhere in New Zealand."* It would be carefully packaged and sealed for at least 40 years before it again saw the light of day. By then he would be in his sixties. Time, he felt, could be expected to have cast its healing veil. In his retirement years he would be able to recall and document the past that he was certain would be whitewashed by Japan's new-age collaborators.

"I have decided," he confided to his diary, *"that I will not be part of the deception instrumented from the Dai-Ichi Building* (SCAP Headquarters, Tokyo) *that proclaims the approaching conclusion of war crimes investigations and trials faithfully pursued by the Allied Powers. What rubbish! Britain abdicated its responsibilities so far as the prosecution of Japanese war criminals was concerned in mid-1948 (that's why ex-Colonel Tsuji is free) I have no doubt that America's misguided pacification programme and democratisation of Japan will endure only so long as the Japanese power brokers want it to. Provided everything falls into place for Japan (favourably), it will go from strength to strength, I understand their psyche too damned well."*

Godwin determined he would resign his commission the following February and return to New Zealand. There, he reassured himself in his writings, was a land where power politics, conspiracies and the perversion of justice were not sanctioned and where sanity and decency prevailed. He would have no hesitation, he noted, gathering the reports he intended spiriting away. "It may be risky taking classified files and documentation out of the Meiji Building for secret transfer to the southern hemisphere, but then and in context, it's a certainty that much of this material will be destroyed when deals between Washington and Tokyo are signed prior to the envisaged peace treaty."

Records of historical significance, he said, should endure for posterity and be available as indisputable testimony to what in future years may be denied. *"Historians and archivists will, I feel sure, agree with the valediction as hard documented evidence is more acceptable and irrefutable than most other forms of testimony — usually branded as conjecture. To this end, therefore, and as a forewarning to future generations, I will gather whatever documentation, classified or otherwise, that I can safely lay my hands on as I am now utterly convinced that with cover-ups and wheeling and dealing, the worst of Japan's wartime excesses will forever be suppressed if only for the political convenience of the United States and Japan, and to a lesser extent, the Allied Powers."*

Godwin, naive and nefarious, had considered his outlandish theft of files very carefully. He knew he would be courting serious problems if he attempted to reveal in book form what he termed his *"clandestine cache."* He correctly surmised: *"I would place my future at risk and could well be the subject of prosecution for unlawfully possessing classified documents, no matter my best intentions."*

On February 10, 1950, Godwin penned a final entry in his diary before winding up his job. He was, he said, looking forward to the next few days at the Meiji Building if only because they would be his last as a war crimes investigator. *"Probably it's because I won't be able to nail any more of those mongrels who fought so blindly for their criminal Emperor and who, in their fanaticism, stooped to the lowest forms of sadistic depravity previously unknown to mankind. Perhaps the chronicles I have faithfully set down will at least provide a glimpse of the deceptive psyche of the Japanese."*

He concluded: *"My main regret will be that a hell of a lot of these evil killers will walk free when the San Francisco*

Captain James Godwin is wearing a New Zealand Army uniform in this 1947 photograph taken during his service as a war crimes investigator with the Australian Military office in Tokyo. He was instrumental in amassing a large portion of the documentary evidence that sent General Nishimura to the gallows. When the controversial Godwin departed Japan in early 1950, he stole more than 80 folders of highly classified Australian war crimes files. He referred to these as his "clandestine cache."

Document evolves into reality as a bloody Peace Treaty. This is a prediction I feel convinced will eventuate."

Thus did the man, entrusted with the task of building a war criminal's case against Nishimura, depart Tokyo with his stockpile of stolen classified papers. For all his pent-up hatred and unresolved revenge, Godwin could quietly luxuriate in at least one accomplishment. The last batch of affidavits that he had fabricated as an investigator with 2 Australian War Crimes Section would most assuredly "nail" Nishimura.

Paradoxically, one of the reports Godwin removed from the Meiji Building could have gone a long way to clearing Nishimura from the stigma of guilt over the Singapore Chinese Massacre. Originally written by Major Arthur D. Pettigrew, from the British War Crimes Section, Tokyo, the document (See Appendix B, page 334.) amounted to a synopsis of the dossier held by his department on the activities of 25th Army Staff Officer Colonel Masanobu Tsuji, the real mastermind and instigator of the Singapore killings. "We are aware that there were many evil Japanese but clearly, Colonel Tsuji was the most evil of all," reported Major Pettigrew.

Nishimura had attempted to explain to the British Military Court trying him about the role played by Tsuji in the killing of Singapore civilians. The prosecution had responded by roundly denying Tsuji had anything to do with the affair. The bench, for their part, chose to ignore all Nishimura had to say about this "most evil of all" Japanese military figures.

The Pettigrew document, pilfered by Godwin and only recently sighted in New Zealand, reveals: "Colonel Wild had amassed a considerable dossier on Colonel Tsuji that if successfully prosecuted would most certainly have guaranteed his execution as a war criminal. All of this vital information and documentation was destroyed in the plane crash." And therein lies the reason for Nishimura's arraignment and conviction in Singapore.

At least two other documents lifted from the Australian Army office in Tokyo and secreted away in New Zealand had direct and vital bearing on the veracity of the prosecution evidence Godwin had engineered against Nishimura. One was his initial report on the Nonaka interrogation referred to earlier in this chapter. The other was a report he made after his interrogation of former staff officer Hinokuma. (See Appendix B, page 332.)

In it Godwin, quoting Hinokuma, provides a graphic account of how the Japanese carried out their massacre at Parit Sulong. The details were purportedly given to Hinokuma by fellow Staff Officer Eisaku Morioka whom, the prosecution would allege, supervised the slaughter.

The Hinokuma affidavit (See Appendix A, page 303.) prepared by Godwin for submission at Nishimura's trial makes no reference whatever to these important details. There is merely passing mention of Morioka speaking about the massacre to Hinokuma during dinner the next day on the outskirts of Batu Pahat.

In essence, the massacre report removed from the files by Godwin provided a very different account of the horror to that outlined by lone survivor Ben Hackney. The Australian and Indian prisoners had not been tied up with rope and wire, with their hands behind their backs, as described by Hackney. According to the Japanese account, those able to walk had been made to carry the immobile wounded to the execution ground. In addition, the walking wounded were also made to carry the bodies of their dead comrades.

Hackney claimed the firearms used for the killing had included rifles and machine-guns. According to the second account only three machine-guns had been employed. The Australian lone survivor had insisted that the bodies had been set afire with gasoline with many of the victims still alive. The Japanese version was that seven prisoners who still showed signs of life after the machine-gunning had to be bayoneted.

Hackney's affidavit suggested the incineration procedure had begun immediately after the shooting. In contrast, the Japanese account told of handgrenades and mortars being first used to collapse a line of shophouses. Once this had been accomplished 161 bodies were placed amid the tinder-dry debris. Paraffin and sixty gallons of gasoline were then poured over the corpses. In addition, tyres and demolition material were piled onto the pyres. At 8 pm Major Morioka gave the signal for everyone to stand clear and then flung down a flaming torch. The resulting fire had been so intense that four adjacent dwellings and nine shops had burned to the ground before midnight.

In the stolen document Morioka is described as being "*self-satisfied*" the morning after the massacre. Yet in the Hinokuma affidavit the same man is quoted as saying "*this whole incident was pitiful to see.*"

For all the inconsistencies in the prosecution evidence highlighted by this report from Godwin's clandestine cache, none has greater impact in demolishing the case against Nishimura than the implications of its final sentence. Morioka is there said to be required to report on the massacre to Chief of Staff Imai. Nishimura's name is unmentioned.

The significance here is that under the Japanese military code, completed order reports could only be made to the initiating officer. By the time Hinokuma's final affidavit was prepared, however, subtle changes had appeared in Morioka's requirements. It had then become necessary for the staff officer to make his report to both Imai and Nishimura.

The stolen document poses several important questions. Why did Godwin choose to withhold this most pertinent information from the evidence to be presented at Nishimura's Manus trial? As we will soon discover, hearsay or not, it would have been readily acceptable under Australian Military

Court regulations. Was it because the details supplied by the man who allegedly oversaw the mass killing were so different from those given by key prosecution witness Hackney? Did Godwin fear that introduction of such seemingly contradictory evidence would further undermine the reliability of Hackney, the mainstay of the prosecution case?

Why did Godwin select the Hinokuma and Nonaka interrogation reports for inclusion in the huge assortment of classified documentation he lifted from the Australian office at the Meiji Building? Was he concerned they undermined the case he had so carefully manufactured against Nishimura, the target of his quite overt vendetta?

Finally, just how many other historically important war documents remain hidden in the Godwin hoard which consisted of more than 80 large folders, included numerous photographs and weighed some 200 pounds? Packed together they completely filled a large plywood tea chest. When Godwin returned to New Zealand following his Tokyo assignment, he placed his illicit haul with relatives living in Napier, on the east coast of New Zealand's north island. The collection is known to have been intact as late as 1973.

Godwin died in Sydney in May 1995 after suffering Alzheimer's disease for more than five years, an affliction almost certainly attributable to his treatment in POW camps. In 1989, prior to falling ill, he had been restructuring his diary and working on some of the stolen documents at his home in the Sydney suburb of Wollstonecraft. It was then just a few months short of 40 years since he had walked out of the Meiji Building with his clandestine cache, the very time frame he had set himself for its public release.

With only a quarter of his diary completed, he suffered a stroke. Early signs of Alzeimer's then set in and Godwin had to abandon the mission he had begun four decades earlier. Following his death, all papers he had transferred from New Zealand were returned there.

Chapter 9

Manoeuvres and manipulations

———— ◆ ————

I t was only when the Australian Army began finalising its
Manus Trials programme in early February, 1950, that
the true dimensions of the logistical problems ahead
were suddenly revealed. Another 11 cases demanded by the
military had been added to the original nine recommended
by General MacArthur. A trial schedule that had been
measured in weeks would now be requiring months.

Onto Los Negros Island would converge 94 Japanese
suspects, a team of Tokyo defence lawyers, a Buddhist priest,
a contingent of PNG prison guards, 24 native labourers also
from PNG and eight Australian Military Court members
ranging in ranks from brigadier down to captain. Also
involved in the transfer would be the regular staff members of
1 Australian War Crimes Section — interpreters, clerks,
stenographers, typists, mess stewards, cooks and the like —
to keep the show functioning.

There had been problems of one sort or another almost
from the moment Cabinet ordered the Army to get its show
on the road. Quick to surface had been New Zealand's flat
refusal to make Captain James Godwin available.
Complicating the issue was Godwin's equally strong personal
antipathy towards attending the hearings — an
understandable reaction in view of what we now know about
the heisted documents and manipulated affidavits. For the AG
in Melbourne, it amounted to a major dilemma. Godwin had

been responsible for investigating no less than eight of the cases to be heard. The Parit Sulong Massacre topped this list.

After considerable difficulty, the New Zealand authorities agreed to Godwin's posting to Manus, but only up to September, 1950. The Military Court seemed unlikely to begin deliberations before early June and even the optimists were predicting eight months of hearings to clear the work load. Thus Godwin's effective participation still seemed in jeopardy. The only solution was to adjust the entire trial schedule to suit the New Zealander's Manus posting. Cases likely to encounter Japanese challenges to evidence obtained by him would be heard first. The AG's department well recognised file No 42, the Parit Sulong Massacre case, would have to be high on the hearing schedule.

There were problems, too, when it came to forming the Military Court. Most officers who had sat on war crimes hearings during the immediate post war period had now left the services, returned to civilian life and were no longer available. There was, however, one notable exception: Norman Frederick Quinton.

From the Army's viewpoint, Quinton seemed ideal for Manus. After his Singapore posting he had gone on a year's medical leave. But in February, 1948, he was back with 1 Australian War Crimes Section, this time posted to Hong Kong. In the Crown Colony Quinton served as a member of another Australian Military Court and deliberated on no less than 11 separate trials. In nine of these he was court President.

Would Major Quinton consider leaving the MMBW where he had returned and transferring from the Reserve of Officers to the active list with the rank of Lt. Colonel? Would he consider undertaking nationally important work as a member of Australia's last ever Pacific theatre Military Court?

Quinton certainly would. Nothing would give him greater pleasure.

On January 27, 1950, the Army's interviewing panel recommended Quinton be appointed court President for the *Manus Trials*. But the politicians were less than satisfied with this nomination. They felt the top judicial post on Manus required a figure of more substantial legal standing. In late March, Prime Minister Menzies wrote to the Queensland state premier seeking the temporary release of Justice Kenneth R. Townley, a senior judge of the Queensland Supreme Court, so he could be appointed Court President for Australia's final war trials.

The Prime Minister's letter noted: "It may be anticipated that the trials will arouse a great deal of public interest both in Australia and abroad. The crimes alleged are grave, and if the accused are convicted, they will be liable to the death penalty. Furthermore, the accused include a number of Japanese of very senior rank. Consequently it is highly desirable that the President of the Court should have had experience of the special jurisdiction created by the War Crimes Act, and also of the techniques of prosecution, defence and procedure generally, which have already been evolved."

Townley, an ex-serviceman and well versed in military law, received the appointment. To facilitate the task at hand, his rank was rather spectacularly raised from major to brigadier. In the brief round of negotiations preceeding these moves, the judge had only one request. He needed an associate to assist him in Manus. Townley recommended 22-year-old Frank Brennan from Rockhampton. Frank was the son of Townley's former judicial colleague, the late Mr Justice F. T. Brennan. The recent death of his father left the young Queensland University graduate with enormous responsibilities, among them the care of his mother. Frank Brennan needed a job. Army Minister Francis quickly acquiesced to Townley's suggestion and confirmed that Brennan would go to Manus as a civilian but with full officer

145

status. It was the first stepping stone in an illustrious legal career for the present Chief Justice of Australia, the Honorable Sir Francis Brennan AC, KBE.

For all the same reasons why Australian political leaders demanded a Court President of substance, they also saw the need for an equally qualified Chief Prosecutor. The advice of the Federal Solicitor General, Professor Kenneth H. Bailey, who had helped recruit Townley, was again sought. Professor Bailey recommended Mr Charles Vincent Rooney, KC, Senior Crown Prosecutor in New South Wales. Arrangements were concluded with the state government for Mr Rooney to take six months' leave of absence during which time the Commonwealth Government agreed to pay him at the rate of A£35 per day.

Far from being lost in the re-shuffle, Norman Quinton would ultimately emerge extremely well placed in the *Manus Trials* pecking order. He had certainly missed out on the top judicial job, but since he lacked any legal or other qualifications this was, perhaps, understandable. When the court membership list was released, there in No 2 slot was the freshly promoted Lt. Colonel N. F. Quinton. Apart from the brigadier judge, Quinton would be the highest ranking officer on the island.

As preparations for Manus continued, the Army, through the AG's office, went about ensuring arrangements advantageous to its trial interests. The subject of witnesses — both prosecution and defence — was given particular attention. When first considered in the heady days of early January, estimates placed a possible requirement for moving 30 or more Japanese defence witnesses from Tokyo to Los Negros.

But by late February the Army's position had undergone an appreciable change. Planning documents now emphasised the impracticality of committing to any specific number of defence witnesses. Only when the trials commenced would these requirements become clear. Requests by the defence for the production of witnesses, the Army decided, could then be examined by the court on a case-by-case basis. If considered reasonable, such requests could be channelled via 1 Australian War Crimes Section on Los Negros, down to Melbourne and back up to SCAP headquarters in Tokyo. Those summoned would be transported to Los Negros on Australian service ships returning home from Japan. Arrangements with the RAN would have to be secured. The RAN would then make sure that vessels carrying Japanese witnesses would avoid calling at any port in Australia prior to discharging their passengers at Manus.

Anyone conversant with military double-talk — let alone realistic trial arrangements — quickly recognised official intentions here. No defence witnesses from Tokyo would be giving evidence at Australia's final war crimes trials.

Keeping the politicians abreast of arrangements, Adjutant General Anderson despatched a confidential Minute Paper to the Ministry. Dated March 7, the paper highlighted the whole subject of witnesses — or, rather, the lack of them. "So far as can be foreseen at this juncture," the AG reported, "no witnesses other than the two Japanese mentioned in sub-para 7(d) of my minute of 1 Mar 50 will be required by the prosecution in the trials at Manus." Within a matter of days the AG would be reporting that even these two witnesses were now considered unnecessary and would therefore not be travelling to Manus.

On March 15, Lt. Colonel Flannagan wrote an advisory to the AG. It set in motion the Army's final policy on defence witnesses. "The production of live witness by the defence," said Flannagan, "cannot be prevented and if material witnesses are required by the defence, I consider arrangements would have to be made for their movement to Manus.

"However," he added, "whenever it is practicable, evidence at war crimes trials is limited to documentary evidence and the production of live witnesses by the defence should not be encouraged. It is proposed to advise 2 Australian War Crimes Section, Tokyo, on this aspect along these lines."

Australia's Tokyo office quite understood the implications of Flannagan's advisory. If it could be avoided, why have defence witnesses complicating proceedings? Military transport was the only means of getting to Los Negros. It was a simple matter to ensure no defence witness ever would.

Adjutant General Anderson's official explanation for effectively barring witnesses from Manus had a decidedly hollow ring. "Having regard to the provisions of the War Crimes Act, and with the object of eliminating unnecessary travel by witnesses," he told his Minister, " it is the practice to require the appearance of a witness before an Australian Military Court only when the prosecution or defence considers that his appearance in person is essential. It is usual, therefore, to obtain the evidence of witnesses when a case is being investigated and to tender that evidence as sworn statements to the court during the trial."

The joint position of Flannagan and the AG on the preference for documentary evidence issue was actually unrelated to the provisions of the Australian War Crimes Act of 1945. Its roots were more in historical legal precedence; what Prime Minister Menzies had aptly described as "the techniques of prosecution, defence and procedure generally, which have already been evolved." By applying these "techniques" to the provisions of the War Crimes Act, the Army's legal experts were able to create for themselves a highly advantageous murky area for *Manus Trials* operations.

Back in 1946, when there appeared strong prospects of Hackney identifying Nishimura, signal wires in Melbourne had run hot with repeated messages seeking the Bathurst grazier's presence in court as a witness. It was then hoped the trial would be in Singapore. But once Hackney had been unable to recognise Nishimura, requests for his live testimony immediately ceased. Pointedly, they were never revived.

As far as the *Manus Trials* were concerned, Hackney's evidence remained the backbone of the prosecution case. Obviously, the Army's legal advisors couldn't fail to recognise the inherent vulnerability of the story he had to tell. Its intense portrayal of cruelty and torture, the minute detail of the word pictures painted and the frightful emotions interwoven therein all reacted to produce a dramatic focus on the pivotal god-like officer described so fully. The insinuation was clear. This was the man who had commanded the massacre.

Yet for all the emotion, there was the cold, case-crippling fact that Hackney simply couldn't identify the man he had described so vividly and was accusing so forcefully. Cross-examination of Hackney in the witness box would almost certainly unearth this fact. It was also likely to establish the witness' proficiency in the Japanese language. If Hackney couldn't speak Japanese — which he couldn't — how could he possibly make insinuations of guilt based on a conversation he had overheard in a language he didn't understand?

The reality of Hackney's weakness as a witness, as destructive as it seemed to the evidence insiduously scraped together by the Army, was but the beginning of the prosecution's worries over case cohesion. The unsigned Fujita statement was a disgrace. The fact that Fujita had been allowed to abscond was scandalous. The continuity of vast slabs of identical testimony across supposedly individual affidavits was acutely embarrassing. In any regular Australian court, the conspicuously assailable case against Nishimura would have fallen apart, probably before the hearing even began. And the Army knew it. The Army also knew that the Australian Military Court at Los Negros would be far from a regular court.

To appreciate the extent to which the Army could manipulate the *Manus Trials* system requires an understanding of Clause 9(1) of the 1945 Act. It read:

"At any hearing before a military court the court may take into consideration any oral statement or any document appearing on the face of it to be authentic provided the statement or document appears to the court to be of assistance in proving or disproving the charge, notwithstanding that the statement or document would not be admissible in evidence before a field general court martial."

From this it followed that the fewer witnesses in court capable of undermining the authenticity of the documentary evidence the better it was for the prosecution side; particularly with a case as tenuous as the one against Nishimura . It could even be argued that a prosecution case based entirely on documentary evidence, without any witnesses, was the one most likely to succeed. This was how the Army's legal experts planned the Parit Sulong Massacre trial. The defence could only cross-examine if prosecution witnesses testified in court. It was clearly impossible to question an affidavit — signed or otherwise. The experts understood the "techniques" for blocking the appearance of witnesses at Manus. It was just a matter of manipulating the system.

When it came to handling Japanese defence counsel on Los Negros the Australian Army followed the British handbook. The British had made no bones about their policy in this respect. Japanese civilian barristers appearing in war crimes cases would be treated as "surrendered personnel." As such, they were at a perpetual psychological disadvantage to their prosecution opposite numbers. The disadvantage overflowed quite naturally into the courtroom. In Melbourne the AG's legal advisors understood the benefits inherent in retaining the psychological high ground. In remote and confined environments — like Los Negros — psychological advantages could prove especially powerful tools. And the advisors knew this, as well.

The Australians stopped short of formally categorizing the defence team as "surrendered personnel." But conditions imposed on the men from Tokyo made the same point, anyway. On departing Japan for Los Negros, lawyers and their clerks and interpreters were all under six month contracts to the Japanese Government. These included options for extentions to 12 months should the trial schedule so demand. In other words, every team member faced the possibility of having to live for the next year away from family contacts on an equatorial island where conditions imposed by the victor nation would be distinctly oppressive.

Once on Los Negros the Japanese lawyers would be officially under the control of the OC 1 Australian War Crimes Section. They would be housed in separate accommodation, surrounded by barbed wire and under armed guard. Throughout their stay on the island they would be prohibited from moving outside the precincts of the court and their quarters, except under military escort. Contact with the outside world could only be processed through the island's military facilities. This meant the Japanese legal team would be deprived all benefits of confidentiality when it came to seeking legal advice, support or direction from Japan-based sources.

Strangely, they would also be deprived of money in their pockets. The Australian orders directed: "In accordance with the established practice, the Japanese government will pay the salaries of members of the defence team direct to their dependants in Japan and, therefore, the members will not receive any payment during the period of their engagement." Instead, each would be permitted to withdraw canteen goods to the value of twenty shillings a week. The goods would be purchased by the Australian Army on their behalf and distributed to them in their quarters. In short, there would be no need for the Japanese to enter the Australian canteen.

Psychological pressures were such that no Japanese defence lawyers on Los Negros ever felt constrained to lodge formal complaints about the disparity in work and living conditions between their team, on the one hand, and the prosecution on the other. What was the point? The all pervasive anti-Japanese mood of the place was bad enough without adding to it. So, when asked by journalists for their comments on trial arrangements, the Japanese lawyers inevitably praised the organisers and predicted the fairest of all possible hearings. It was in court that they voiced their complaints about the uneven playing field. But these remarks were never reported and had no effect, anyway.

Ninety-two Japanese war crimes suspects sailed from Tokyo aboard the *SS Sinkiang* bound for Manus on February 20, 1950. The finalised charge sheets showed that the Australians intended arraigning a total of 102 suspects. However, two had died before arrests could be effected, seven were avoiding apprehension and the remaining one — Lt. General Nishimura — was in prison in Singapore. The original plan had been to fly Nishimura to Tokyo and there place him aboard the *SS Sinkiang* with the other 92 suspects. A garbled version of this reached Nishimura in Outram Road Prison where he underwent a physical check-up and was pronounced fit to be moved to Japan. His heart leaped with expectation. Perhaps his case was under review. Perhaps he was being considered for early release. Could the British have finally uncovered the truth about the Chinese Massacre in Singapore and the role of the real mastermind, Colonel Masanobu Tsuji?

Nishimura felt certain he was being transferred to Sugamo Prison. At worst, if he had to serve out the rest of his sentence there, he could at least look forward to occasional visits by members of his family. The weeks dragged by and he remained in his cell. In Japan, the defence team, overloaded with translation work on more than 200 documents, had been granted a month's delay in their departure for Manus. Instead of leaving aboard the *SS Taiping* in early April they were now booked to depart aboard the *SS Changte*. This vessel, scheduled to sail on May 11, would call at Hong Kong enroute.

On March 9, Nishimura, still convinced he was heading for Japan, was taken under armed guard from Outram Road Prison and placed aboard the Hong Kong-bound transport ship, *SS Orwell*. In Hong Kong he was transferred to the colony's Stanley Prison and remained there until May 21 when he went aboard the *SS Changte*. There Nishimura found himself sharing a cell with former Japanese Imperial Navy seaman, Shikao Nakamura, the only member of the fugitive seven the Tokyo authorities had been able to arrest.

The 36-year-old Nakamura told a deeply puzzled Nishimura how the *Changte* had departed Yokohama 13 days earlier. The vessel was enroute to Manus Island, not Japan. Nakamura explained he and four other former navy personnel faced trial before a Military Court in Manus, jointly charged with executing Australian prisoners of war at Ambon. Later that afternoon Nishimura would learn for the first time that he, too, was enroute to a Manus trial. An elderly, balding Japanese civilian came to the cell and introduced himself as Choji Nakayama, one of the officially appointed defence counsel. The lawyer informed the now devastated Nishimura that he was to be charged before the Australian authorities with responsibility for the massacre at Parit Sulong.

Counsel and client continued their discussions in the

cramped confines of the narrow shipboard cell. Nishimura insisted he knew of absolutely no reason why he had been charged with the killing of Australian and Indian prisoners. He recalled how, three years earlier, he had been interrogated in Changi Jail about the same incident. He had made a statement then to the effect that he simply had no knowledge of it. He stood by that statement.

Casting his mind back more than eight years, Nishimura said he remembered passing through Parit Sulong by car. He insisted, however, he had not stopped there. Nakayama then asked Nishimura in view of his claims, to read four sworn affidavits by former Imperial Guards officers. Each placed the commanding general firmly in Parit Sulong prior to the massacre. The statements flatly asserted that the Imperial Guards' CO had personally issued orders on the spot to kill all the Australian and Indian prisoners held there.

After reading the four accounts, an exasperated Nishimura turned to his lawyer and exclaimed it was clearly pointless for his lone voice to maintain innocence against such a barrage of claims. "All right then, if my neck is wanted so badly, I will give it," he shouted.

Nakayama attempted to calm his agitated client by returning coldly to the contents of the statements.

"Do you remember getting out of the car at Parit Sulong?" he asked.

"I do not remember getting out of the car," came the flat response.

The lawyer then drew Nishimura's attention to a statement by a fellow accused in the same case. This had gone into some detail about the commanding officer's movements once he had stepped from the vehicle. A seemingly resigned Nishimura still maintained he had not the faintest memory of these events. But as all the statements appeared to agree with one another, he saw no alternative but to admit he had alighted there.

Before Nakayama left, he explained Australia's intention of jointly trying the former Imperial Guards commander along with onetime aide, Nonaka, and Fujita, the self-confessed executioner, if the latter was traced in time by the Japanese authorities. Nakayama urged Nishimura to speak to Nonaka when he got to Manus and decide, one way or the other, whether he would admit to getting out of the car.

Ten days later, Nishimura and his cell-mate were being hurled bodily into the back of a military lorry parked by the Los Negros Island wharf and driven off round Seeadler Harbour to the Lombrum Point prison compound. A handful of Australian journalists was there to record the scene. If nothing else, their reports captured the mood of the moment rather accurately. In a curtain-raiser feature on the trials the Sydney Sun on June 2 described how the accused general, handcuffed to Australian provosts, had stepped ashore in Manus from the steamer *Changte*. It talked derisively of a "dazed and stupid-looking Japanese ordinary seaman, in company with big-shot Lt. General Takuma Nishimura, onetime commander of Japan's elite Imperial Guards Division which conquered Singapore, under the supreme command of the notorious Yamashita." (The "dazed and stupid looking " Nakamura, would later be acquitted of all charges.)

What the Sun's account lacked in historical accuracy was more than compensated for by purple prose. Nishimura, described as "scowling, unshaven, bullet-headed," had been "pushed into the back of a five-ton truck unceremoniously and by the buttocks by native police."

The feature was headed "**JAP GENERAL HOPES HE WILL BE HANGED**." The author made no attempt to explain the obvious dichotomy between Nishimura's supposed death wish at the hands of his captors and the announcement he would be pleading not guilty. The Sun's correspondent went on to editorialise: *"On the evidence which the prosecution intends bringing before the court, including some of the most* *shocking atrocities of the Pacific war, it seems certain that many of the defendants will be unable to escape the ultimate penalty — death by hanging."*

Having set a decidedly hardline tone, the correspondent tempered his observations with the reassurance that death sentences could only result from a two-thirds majority finding by the court, followed by final authorisation from the Australian Military Forces' Adjutant General himself. The clear implication here was that despite the prospect of "many" hangings on Los Negros, the ever vigilant overseeing role of the AG ensured all necessary safeguards were well in place. Justice would be done and would be seen to be done come the inevitable executions.

The Sun's reporter explained that based on discussions he had held on the island and his preliminary examination of prosecution briefs, he had formed the opinion *"this will be a tough court, unlikely to show the remarkable leniency displayed in certain war crimes trials conducted overseas."* The jibe, directed at both the Americans and the British, reflected widespread rancour within Australian military circles. Washington and London had gone soft and deserted the war crimes crusade. Manus would show them.

None of the Australian press accounts of the day saw merit in delving into Nishimura's background — be it from personal or military viewpoints. Newspapers were looking at far simpler approaches to the story. At long last the *other Tiger* of Malaya had fallen into Australian hands. A solid record of his final humiliation seemed the pressing journalistic requirement.

Nishimura entered Los Negros Island's Lombrum Point prison compound on May 31, 1950. His trial would begin 19 days later.

Chapter 10

No witnesses
for the prosecution

———— ◆ ————

The Chifley Labour government struck an excellent deal when it agreed to pay the United States A£1.25 million in 1948 for all American war surplus property in the territory of Papua-New Guinea. It gave Australia title to all left-behind US military paraphernalia on the New Guinea side which alone had a declared value of A£13 million. Also included in the arrangements were all US "fixed installations and moveable components" on the twin islands of Manus and Los Negros. These were estimated to be worth at least another A£16 million.

Best of all, the deal enabled Canberra to create a single, centralised war criminals' compound outside Australia. What had formerly been part of the large US naval facility at Lombrum Point was utilised to house war criminals convicted during separate military court hearings at Labuan, Wewak, Morotai, Rabaul and even Darwin. When preparations for the final Los Negros trials began, 226 Japanese convicts were on hand as ready labour along with resident Works and Housing construction crews totalling another 200 men.

The A£7,000 budget set aside by the Menzies government to provide temporary accommodation on the island for the suspects, the Japanese Defence Team and 1 Australian War Crimes Section was stretched to include costs for construction of the condemned cell block next to the main prison compound at Lombrum. A large US military hall at Nutt Point was chosen as the best location for the court. Japanese war criminals were trucked across daily from their compound to convert the 100 ft by 40 ft wood and fibro-cement structure into a courtroom incorporating a small holding cell at the rear. Labouring under the direction of Australian civilian engineers, the Japanese completed their renovations with less than a week to spare before the scheduled June opening of the trials. As a parting gesture they scrawled the English words "no guilty" on one of the courtroom walls and on a post outside. These were hastily painted out shortly before the first session commenced.

During the lead-up to the trials, international press reports were overwhelmingly critical of Australia's handling of the whole issue. Reporting from Hong Kong, the Manchester Guardian on April 10, 1950, maintained that the "bitterest opposition to General MacArthur's parole board for Japanese war criminals comes from Australians, always anti-Asiatic in tradition and principle." The newspaper quoted a Liberal member of the House of Representatives in Canberra as declaring the Japanese "sub-human creatures and their complete elimination as a race would in no way detract from the future prospect of the world's development and prosperity." Recognising this as an extremist view "scorning not only humanitarian concepts but also those of practicability" the account went on to argue the case for restoring the Japanese to self-sufficiency and self-respect.

"The Western way is to season justice with mercy; the Japanese had expected something quite different; this makes a strong impression not only on the Japanese but on Asiatic thought generally. They contrast this magnanimity with the hate-inspired policy of Russia, which has been shown again lately in the demand for the trial of the Emperor." continued the Guardian.

Story after story emanating from Tokyo's international press corps lambasted both Canberra and the Australian Army for insensitivity, vindictiveness and incompetence. Comparisons were drawn between Australia and her trial preparations and the Netherlands, then repatriating over 600 convicted war criminals back to Japan from the Dutch East Indies. The Dutch had concluded arrangements for the prisoners to serve out the remainder of their sentences in Sugamo Prison.

Among those to be repatriated was General Hitoshi Imamura, former commander of Japanese forces in the South West Pacific. The Australians had separately sentenced Imamura to ten years' imprisonment for war crimes in New Britain. As soon as they got wind of his repatriation they had the then physically frail and feeble-minded general seized and despatched to Los Negros to begin his Australian imposed term of detention.

Typical of the Tokyo-sourced reports was one published by the Melbourne Argus just prior to the *SS Sinkiang's* departure for Manus with the main batch of 92 suspects. Under the heading **SECRECY HIDES TRIAL PLANS** the Melbourne Argus' special correspondent in Japan complained that war crimes suspects had been held in jail for years and Australian authorities would make no statement about them. His story continued:

No official information is available and the silence in Tokyo about details of the impending transfers and arrangements for the defence of the accused indicates uneasiness about possibly maladroit handling of the whole war criminal question.

One Australian commented: "It was a good thing for Australia last year that no writ of habeas corpus operates here."

Allied circles remain politely silent, but it is the general opinion that Australia has badly bungled the closing stages of the war crimes investigations.

It was fortunate for the Army that the Argus correspondent had not learned of Fujita's disappearance, the role he'd played at Parit Sulong, the statement being accredited to him, or the orchestrated affidavits of the three Japanese staff officers and divisional aide Nonaka.

Happily for Canberra and the Australian Army as well, the barrage of criticism would soon cease. At this point the propaganda advantages inherent in Los Negros' remoteness — and so fortuitously forecast by the AG in his advice to Cabinet — would come sharply into play. And what a difference they would make.

The Melbourne Herald ran its curtain-raiser to the trials headed **MILLION-MILE HUNT FOR EVIDENCE**. It began:

Almost five years' work, involving journeys totalling almost one million miles and packed with adventures and peril, lies behind the presentation of the prosecution's case at the Australian War Crimes trials beginning here today.

It is one of the least-known stories of the war. It involved remarkable detective work by a comparative small group of Australian servicemen — mainly belonging to the Australian War Crimes section.

The report gushed on:

Members of the teams have usually been army lawyers and special agents. They combed tens of thousands of square miles of the Asiatic mainland and Japan and searched thousands of islands in the Pacific and China Sea.

Many were constantly in danger; some were ambushed and murdered.

When compared with the realities of Australian investigative activities in Singapore, Hong Kong and Tokyo, these claims were, of course, barking nonsense. Along with it and other stirring accounts in the Australian press came an interesting half-column published by the Melbourne Herald on June 2 under the heading **JAP LAWYERS ARE BEHIND BARBED WIRE.** Padded with praise for work accomplished by 1 Australian War Crimes Section it noted: *"As the Japanese lawyers are still enemy nationals and in a defence area, they are confined strictly to a small wired compound."* Senior defence counsel Choji Nakayama found the barbed wire irksome, said the news story. He contrasted conditions under the Australians with the "wonderful" treatment Japanese defence lawyers had received from the American Army in Tokyo, Guam and elsewhere.

"I will be patient," Nakayama was quoted as saying philosophically. "Perhaps it will improve; after all, we are not prisoners."

At the same time Nakayama and his colleagues were reported as having nothing but praise for trial arrangements. Allied war trials were conducted with scrupulous fairness. Any similar trials held in Japan "could not match them." The newsman rounded off his story with a personal observation. "I have not the slightest doubt," he said, "that the Japanese expect lenient judgements in these trials. Their theory is that because the crimes of which they are accused occurred from six to eight years ago, Australians will be more inclined to 'forgive and forget' than they would if the trials had been held immediately after the war." If ever an observation was geared to raise the hackles of Australian returned servicemen, this was it. If the account was accurate, the Japanese were only days away from dramatic enlightenment.

At precisely 1330 hours on Monday, June 19, 1950, Lt. General Nishimura and Captain Nonaka, were escorted into the freshly painted eggshell green courtroom and placed side by side in the dock.

Two pieces of important legal spring cleaning had to be undertaken before the official order for the assembly of the court could be read and the hearing commenced. "May it please the court," said the prosecuting counsel, Mr. Charles Rooney, rising to his feet. "I have an instruction from the convening authority that the charge against Seizaburo Fujita is to be withdrawn and no evidence will be given against him and the court will not be asked to make any finding against him."

Judge Kenneth R. Townley, a former Army major, was temporarily released from Queensland Supreme Court duties so that he could sit as the senior judicial figure on the Manus Island Trials. With the rank of brigadier, he presided over a total of 24 of the last 26 Australian war crimes hearings — including the Nishimura trial. The above photograph shows him in his official robes as a senior judge in the Queensland Supreme Court.

There had been vague efforts by some Army legal officers to have the missing Fujita tried *in absentia.* But Adjutant General Anderson had stepped in and firmly blocked these. Was the AG simply baulking at the prospect of an unsworn, unsigned statement convicting a suspect who wasn't even in court? Or were there other explanations? Were these possibly linked to a desire to avoid complicating a system that was already assuring the formal submission of an unauthenticated confession with built-in immunity from any protest by the defence?

The second item of pre-trial business concerned Major N. McLeod, a former war crimes investigator and one of the listed court members. Brigadier Townley announced that Major McLeod would not be sitting as he had been previously involved with enquiries into the case. His place would be taken by Major H. F. Hayes from the Army's special list, the only member without previous court experience. Unlike Major McLeod, Lt. Colonel Quinton, ensconced on the bench, was apparently satisfied his position had in no way been compromised by previous War Crimes Section activities in Singapore, Hong Kong or anywhere else.

In addition to Townley, Quinton and Hayes, there were two other members on the military bench line-up. One was Major W. E. Clarke, an intelligence officer and Japanese speaking linguist whose impressive credentials listed service as chief of the US Language Bureau during the IMTFE's trial of "major" war criminals in Tokyo. The other was Major E. J. Gerling, who had served on Australian Military Courts in both Rabaul and Hong Kong.

Nishimura and Nonaka each pleaded not guilty to the formal charge of having committed a war crime in that they, at Parit Sulong in Malaya on January 22, 1942, murdered a number of Australian and Allied prisoners of war.

Brigadier Townley then asked senior defence counsel Nakayama if he wished to apply for an adjournment on grounds that the accused may have been prejudiced in any way or that there had been insufficient time to prepare their defence. Nakayama responded that he had no wish to apply for such an adjournment.

Prosecutor: If the court pleases, I would like to ask permission for Captain Godwin to remain in court and to be seated at the bar table. Captain Godwin investigated this matter but it is not anticipated that he will be required to give evidence at any stage. If that happens, I will ask him to leave the court.

There were no objections from Nakayama. Captain Godwin moved into his place at the bar table as Mr Rooney prepared to read his two-page opening address. The chief prosecutor's remarks made it clear the Army's case against Nishimura and Nonaka would be argued purely on documentary evidence. No prosecution witnesses would be called. Affidavits would be produced, one by one, tendered to the court, allotted an exhibit number and then read aloud by Mr. Rooney.

As each was produced, the President asked whether the defence had "any objection to the submission of this document, or any portion of this document?" Nakayama raised no serious objections to any of them.

There were one or two minor variations to this rapid system of locking in the prosecution case. When it came to presenting Ben Hackney's evidence, for instance, large sections of the long typewritten document were struck out. They were eliminated by a single ink line through the text which effectively removed large segments of the documents from any possibility of defence objections. The single line deletion, however, made the complete text eminently readable for those adjudicating the case. Among the paragraphs deleted in this manner were glaring inconsistencies that could have given the defence ample ammunition to bore holes in Hackney's evidence. Mr Rooney maintained the deleted parts had no relevance.

Nakayama tentatively questioned a segment of Hackney's

account which began with the words "I have heard subsequently." Surely, this was hearsay? Under the constitution of the court there could be no objection to its admissibility, argued Mr. Rooney. The court saw it Mr. Rooney's way.

The procedure for submission of documentary evidence ensured a most curious aspect of Hackney's testimony would pass into the court record unchallenged. For all the minutiae of his affidavit's description and the definition of a subsequent Parit Sulong diagram he drew for the prosecution, Hackney had notably omitted from his testimony one essential element. The location of the massacre site. He had identified the positions of the main bridge, the coolie quarters in which the prisoners had been held and a subsidiary bridge capable of carrying Japanese tanks. He had provided distances of various points from the road and even the location of the village police station.

What was the explanation for this curious oversight? Had no investigating officer sought such an important detail from the lone survivor? Or had Hackney, for some reason, been unable to supply the information?

It took the prosecution something less than two hours to complete its case. Hackney's evidence which provided the foundation of the presentation had been tabled first. This was followed by the largely corroborative affidavits of the three staff officers, Inagaki, Sono and Hinokuma. Then had come a joint affidavit by Captain Godwin and US Sgt. Dix Asai attesting to the authenticity of the most irregular Fujita statement. The prosecution had concluded with the tabling of Nonaka's affidavit sworn before Captain Godwin on October 28, 1949, and Nishimura's Changi Jail statement dated August 27, 1947. (See Appendix A page 316 for the full documentary evidence submitted by the prosecution.)

In less than half a day the Army had laid the charges against Nishimura and Nonaka, provided evidence of the alleged circumstances under which the massacre had taken place, and produced several eye-witness accounts linking the two accused directly to the crime. Not a single witness had been called. Although the two accused had pleaded not guilty, their defence counsel had been unable to contest a single word of the prosecution case before it closed.

A severely disadvantaged Nakayama had been effectively neutralised by the "techniques" employed under the War Crimes Act. The railroading of evidence was bad enough. This had ensured the uncontested presentation in court of highly selective material. Worse, though, was the way the system had been employed for the calculated suppression of information that would otherwise have been vital to the court's ultimate findings.

The AG's department and every functioning Australian war crimes operation had known since September, 1946, that Hackney was incapable of making the critical identification of Nishimura. The same offices knew that the Army, when first confronted with this fundamental flaw in Hackney's evidence, had ceased investigating Nishimura for the crime. It was widely recognised there were just too many inconsistencies in Hackney's recollections, not the least of which was his physical description of the senior officer at Parit Sulong that positively eliminated Nishimura from suspicion.

Yet, when Hackney's evidence was tabled in court, the prosecution provided not the slightest indication of this relevant background. Hackney's failure with the photographs of Nishimura was never revealed openly in court or privately to Nakayama. Nor was there ever a chance of the Japanese lawyer unearthing such details. No prosecution witness ever entered the witness box to become available for cross-examination.

Directly linked to this effective suppression of vital evidence is another disturbing aspect of the proceedings. One member of the Los Negros Military Court trying the case

With General Nishimura's trial underway at Los Negros, the Sydney Sun flew photographer Bob Rice to Bathurst to meet Ben Hackney. This photograph resulted from the assignment and shows the Parit Sulong survivor, back on the land as a grazier, at his Wonalabee property.

had full knowledge of Hackney's inability to identify Nishimura. Lt. Colonel Quinton had been attached to 1 Australian War Crimes Section in Singapore in 1946 when the devastating news of Hackney's failure had been signalled from Melbourne. Furthermore, at the bar table with the prosecution team, sat another man who also appreciated the full implications of the evidence being suppressed. Captain Godwin had, for months, worked from files containing full details on the matter. In fact, all the affidavits he had produced for the prosecution had been created specifically to overcome that one gaping flaw in Hackney's testimony. Captain Godwin remained silent.

At no time during the trial did the bench seek to establish whether Hackney had ever been asked to substantiate his evidence with an identification. It would have been a valid question. Such an enquiry — certainly by the cognizant and involved Lt. Colonel Quinton — would have been consistent with the concepts of fairness and justice. Lt. Colonel Quinton also chose to remain silent.

The importance of the identification question to the Parit Sulong Massacre case cannot be over-estimated or over-emphasised. Had Hackney, from the outset, never alluded to the possibility of a senior Japanese officer personally delivering orders at Parit Sulong, Nishimura would never have been under suspicion. Hackney's statement, when first shown to a sympathetic and admiring Major Wild at Changi in August, 1945, established a permanent direction for investigations. This was predicated on the rigid theory that events at Parit Sulong simply had to have resulted from orders handed down by the senior officer described by the lone eye-witness.

Wild proclaimed as much in written directives and inter-departmental advisories. These, in turn, determined that an incompetent team of Singapore-based Australian investigators, subordinate to the British and largely in awe of them, would unquestioningly follow their lead. Wild's death in the Hong Kong air crash removed the one person capable of rescuing the misdirected investigations and repositioning them on legitimate tracks.

Consequently, Hackney's account was never subjected to any form of critical analysis. It was as though it might be construed as unpatriotic or ungrateful to question the word of a brave survivor who had endured so much. The fact that the wounded Australian lieutenant lacked any knowledge of the Japanese language never became a point for consideration within the context of his claim to have "witnessed" what appeared to be killing orders at their point of delivery. The degree to which Hackney's massive physical injuries, not to mention the mental trauma he suffered, might have impinged on his capacity for accurately recalling his experiences was also totally ignored. So, too, was the possibility that an entirely different set of circumstances, unrelated to orders in any way, could have triggered the massacre. These failures ensured all other legitimate lines of enquiry would remain untapped during the four-year span of investigations

For the first year the emphasis was exclusively on proving that the senior officer described by Hackney and the Imperial Guards Divisional Commander were one and the same person.

When the identification failure saw the immediate collapse of this approach, Australia's bumbling investigators merely switched tactics to a desultory search for other possible Japanese "senior officers" to fill the void. The fact that Hackney actually saw a resemblance in one of the alternate candidates, but was unprepared to stand by a formal identification, reflects the level to which investigations had then sunk. Thereafter they came to a standstill.

Hackney's statement remained on official files and subsequently became the basic document for revived investigations in Tokyo. Once again, without the clear suggestion of Nishimura's involvement it would have been impossible for Captain Godwin in late 1949 to have organised three closely parallel statements from separate staff officers corroborating the theory that the divisional commander had ordered the killing.

The theory itself was outlandish. It may well have fitted Australian public perceptions of the behaviour of senior Japanese military officers at that time. In reality, there was about as much chance of a Japanese divisional commander driving onto a battlefield and ordering an on-the-spot massacre of 150 wounded prisoners, as there was for a British or Australian counterpart to behave similarly.

There is no question that the Japanese perpetrated an

horrific mass killing at Parit Sulong. But Lt. General Nishimura was not the culprit. It is legitimate to consider what course the trial might have taken had Ben Hackney been brought into the witness box and subjected to cross-examination. Of course, the onus then would have been on the defence to uncover the critical identification evidence being wilfully suppressed by the Army. But once this had been done, the knock-on effect for the rest of the prosecution case — all of it firmly rooted in the Hackney statement — would have been devastating.

It is equally legitimate to ponder the implications for the prosecution case had the court become privy to the practices, designs and motivations of Captain Godwin. What would have been the court's opinion of Godwin's October 1949 Investigating Officer's Report, quite aside from the fact that he had stolen it and was concealing it? This document, it will be recalled, provided an account of the massacre as seen through the eyes of Major Morioka, the staff officer who, the prosecution was now alleging, oversaw the slaughter. The details here provided by Morioka (See Appendix B, page 332) were brutally plausible. But they were also substantially different to those outlined by Hackney. As such, they would have further seriously undermined the accuracy of testimony by the prosecution's star witness.

Chapter 11

Nishimura takes the stand

———— ◆ ————

Deprived of any opportunity for directly attacking prosecution evidence, Nakayama faced an impossible task as the second day of the hearing opened the following morning at 0900 hrs. At the outset Nishimura and Nonaka indicated they would both be giving evidence on oath. While it was well appreciated that Army arrangements had precluded the presence in Los Negros of defence witnesses from Japan, the court still curiously went ahead to establish whether Nishimura or Nonaka intended calling any. Nakayama informed the court that neither did and thereafter the day's proceedings got underway with Nishimura stepping forward and swearing his oath.

Under examination by Nakayama, the one-time Imperial Guards commander first provided a thumbnail sketch of his 40-year military career beginning with his entry into Japan's Preparatory Military Academy in 1903 and ending with his retirement to the Reserve List and appointment as military administrator of Burma in 1943, and then of Java until hostilities ceased.

Nishimura went on to recall how an investigating officer had interrogated him in Singapore in the autumn of 1947. This was when he had first heard vaguely about an incident at Parit Sulong. "But I was not given any concrete idea about it. If such a case had happened, I thought it might have happened at the front with a combat unit." Nishimura said he had continued serving his sentence in Singapore, giving no further thought to the Parit Sulong affair as he felt he had been in no way connected with it. "However, when I was shown the abstract of the Charge Sheet on May 21 on board the ship coming to Manus Island I was very much surprised." Only then had he learned he was to be charged.

The complication of speaking through an interpreter and the inherent disparity between the translated words and the original thought patterns in Japanese imparted a halting, diffident quality to Nishimura's evidence. One of the key points he tried to get across was the difficulty he faced searching his memory over a timespan of more than eight years. After all, he had made only the briefest of stopovers in Parit Sulong on January 22, 1942; somewhere between five and eight minutes. To cynics he sounded evasive and the longer he was forced to fall back on a failing memory the worse his predicament became. Compounding problems was the constant pressure on him to recall matters of significance arising from an interlude in his life where, in fact, nothing substantial had occurred. The frightful events on which the charge against him was based had taken place some hours after his departure from Parit Sulong. He hadn't seen what Hackney had seen. The other affidavits directly linking him to the massacre were untrue.

Defence: What were the circumstances of your inspection of the prisoners of war?

Nishimura: My memory is that I had just gone down from the car and had a look at the prisoners so I do not remember any particulars.

Defence: Did you receive any report from the officer in charge of the prisoners of war?

Nishimura: I believe I had naturally received some sort of report from him but I do not remember the particulars.

Defence: What were the conditions of the prisoners

when you went for inspection?

Nishimura: I do not remember clearly.

Defence: What was the number of the prisoners.

Nishimura: I thought there were some but I do not remember the number.

Defence: What were the conditions of the place where the prisoners were interned?

Nishimura: I thought they were interned in a building but I do not remember the particulars.

Defence: Did you know that the prisoners were executed?

Nishimura: I did not know.

Defence: When did you come to know that the prisoners had been executed?

Nishimura: I came to know on May 21 at Hong Kong when I boarded the ship to come to Manus Island when I saw the abstract of the Charge Sheet.

Defence: Why did you not know of the execution of the prisoners?

Nishimura: I did not know because I do not remember giving such an order and I do not remember receiving any report of such an execution.

The question and answer evidence continued with Nishimura drawing the distinction between the separate meanings of the Japanese words "shobun" (dispose) and "shokei" (execute). "I remember giving the word 'shobun' but I do not remember saying such a word as execute — 'shokei.' The meaning of 'shobun,' as I have formerly stated is to take steps to send the prisoners back to the rear," he added.

Nakayama then asked what explanation Nishimura could give for the fact that all prosecution statements indicated his order had been to execute by firing squad. If the truth were known, the one man capable of responding to that question was Captain James Godwin, sitting there at the court's bar table.

Nishimura, who naturally lacked any insight into what had transpired in Tokyo during the frantic final weeks of Godwin's enquiries, struggled to supply a plausible answer. In the end he offered a rundown on the procedure that would have been required if he, the divisional commander, had chosen to give an on-the-spot order to execute prisoners. As his standing instructions had been to ensure prisoners were sent back to Yamashita's rear headquarters, there would have been a need to rescind this original order. Consultations would have been mandatory with divisional Chief of Staff, Colonel Imai, and Staff Officer Morioka, who together were in charge of prisoners of war. The new execution order would then have been released by General Imai to the regimental commander concerned, down to the battalion commander and finally to the officer in charge of prisoners. Nishimura argued it would have been impossible for him to side-step this protocol by slipping new on-the-spot execution instructions to his aide Nonaka.

Defence: Will you tell the circumstances why you had ordered or you had given advice "shobun seyo" or "disposal?"

Nishimura: When this case at Parit Sulong occurred it was in the midst of the operation and I was quartered in a certain small hut within the Bakri district. In these quarters were my personal aide Nonaka, Adjutant Toda, our chauffeur and orderly. One day while the operation of Parit Sulong was going on, Staff Officer Morioka came to me and he told me the following facts. He said: "The battle of Parit Sulong is progressing and at the north of the bridge which the Japanese have taken there may be some prisoners of war and what shall we do with the prisoners of war when captured?" Then I answered as follows: "If they were to take some prisoners of war, then take steps to send them back to the rear at Yamashita Headquarters."

Nishimura said he had explained these arrangements to the officer who interrogated him in 1947. He was quite sure Staff Officer Morioka had conveyed his intentions to Chief of Staff Imai and also to Adjutant Toda. Furthermore, Morioka had conveyed the divisional commander's order to the 5th Infantry Regiment to which the officer in charge of the prisoners belonged. As proof that the order had travelled effectively down the line of command Nishimura drew the court's attention to the fact that Fujita himself had made reference to the requirement to transfer prisoners to rear areas.

Nakayama came back to the delicate question of the meanings of the words "shobun" and "shokei."

Nishimura: "Shobun" or "disposal" not only means execute, but fundamentally it means to dispose of, deal with or to put things in order. In this case the word "shobun" or "disposal" means to dispose of the prisoners by sending them back to the rear.

Defence Counsel Nakayama then asked whether Nonaka could have passed on the order "to execute" rather than "to dispose" against the divisional commander's will?

Nishimura: I absolutely do not think such could happen. I firmly believe that Nonaka relayed my instructions to "dispose of."

As Nishimura explained it, Nonaka's functions as a personal aide set him apart from divisional duties. The aide had no voice in operational affairs and acted purely as a "speaking tube" for the commander.

Nakayama then drove to the heart of the dilemma and asked Nishimura to provide an explanation for Fujita's action in executing the prisoners. It was an impossible question which underlined the desperation of the defence. Certainly

Nishimura was in no position to provide the answer. He had not known Fujita nor could he have even guessed at the lieutenant's motivations. He had been nowhere near the scene when the crime occurred and had only come to learn its details aboard the *SS Changte* a month earlier. Since then he had been incarcerated at the Lombrum Point compound.

Nishimura endeavoured to piece together a response to Nakayama's question. "I am not sure," he said, "besides I do not mean to blame others but I had doubts on such a situation even considering the fact that Chief of Staff Imai and Staff Officer Morioka were at the spot." It was a stumbling reply made to sound all the more inept by what was lost in translation. Nishimura was struggling to come to terms with a military code imbued over four decades. It was deeply degrading for him to offer the possible actions of subordinate officers as his means of evading responsibility. But from his restricted viewpoint, he could provide no logical explanation for the barbarism that had erupted other than it must have resulted from the involvements of Colonel Imai and Major Morioka, the two officers responsible for prisoners of war.

Reflecting on those days, said Nishimura, two major doubts arose in his mind as far as the prosecution evidence was concerned. The first was his earlier observation that any execution order could only have followed consultations between himself, Imai and Morioka. As it was, he had "no recollection whatsoever" of such consultations having taken place. His second concern involved that section of a prosecution statement (Inagaki's affidavit, Appendix A, page 294) indicating Morioka had ultimately reported completion of the massacre to Imai who had responded with the words of praise "well done." The implication here was that if Nishimura had indeed ordered the massacre, Morioka would have had to report directly back to the divisional commander himself. He would have had no alternative. Japanese military procedures were unyielding on this requirement. Nishimura maintained he had never received such a report. Here again, the stolen report of Hinokuma's interrogation and Morioka's recollections strongly supports Nishimura's contentions.

Asked what he thought of Hackney's sworn statement, Nishimura observed that as he did not know the truth of what happened at Parit Sulong he couldn't say anything. But he went on strongly to refute Hackney's description of the motor convoy. Unlike Hackney's account, his convoy had contained fewer vehicles and had functioned without tank escorts. Nishimura completed his evidence with a further rundown of the duties of Nonaka, his "personal aide." It was the custom in the Japanese Army, he said, to have personal aides for brigade commanders, divisional commanders and Army commanders. "As I have previously stated the duties of a personal aide included looking after the personal affairs of the commanders and carrying messages and things private. The rest is as I have stated before."

All in all, Nishimura's attempt to convince the court of his innocence had been a pathetic spectacle. Deprived of the normal basic rights of an accused person and faced with the prosecution's selection and suppression of evidence, he had no credible counter to the charges laid against him. Cross-examination, under the circumstances, seemed almost unnecessary.

Questions posed by Prosecutor Rooney delved into Nishimura's views on what constituted clear and acceptable orders. He put it to Nishimura that the Japanese Army's ideal of service was "immediate and unquestioning obedience of an order from a superior officer." Nishimura corrected this by insisting that unambiguous orders were to be obeyed and ambiguous orders clarified.

Long and convoluted probing on details of the convoy that carried Nishimura to Parit Sulong appeared to raise more questions than it answered.

Charles Vincent Rooney took leave of absence from his post as senior Crown prosecutor in New South Wales to serve as chief prosecutor at the Manus Trials. He was personally recommended by Australia's Solicitor General, Professor Kenneth Bailey.

Prosecutor: Did you ask the officer in the first vehicle directing the convoy to stop at Parit Sulong?

Nishimura: Although some sworn statements say so I do not remember my giving the order to that effect.

Prosecutor: Is this then the position, that you are unable to affirm or deny that suggestion, that you had given orders for the convoy to stop at Parit Sulong?

Nishimura: My memory is so vague as to remember only that I heard there were prisoners of war there and I got out of the car to see them.

Prosecutor: Are you able to affirm or deny the suggestion that you gave the order to stop the convoy at Parit Sulong?

Nishimura: I am not quite sure of it.

Prosecutor: The convoy did in fact stop there on that occasion?

Nishimura: To tell you the truth I thought the convoy had not stopped near that spot and when I saw some sworn statements I come to think that I stopped there and got out of the car to see them.

Prosecutor: Have you any doubt now that the convoy in fact did stop there on that occasion?

Nishimura: As to that point, as I stated before, after seeing the charge sheet and some evidences I remember that I had got out of the car there and went to see them.

It is fair to note the consistency between Nishimura's answers to the prosecutor in this exchange and remarks he made during the first meeting with his counsel aboard the *SS Changte* the previous month. The third person in the shipboard cell at the time of this encounter, former seaman Shikao Nakamura, would later make a statement verifying the substance of that lawyer-client conversaion. But by the time the Nakamura document surfaced, the Army's reviewing authorities had no interest in the consistency of Nishimura's reaction to the allegations. They wanted him hanged as expeditiously as possible.

To those convinced of his guilt, Nishimura's performance under cross-examination came as full justification of their cause. How could anybody who had witnessed a scene such as that portrayed by Hackney have forgotten about it? Impossible! But the question raised here is whether Nishimura did witness the scene described by Hackney. If he had only been exposed briefly to a small portion of it, would this have imprinted itself on his memory? If, indeed, that was the truth of Nishimura's involvement, to what extent had he later become influenced by the documents prepared by the prosecution?

By the afternoon of the trial's second day Prosecutor Rooney was still attempting to pin down details of Nishimura's movements during the convoy's Parit Sulong stopover, and his inspection of the prisoners.

Prosecutor: Did you swear this morning that you remember nothing about their condition or the condition of the building?

Nishimura: Yes, I swore so.

Prosecutor: Do you remember if there was a stench of blood and wounded flesh that could be smelt from some feet away from the building before you entered the building?

Nishimura: I did not notice it and I do not remember it.

Prosecutor: Did you hear any groans from grievously wounded men?

Nishimura: Such a thing is not in my memory.

Prosecutor: Would you be likely to have forgotten it if the conditions were as I have suggested?

Nishimura: I do not quite understand your question.

Prosecutor: I withdraw it.

Later in the cross examination Rooney returned to the purpose of Nishimura's visit to Parit Sulong.

Prosecutor: May I assume that the sole purpose of the convoy stopping was for you to inspect the prisoners of war?

Nishimura: Yes, you may.

Prosecutor: Yes, now when you told us earlier this afternoon that you had given instructions to a staff officer about your views on the treatment of prisoners of war and that you assumed he would broadcast that amongst your division, what was the name of that officer, that staff officer?

Nishimura: Staff Officer Morioka.

Prosecutor: And when was it you gave him those instructions?

Nishimura: I gave that instruction at my quarters at Bakri.

Prosecutor: How long before you left Bakri? How long before the 22nd of January?

Nishimura: One or two days before the 22nd of January.

Prosecutor: So may I assume then that you gave no instructions about the treatment of prisoners of war until after you had come to grips with the enemy, until after the actual fighting had commenced with your unit?

Nishimura: No, you might not assume like that. Before the Malaya operation started I gave general instructions on that matter.

At the outset of the trial's third day Nishimura was still under cross examination. The previous day's verbal manoeuvrings had failed to clarify substantive points for either side. Prosecutor Rooney was keen to explore information he had received about Nishimura finally dismissing Nonaka. Perhaps this had a connection to the massacre. He began by posing general questions about Staff Officer Morioka and personal aide Nonaka then zeroed in with the specific query.

Prosecutor: Did you ever take steps to have either of these officers removed from your staff or from headquarters?

Nishimura: Yes, I did.

Prosecutor: Which one?

Nishimura: It was Chief of Staff Imai.

That was not the answer Prosecutor Rooney had expected. Rather, it was precisely the answer he had tried to avoid when he purposely limited discussions to Morioka and Nonaka. The ploy had failed and Nishimura had drawn attention for the first time to the animosity that had existed between himself and Colonel Imai.

Prosecutor: I was only asking you about Morioka and Nonaka. Had you taken steps to have either of these officers removed from your staff?

Nishimura: Because First Lt. Nonaka desired to be transferred and I ordered to transfer him.

Prosecutor: Did you ever take steps to have either of these officers removed on the grounds of incompetence or misconduct?

Nishimura: I transferred for that reason Chief of Staff Imai, but Nonaka was not.

Prosecutor: I am not asking you about Imai, I am asking you only about Nonaka and Morioka. Did you ever lose confidence in them or take steps to have them removed from your staff for reasons of incompetence or misconduct?

Nishimura: I feel quite sorry to say the following matters in front of Nonaka, who is accused. In fact he was not sufficient in his ability, and also I thought that it might be better for him to transfer to the front unit rather than to remain in the divisional headquarters, because it might be better for his military attainment.

With the prospect of the cross examination soon running out of territory to explore, Rooney decided to pin down, once and for all, the basic plank of the prosecution case. The massacre had resulted from an order and — irrespective of how the defence chose to portray events — the order had originated with Nishimura. Rooney asked whether Nishimura believed the killings "were the result either of a mistake regarding the order, or wilful disobedience of the order by sub-ordinate officers."

Nishimura: I believe it took place by such a mistake, although I am not very sure if it was by a mistake or a wilful disobedience.

Prosecutor: If the killings were due to wilful disobedience that would be a very evil act by the officer responsible, would it not?

Nishimura: If my order had been issued and my sub-ordinate officer disobeyed my order, it would be very bad conduct.

Prosecutor: Will you agree that the killings were not only against your orders but were also quite unnecessary?

Nishimura: I am not sure that the killing took place against my will or by the mistake on the part of the sub-ordinate officer, but such killing occurred by a mistake and was very bad conduct.

Prosecutor: I am only asking you now the theory that the killings may have been due to deliberate disobedience by your sub-ordinates. Will you not agree that the killings were not only against your orders but entirely unnecessary?

Nishimura: If it was carried out wilfully, I think I agree with you.

Prosecutor: Will you further agree that the method and the details of the killings were atrocious and barbarous?

Nishimura: I do not know about the scene of the killing.

Prosecutor: If the details of the killings are as stated in the documents and in the evidence of the prosecution, were not such killings atrocious and barbarous?

Nishimura: If it had taken place as appeared in the

statements, I agree with the words of the prosecution.

Prosecutor: And had you learned about those details the following day would you not have severely punished the officer who had so disobeyed your orders?

Nishimura: Naturally I would have punished him.

Prosecutor: With severity?

Nishimura: I think he would have been tried by a Court Martial.

Prosecutor: And if he was found guilty of such disobedience would not the punishment have been severe?

Nishimura: I think it would have been severe.

Prosecutor: And that would be because of not only the disobedience but also because of the atrocious nature of the details?

Nishimura: I think the main reasons might have been so.

Prosecutor: In your opinion was either Major Morioka or Captain Nonaka capable of such disobedience and such atrocious conduct?

Nishimura: I believe Nonaka could not do such things.

Prosecutor: What about Morioka?

Nishimura: Morioka is a little strange and a thoughtless character.

Prosecutor: Morioka, of course, knew better than any other man in your division your views on the treatment of prisoners of war?

Nishimura: He should have known them well.

Prosecutor: And he would also have known the penalties for his actions if he were found out?

Nishimura: I think he would have known it.

Prosecutor: And, of course, Morioka died during the hostilities?

Nishimura: I do not know well about it because I left the military career.

Prosecutor: Have you been informed that Morioka has been dead for some years?

Nishimura: No sir.

With that response the cross-examination concluded. There followed a period of further questions from court members but these, too, failed to clarify any significant point with Nishimura repeatedly being unable to recall specific details.

Court: Did you see with your own eyes any prisoners of war at Parit Sulong?

Nishimura: Yes, I saw so.

Court: Were they Australians?

Nishimura: As far as I recall they were Australians.

Court: Were they in uniform?

Nishimura: My memory became vague so far as such matters.

Court: Were they not naked?

Nishimura: Such special or queer impression as they were all naked does not remain in my memory.

Court: Were any of them wounded?

Nishimura: As stated before I do not remember about that.

Later in the questioning the court probed to see if Nishimura could explain why the three staff officers — Inagaki, Sono and Hinokuma — should have chosen to lie about orders seeing there was no suggestion they had taken part in the killings

Nishimura: I think something what I felt but I do not like to state it.

Court: Well, you need not be frightened to say it here. If you can give any reason as to why they should lie, you are at perfect liberty to do so.

Nishimura's reply rambled but the thrust of it was that the

three had done so because they feared being ultimately accused of the killings, even though they had no direct connection to them.

There was one telling moment as the court's questioning drew to a close. Nishimura was asked whether he remembered giving advice to Nonaka or Fujita to ensure the prisoners of war would be taken to the rear.

Nishimura's reply was: "Reading the charge sheet and also the statements, I recall I did so."

It was an oblique response that escaped the court's attention. At this point, however, Nishimura was revealing the torment of trying to provide reactions to the prosecution's clear and undoubtedly horrifying portrayal of events that any truthful man, who had witnessed them, should have readily recalled. But his presence in Parit Sulong had been fleeting and the passage of years had quite reasonably taken their toll on his memory for such brief moments. Thus, he found himself unable to comply. In this instance, as with much of his testimony, his recollections had been heavily influenced by his reading of the prosecution documents. He was a perplexed and frightened man trying to explain himself before a hostile system. At the same time, of course, he was attempting to grapple with a shamefully concocted case.

Chapter 12

The inevitable convictions

———————◆———————

The Australian Army's primary objective in pursuing the Parit Sulong Massacre case was to snare Nishimura. But the time-pressed Captain Godwin had, in the process of organising his documentary evidence, created one serious dilemma. It became impossible to proceed against Nishimura without jointly charging his aide Nonaka as well.

Godwin had supposedly secured the affidavits of Staff Officers Inagaki, Sono and Hinokuma on October 3, 14 and 18, 1949, respectively. In each case, he had clearly worked from the basic statement of massacre survivor Ben Hackney. In addition, he had undertaken an immense amount of cross referencing with the staff officers' statements. All three provided almost identical allegations on Nishimura delivering the killing orders via his personal aide.

It wasn't until October 28 that Godwin concluded his interrogation of Nonaka who then signed a separate, albeit very similar, document to the other three. Given the circumstances of the investigations and Fujita's disappearance, failing to charge Nonaka would have risked exposing the Army to criticism of selective indictment. This, in turn, could have developed a life of its own at the trial stage. Stuck with charging Nonaka alongside Nishimura, the Army's legal advisors realised that, once in the witness box, the former junior officer could rapidly become the one weak link in their otherwise impervious chain of evidence.

They weren't wrong. Within seconds of taking the oath Nonaka had launched into a stinging attack on the way interrogator Godwin had manipulated his October 28 affidavit. Nonaka sought to correct its wording. Nishimura had not given the order to "execute by firing squad." He had used the word "shobun" which translated was equivalent to the English word "dispose" and his intention was to remove the prisoners to the rear. Furthermore, Nonaka had no memory of Chief of Staff Imai ordering the cremation of prisoners' bodies. "At the time of the investigation I did not know that my statement would be employed in such case as this and I did not know that I would be placed in such a place as I stand now, " Nonaka added.

Clearly taken aback, Court President Townley turned to Nonaka and interjected: "What did you think your statement was being taken for?"

"At that time I could not understand the purpose," Nonaka shot back.

Defence Counsel Nakayama sought to calm matters by temporarily diverting the accused to a less controversial examination of his military career with the Imperial Guards and a review of his duties as Nishimura's personal aide. Emphasising the difficulties he had recalling events over an interval of eight years, Nonaka proceeded to describe what he could of the convoy that transported Nishimura to Parit Sulong and the scene there when they arrived. He had accompanied Nishimura in the divisional commander's car.

On alighting from the vehicle Nishimura had walked to the right hand side of the road. Nonaka could vaguely recall two or three dead bodies in the area but had not immediately seen any prisoners.

Defence: Did you go to the building where the prisoners of war were kept?

Nonaka: I went there.

Defence: What kind or style was the building?

Nonaka: My memory is vague and accordingly reading the statement at the time of the investigation I recall that it was a flat one-storey building.

Nonaka went on to claim his memory had been influenced and confused when Godwin introduced the statements of other witnesses during the interrogation sessions. As with Nishimura's complaint about prosecution statements, there was no digression or discussion of the matter and the evidence continued. Nonaka described how he and Nishimura had advanced towards the building and glanced briefly inside.

Defence: Did the divisional commander speak to anybody else while inspecting there?

Nonaka: I do not remember about it at all.

Defence: How did the divisional commander give that order or advice?

Nonaka: When we were about to come back to our cars, the officer in charge of the guarding asked the commanding officer as to how to handle the prisoners of war. That is my memory.

Defence: What did the divisional commander do then?

Nonaka: Then the divisional commander stopped for a while and looked back to me and told me to dispose of them.

Defence: Other statements say that the divisional commander said to shoot the prisoners of war to death, what do you think about it?

Nonaka: I do not care what other people say in their statements but, as for me, I was told by the divisional commander to dispose of them and I transmitted the order to the officer in charge of guarding the prisoners of war.

Defence: Your sworn statement also says that the divisional commander told you to shoot the prisoners of war by shooting squad, and you made a correction this morning about it; will you please explain why you made such a correction?

Nonaka: Even when I was interrogated I clearly stated that I was ordered by the divisional commander to dispose of the prisoners of war and I conveyed that order to the officer in charge of guarding the prisoners. Then the interrogator repeatedly told me that the divisional commander had ordered to shoot the prisoners of war and he put that suggestion to me repeatedly. When the sworn statements by Sono and Hinokuma, who had been interrogated before I was, were read to me . . . .

At this point, Prosecutor Rooney interrupted with a somewhat belated suggestion. It had been obvious from the outset of Nonaka's evidence that Godwin's method of interrogation would be attacked. By rights the New Zealander should then have left the courtroom. The prosecution had chosen to let him remain.

"If the court pleases," said Rooney," it might be better if Captain Godwin left the court now as he may be called later on." Brigadier Townley readily agreed. With Godwin's departure the proceedings continued. Nonaka had been explaining how, during his interrogation in Tokyo, the statements of Sono and Hinokuma had been read to him by Godwin. As the interrogator had repeatedly insisted that the word "shobun" might have meant to shoot the prisoners, Nonaka had been persuaded — given the undeniable fact of the massacre — to go along with the suggestions being put to him.

Defence Counsel Nakayama then turned to Nonaka's opening evidence dealing with Chief of Staff Imai's involvement at Parit Sulong. Why had he corrected his statement's original claim that Imai had ordered the prisoners' bodies be cremated?

Nonaka explained his initial reaction to Godwin's

questions on Imai's role had been identical to his reaction when asked about Nishimura. He simply couldn't remember. The interrogator had again repeatedly put to him suggestions about Imai. Again sworn statements by witnesses questioned previously had been read over to him. As a result, he came to believe that perhaps what was being suggested to him was correct. But he had absolutely no recollection of those events.

Nonaka then made a most revealing observation: "The Chief of Staff never used me as a messenger when he wanted to have somebody to convey his order. I remember that he used the Staff Officer or Inagaki who was, more or less, personal aide. When he wanted to have an order conveyed he used to call a man to him he wanted to give the order to."

These remarks were delivered almost as an aside to the main thrust of Nonaka's position. Stripped of their translated clumsiness, they could have provided a key piece to the massacre puzzle. Relations between Nishimura and Imai had become so acrimonious by this point in the Malayan Campaign that each man was functioning with as little contact with the other as possible. Nishimura retained Nonaka as his personal aide. Imai, although strictly unentitled to a personal aide, used Inagaki as his. In effect, the separate personal messengers helped prevent the gulf between the division's two most senior officers from widening to a point where the headquarters became dysfunctional. Imai would never have used Nonaka as his mouthpiece, particularly in the presence of Nishimura. If Imai had been intent on issuing instructions during the divisional convoy's Parit Sulong stopover, he would have done so through Inagaki. This was the point of Nonaka's aside. It is a point that will acquire some significance in the trial's aftermath.

In rounding off his evidence, Nonaka emphasised Godwin had neither tortured nor mistreated him at any time during the Tokyo interrogation.

Nonaka: He did not use any force, nor did he say any bad words. He treated me very kindly, but he put leading questions to me.

Defence: How did you interpret the divisional commander's word "shobun" and how did you convey that word?

Nonaka: It was neither my duty nor right to put a comment on the word of the divisional commander. I had only to convey his order exactly as it was.

Was Nonaka just another Jap war criminal who, when faced with a capital charge, would twist the truth, distort it, blame others, lie and willingly recant sworn evidence; anything to save his neck? To hard bitten Australian investigators this was certainly the stereotypical wartime thug from the land of the rising sun. You just couldn't trust them. Any of them.

Or, on the other hand, did Nonaka's story as related in the Los Negros courtroom have a distinct ring of truth to it? Had he really been manipulated into signing a statement by a skilful interrogator whose job it was to know what effects repetitious suggestions, leading questions, and subtle phraseology could have on an unnerved suspect? And lastly, had the passage of so many years since the events in question made it genuinely impossible for the accused to recall details?

The job ahead of Rooney was now to ensure, through cross examination, that Nonaka's testimony from the witness box lacked all credibility. It was the former aide's original affidavit that must sustain as the apparently truthful account.

In any other Australian court the chief prosecutor would have been facing an impossible task. So many of the answers supposedly provided by Nonaka in response to questions from Godwin (See Appendix A, page 311) conveyed such obviously un-Japanese flows of thought and expression.

Then there were the uncomfortable allegations that Godwin had actually read from other witnesses' statements during the Nonaka interrogation in order to pressure the suspect into compliance with their contents.

Here the similarities between Nonaka's affidavit and those of Inagaki, Sono and Hinokuma seemed only to reinforce such allegations. To say the least, Godwin had conducted a series of highly questionable witness interrogations.

One factor was playing into Prosecutor Rooney's hands. Defence Counsel Nakayama had neglected to exploit the Nonaka affidavit's weaknesses to their full potential during his client's main evidence. To a large extent this failure on the part of the defence would determine the course of the prosecution cross examination.

Rooney began by concentrating on the orders delivered by Nishimura after he had inspected the prisoners.

Prosecutor: And how many people were present when those instructions were given?

Nonaka: I think there were staff officers and the adjutant of the division. I am not sure of it, however.

Prosecutor: Were all the officers of the convoy present at the inspection and later when the orders were given regarding the disposal of the prisoners of war?

Nonaka: I have no clear recollection about it but I think all of them were around there.

Prosecutor: Would you agree that there would be about seven or eight officers present when those instructions were given?

Nonaka: Yes, I do.

Rooney went ahead and tried to identify the officers who could have overheard Nishimura. Nonaka, of course, was one. Colonel Imai was another. Nonaka thought Sono and Hinokuma were also present.

Prosecutor: And immediately before Nishimura gave that

order he had been receiving a report from Fujita?

Nonaka: As far as I can remember on his way back Lt. General Nishimura was asked by Fujita as to how to handle the prisoners of war.

Prosecutor: I see, Fujita asked Nishimura how the prisoners of war were to be disposed of and it was then that Nishimura gave the order?

Nonaka: Yes, that is correct.

Prosecutor: So there was no physical reason why Nishimura could not have given the order direct to Fujita?

Nonaka: I think there was no physical reason.

Prosecutor: And was it for reasons of pride or face that he transmitted the order through you to Fujita?

Nonaka: I do not know about it.

Prosecutor: I see, and did you transmit the order immediately upon receiving it?

Nonaka: Yes I did.

Prosecutor: And did Nishimura remain there in a position to hear your transmission of the order to Fujita?

Nonaka: I think he heard my transmission of that order but I have no clear recollection about it.

Prosecutor: Did you repeat the order faithfully, word for word?

Nonaka: I transmitted the divisional commander's order exactly as it was without fail.

Nonaka went on to claim he had not the slightest memory of Colonel Imai providing instructions for the disposal of bodies. Rooney then switched back to the condition of the prisoners during Nishimura's inspection and asked Nonaka whether the passage he was about to read was a correct description of what he had seen and heard and smelt in Parit Sulong. The prosecutor then began quoting from Nonaka's original affidavit:

"I do remember seeing many Australian prisoners of war in various postures, most of whom appeared to be wounded. There was a nauseating stench of blood emanating from the prisoners of war confined in this room. In addition, these prisoners of war were making a considerable amount of noise, but I do not remember whether I heard any particularly loud groans or screams of pain."

Prosecutor: When you gave that description last October was it a plain statement of fact or was it a piece of fancy fiction?

Nonaka: Concerning some portions of that description I answered when I was not quite sure and when leading questions were put to me.

Prosecutor: Do you mean by that, that at the suggestion of the interrogating officer you put into your statement that which was not true or matters of which you had no clear recollection?

Nonaka: Yes I do.

Later in the cross examination Rooney referred back to the section of Nonaka's affidavit he had read allowed to the court. Had the words "most of whom were wounded" been suggested by the interrogating officer? Nonaka insisted that they had. Had he used the phrase "nauseating stench of blood?" Nonaka had no memory of using that phrase.

Rooney repeatedly probed for reasons why Nonaka had changed his story. Nonaka claimed that even during the interrogation itself he had become concerned and asked to speak to Sono and Hinokuma, whose statements had been read to him. His requests had been refused. He had begun to have serious misgivings about the affidavit he had signed as soon as he returned to his village. He had not known the proper procedure for correcting its errors. He had attempted to track down Sono and Hinokuma in Tokyo in the hopes they could help him. But as the city had suffered so much war damage he had been unable to find them.

The prosecutor's cross examination concluded at the end of the third day's hearing. On the fourth and final day of the trial the bench further examined Nonaka. Was he sure Nishimura had used the words "shobun seyo" and no other? Yes he was. Were any of the prisoners at Parit Sulong naked? He couldn't remember. How long after leaving the township did he learn the prisoners had been executed? After about two or three days when Staff Officer Morioka rejoined the division. Had he informed Nishimura what he had heard about the execution? He did not recall informing him. Well, if he had not informed Nishimura about the prisoners was it because he thought the divisional commander's order had been to execute them? No, operational matters were not his responsibility. After he had made his statement to Captain Godwin, had he ever imagined for what purpose it might be used? When he returned home he thought it might be used against Nishimura, Imai and himself. Was it after realising it could be used against himself that he became anxious to alter it? That is when he thought he should make corrections to it.

At the end of the defence's case Nakayama sought the court's permission for Nishimura to make a last statement from the dock. Rooney was against the idea, arguing that anything the general wanted to say should be incorporated in his counsel's final address.

After considering the implications, Brigadier Townley turned to the court interpreter and said: "Will you explain this, that strictly speaking the accused Nishimura is not entitled to make a statement from the dock once he has given evidence on oath. But seeing that the charge in this case is so serious, the court will, as a favour and in its discretion, allow him to do so. The court does not wish it to be felt that any accused was prevented from placing before it everything he wishes to place before the court."

Nishimura then stood in the dock. "I am very sorry," he intoned, "that due to my carelessness in this case such an incident as this happened. I wish to give praise with sorrow to those who were killed in this case. That is all."

In his final address to the court on behalf of both accused, Nakayama characterised the trial procedure as one of the strangest in modern times. Under the system employed it had been impossible for either Nishimura or Nonaka to produce evidence in rebuttal to the charges laid against them. As a result, Nakayama proclaimed, the court would be passing judgement based on "available evidence" which did not conform with the truth.

As far as Nishimura was concerned, it had been impossible for him to prepare his defence. He had been brought straight to Los Negros from a prison cell in Singapore to face a charge he only learned about a month earlier while enroute. Running briefly through the documentary evidence as presented by the prosecution, Nakayama argued that under the Australian trial system on Los Negros, conviction of the innocent became unavoidable. Los Negros had exhibited "to the fullest extent" the defects of trial by documentary evidence. The real culprit had been the 5th Imperial Guards Regiment. Instead, a group of staff officer "survivors" had manoeuvred to place the entire responsibility on the divisional commander and his personal aide. The testimony presented had not been material evidence. It had been mere hearsay and lacked accuracy. Anyone acquainted with court procedures would be well aware of these facts.

Having lambasted the system, Nakayama went ahead with a point-by-point discussion of the evidence presented during the four-day hearing. But it was a thankless task and the further he continued with it the more fragile his arguments appeared. The system of which he complained so bitterly had defeated him and he knew it.

It was Prosecutor Rooney's closing address that would

make the news columns in Australia the next day. Nobody wanted to read a Nip lawyer's complaints about justice Australian style. Reassurance of the system's integrity and vindication of the righteous cause; these were the requirements. Rooney was ready to provide.

The evidence of Lt. Hackney, he said, reading from his prepared text, had provided a detailed and vivid description of the atrocity. The court was fortunate in having such testimony of a survivor and this evidence, he pointed out, had been "uncontradicted."

The defence of each of the accused, argued Rooney, depended upon one or another of two hypotheses. Firstly, that the killings had been caused by a tragic misunderstanding of Nishimura's order. Or secondly, that it had been due to the deliberate disobedience of Nishimura's order by unspecified sub-ordinate officers.

"Even if it could be argued," said Rooney, "that a military officer of Nishimura's rank and experience could possibly make such an order in terms likely to be misunderstood, that theory is demolished if the court accepts that immediately upon the giving of the order and before it was relayed by Nonaka, Colonel Imai made an additional order to cremate the bodies by gasoline. This is clearly incapable of any mistake or confusion."

The executions had been carried out, argued the prosecutor, within an hour or two of the convoy's departure and no other business was attempted by Nishimura or any of his staff beyond inspecting the prisoners and giving the order. Rooney also offered the observation that no disciplinary action had been taken by Nishimura or anybody else in regard to the massacre. No enquiry had been held to sheet home the responsibility.

Each of the accused, he said, was entitled to a separate consideration of the evidence. Although he was a mere conduit and had nothing to do with the instigation or supervision of the execution, Nonaka must have known the true meaning of the order. He must have recognised it as illegal under international law. His part had been minor by comparison, but he could not hope to escape some responsibility. His deliberate attempts to deceive the court disentitled him to any special claim for clemency.

Nishimura's case, Rooney submitted, was very different. Here was a man in a high position of authority, inflamed with power and intoxicated with temporary success. Out of sheer arrogance and without any possible justification, he arbitrarily ordered the execution of those prisoners of war and accepted Colonel Imai's addition as to the disposal of the bodies after execution.

"I am forced to submit to the court," Rooney went on, "that Nishimura was an evil man, caring nothing for human life or suffering and having no regard for the conventions or for international law or for the dictates of humanity. It is submitted that it would be impossible to find a case which demands prosecution and punishment more than the case against Nishimura and it is further submitted that it is the type of case contemplated by the statute creating this jurisdiction."

At 1420 hours on June 22, 1950, the Australian War Crimes Court at Los Negros Island adjourned to consider its findings. Fifty minutes later Brigadier Townley led his four bench colleagues back to announce that Nishimura and Nonaka had both been found guilty as charged. After another adjournment, this time lasting 20 minutes, the court sentenced Nishimura to suffer death by hanging and Nonaka to be imprisoned for six months.

Lt. Colonel Charles G. W. Anderson made the nightmare decision of leaving behind some 150 severely wounded troops when he ordered a withdrawal from Parit Sulong after four days of savage fighting. He was awarded the Victoria Cross soon after.

Chapter 13

"Take no prisoners; leave no wounded"

——————◆——————

With the guilty verdicts on General Nishimura and Captain Nonaka, the Australian Military Court had concurred with one fundamental theory of the prosecution case. The fate of the prisoners slaughtered at Parit Sulong had been decided during the five to eight minute time frame of the divisional commander's visit.

It was a convenient theory. Its origins, of course, lay in the vital four-paragraph segment of Lt. Ben Hackney's eye-witness report describing the visit of the senior officer, "presumably the commander of Japanese forces in the area."

Mesmerised by these paragraphs, British and Australian investigators alike had limited their enquiries to establishing what might have transpired during this brief interval. Even when Hackney's capacity for recall was exposed as being, at best, highly unreliable, the emphasis of investigations still concentrated on that five to eight minute time frame. The overwhelming requirement continued to be the arrest of a senior Japanese officer fitting the lone survivors' description.

When Australia's War Crimes office in Tokyo resumed investigations into the case in late 1949, after a two-year lull, the exclusive focus of endeavour remained on that 'short, stocky" senior officer. By then the AG's department in Melbourne was urging another attempt at pinning the massacre on Nishimura. This time, there would no longer be a requirement for suspect identification by Hackney.

The cumulative effect of these restricted investigations, stretched across four years and ten months, was questionable, to say the least. In the final analysis, personal recollections of momentary remarks made during the briefest of timespans eight years and five months earlier — the claims and the counter claims — were the details that had preoccupied the Los Negros courtroom.

The convenient theory had immeasurably simplified investigations. The convenient theory had also simplified the legal process. But the convenient theory had most certainly predetermined the verdicts.

As it happened, the Parit Sulong Massacre had not been triggered by any remarks made by Nishimura during those supposedly crucial five to eight minutes. The trigger for the killing lay in the four days of furious fighting that had preceded his visit. Significantly, all details of these events were excluded from the court's attention by the very nature of the investigations undertaken and the presentation of the prosecution case.

Four days prior to the January 22 massacre, Australian forces defending the Muar River western front in northern Johore began a series of battles against invading Imperial Guardsmen. Japanese 25th Army Commander Yamashita would later characterise these as "the most savage action of the Malayan Campaign." His words were well chosen. To this day the degree of combat savagery has never been fully revealed. The Australians went into battle on the Muar Front as the overall British commander, Lt. General Arthur Percival, was struggling to withdraw his entire Westforce frontline defenders through a perilous bottleneck on the main north-south trunk road at the township of Yong Peng. Percival feared the Japanese would continue infiltrating forces by sea in small boats down the Straits of Malacca and eventually cut the roadlink south to Singapore behind retreating Westforce units. The defenders would then be ripe for annihilation.

Australian reinforcements were rushed to the crossroads village of Bakri situated south of the Muar River. Bakri lies some 10 miles east of the rivermouth township of Muar along a winding secondary road that eventually runs to Yong Peng, a further 30 miles away in the eastern hinterland. The Australians initially came within the overall command structure of the 45th Indian Brigade comprising the 4/9th Jats, 7/6th Rajputana Rifles and 5/18th Royal Garhwal. The three indifferently trained Indian battalions were positioned to hold the Muar River natural defence line against the Japanese advance down Peninsular Malaya's western coastal region.

Australia's 2/29th Battalion and a troop of the 2/4th Anti-Tank Regiment arrived on January 17, 1942. They stopped about a mile and a half west of Bakri along the road to Muar. Australia's 2/19th Battalion arrived the following day and was deployed at Bakri itself and in positions defending road approaches leading from the the fishing village of Parit Jawa to the south west and Yong Peng. Attached to the 45th Brigade from the outset had been the 65th Australian Artillery Battery of the 2/15th Field Regiment.

Both Australian reinforcement battalions plunged quickly into bitter hand-to-hand clashes with Imperial Guards troops who had successfully forded the Muar River to rout numerous Indian defensive positions. Bayonets and handgrenades set grim standards for combat to come. Australia's official war history, *The Japanese Thrust,* by Lionel Wigmore, only hints at the viciousness of the fighting when it describes action by B Company 2/19th troops just south of Bakri in terrain lying in the fork of the Parit Jawa and Yong Peng roads. It details how B Company units employed encircling tactics in one action to kill 140 Japanese. The cost: 10 Australian dead and 15 wounded. In the aftermath, the Australians encountered the problem of seemingly dead Japanese troops rising from the battlefield to resume the fight. In the Wigmore account, Lt. P. R. Reynolds, a grazier from Cumnock, New South

Wales, describes standing among a litter of Japanese dead around a gun position and spotting "one of the prostrate figures" attempting to hurl a handgrenade. The Japanese is shot dead but his grenade explodes, wounding Reynolds who then falls close to another not-so-dead Japanese.

Reynolds' recollection is recorded by Wigmore: "I saw him pushing his rifle laboriously towards me so I picked up my pistol from under me and with my left hand took careful aim and pulled the trigger for all my worth, but it would not fire. I can tell you I was extremely annoyed. Luckily my batman saw the Jap up to his tricks, so he shot him. At the same time Captain Harris, 2 i/c, dashed up and kicked the rifle out of the Jap's hands."

This episode is followed by an account of Reynolds' batman, in the same general area, shooting two more Japanese described as "wearing only short trousers." Included in the official history is a subsequent story of two Australian troops searching the same battlefield "to see if all the Japanese were dead." A supposed corpse suddenly sprang to its feet and made a dash, unarmed, at one of them — Private "Bluey" Watkins. A war diarist is then quoted as writing that Bluey, "who had done quite a lot of fighting in Sydney, threw aside his rifle and bayonet and came to grips. A good fight was witnessed for a short time until (Private) Farrel came to the rescue with his .303. The explosion almost deafened Bluey, and some time afterwards he was shouting loudly his story to his mates."

The official history fails to make clear the fate that thereafter befell all wounded Japanese encountered on the Muar Front by Australians. Mr Charles "Chick" Warden was a 17-year-old infantryman with the 2/19th's B Company when he fought in the same battle just south of Bakri and a string of subsequent actions. Now retired and living in the Sydney suburb of Baulkham Hills, Chick Warden has never been under illusions as to what prompted the Parit Sulong

Massacre. He has kept a private account of his Malaya combat experiences.

Under January 19, 1942, the day of the Bakri fighting, Warden records: "During the morning we were given orders to spread out and move through the scrub and bracken fern in which we had been positioned all night. The belt of scrub finished and we were in the rubber charging forward. The enemy were attacking A Company who were positioned along a rise in the rubber. The move of B Company brought us in on the flank and behind the enemy who were completely taken by surprise. The enemy just did not know where to go because they were virtually being hit from all sides. I believe this was the reason a number of them played 'possum' and pretended to be dead, as we were later to find out."

Warden's account continues: "There were some nasty little incidents involving some of B Company coming through behind us doing a body count and gathering up automatic weapons. Some of the assumed to be dead that we had passed suddenly came to life and started throwing grenades around and the enemy wounded wanted to make their last fanatical shot."

He goes on to describe moving through a rubber plantation to an elevated position where his unit became the target for a brief Japanese artillery barrage. "When the barrage stopped we moved off again through the rubber and it was about midday when we took up another defensive position in the rubber about 100 yards in and parallel to the main road. While in this position we were told that as we were on the defensive we were not in a situation to take any prisoners and due to past recent experience we were to leave no wounded. Approach to any assumed dead or wounded enemy was to be done with degree of caution and the bayonet was to be used. In brief the order was: take no prisoners, leave no wounded."

Who issued these orders? Warden has always firmly believed they came straight from the 2/19th Commanding Officer, Lt. Colonel Charles G. W. Anderson, who had personally directed tactics for this Bakri action. Pointedly, there are no indications in the battalion's War Diary that Anderson formally issued such instructions. However there has long been wide acceptance among Australians who fought on the Muar Front that "take no prisoners, leave no wounded" was at least the officially sanctioned "word" given the extreme emergency of the situation. Even those uneasy about the source of the directions concede these were certainly the tactics employed by the Australians during the desperate 72-hour period from January 19 - 22. Put very simply: there was no alternative course of action open to them if they were to survive, let alone tie down the Japanese for the estimated seven days it would take to withdraw Westforce through Yong Peng.

With every passing hour the predicament of the 45th Indian Brigade and its Australian reinforcements intensified. British officers lost control of some Indian units which broke and ran. Other Indian units became cut off and lost as Nishimura sought to confuse the battlefield, driving as many wedges as he could between defending forces then employing encircling manoeuvres to disrupt their cohesion. Australia's 2/29th itself became isolated and in a 24-hour period lost first its commanding officer, Lt. Colonel J. C. Robertson, then its deputy commander, Major S. F. Olliff.

Endeavouring to capitalise on his absolute superiority in tanks, Nishimura sent the Gotanda tank company into battle. In the fury of the next few days the company's entire complement of 10 vehicles would be destroyed and every crew member killed. The Australians were less successful, however, when it came to dealing with the enemy's superiority in the air. At 1000 hrs. on January 19, a Japanese bomber pilot scored a direct hit on the 45th Indian Brigade

This picture of Lt General Takuma Nishimura was taken in Malaya in January 1942 and almost certainly while he was directing his Imperial Guards against Australian forces in the Muar Front action.

headquarters at Bakri killing or severely wounding every attached staff officer except two. One survivor was the CO, Brigadier H. C. Duncan, who was heavily concussed. The other was the brigade major. Also killed in this bombing was the CO of Australia's 65th Artillery Battery, Major W. W. Julius, who was visiting the HQ at the time. As the official history points out, Australia's 2/19th commander, Lt Colonel Anderson, then assumed command of the 45th Brigade which had practically ceased to exist, except as a liability.

Anderson quickly sought to re-group what was left of the brigade and its reinforcements in preparation for a withdrawal down the road eastwards to Yong Peng. He ordered the 2/29th back to Bakri. In the ensuing confusion the battalion suffered terrible casualties from enemy fire, their own artillery and 2/19th mortars. When the battalion assembled at Bakri its fighting strength was listed: A Company, 0 officers and 45 men; B Company, 4 officers and 100 men; C Company, 3 officers and 45 men.

Orders for the withdrawal from Bakri called for the advance-guard to move off at 0700 hrs on January 20. Unnecessary gear was to be dumped and destroyed and various trucks set aside for carrying the large number of wounded. Anderson organised his force as a battalion of five rifle companies to which he attached two companies of Jats and a combined force of Rajputs and Garhwalis.

An hour out of Bakri, the advance-guard struck its first Japanese road ambush. The enemy had dug into a slight rise on the south side of the road and heavily resisted all Australian attempts at dislodging them. The official history tells how Anderson finally decided a "rapid and spirited" assault was needed to break through the Japanese position. The assault was organised and a group of Australians charged the Japanese singing:

Once a jolly swagman camped by a billabong,
Under the shade of a coolibah tree . . . . .

The history notes that "'Waltzing Matilda', never sung by Australians with more enthusiasm than when they meet in surroundings strange to them, had become a battle song." The same rousing scene becomes suddenly transformed when viewed from the vantage point of the battlefield itself. "Chick" Warden was there and records it this way:

"Our two forward scouts were shot dead and our section on the road came under heavy machine-gun fire. The enemy machine-gun nest was somewhere on the top of the cutting on the right hand side of the road and our section on that side went in to attack but were pinned down. 11 section was withdrawn back along the left side then across the road and up the right side. As we charged up we were under fire but we were not exactly sure where it was coming from as the enemy were pretty well concealed. I was about to go over the top of a rotting tree trunk that was across my front and looked down and saw a Jap under a small personal camouflage net on the other side. I gave him a quick

Charles "Chick" Warden faked his age to join the Australian Army prior to the outset of the Pacific War. He was 16 years old when he went to Malaya with Australia's 8th Division and barely 17 when he fought General Nishimura's Imperial Guards in the ferocious Muar Front battles. Warden, now retired and living with his wife, Leonie, in Baulkam Hills, Sydney, is adamant that the order "take no prisoners, leave no wounded" was issued personally by Colonel Charles Anderson, Australian commander of the Allied column which attempted to break through Japanese lines at Parit Sulong.

effective shot. At the same time I saw a Jap with a light machine-gun who had just shot my mate on my right and in his haste to bring the gun around onto me it fell over on its legs giving me the split second to get my shot into him at a distance of about eight feet.

"I momentarily took cover behind the old rotting tree trunk because I knew for sure now where the enemy was and we were among them. I took a quick look over the top and saw a pair of legs and backside about six feet to my right so I shot him in the hip. He gave a yell and was certainly not dead but it slowed him down and gave him something to think about for the present. I then saw the face of a Jap lying down beside a rubber tree about 12 feet away directly in front. I fired a quick shot at him and at the same time I was knocked backwards off balance and felt a terrific burning pain in my left shoulder as a bullet went through. All of the aforementioned happened within about two minutes of me first reaching the old tree trunk.

"We were pinned down now, my mate on my left threw two grenades forward. As he got onto his knees to throw the second grenade he was hit and badly wounded. The bullet went through his body and right lung and out his back leaving about a three-inch diameter hole. I threw one grenade forward. Our 12 platoon commander was about 10 feet behind me throwing grenades over us into the machine gun post but was required to break his cover from behind a rubber tree to do this. In so doing he was hit and badly wounded.

"During this time A Company had worked their way round to the right and put down a covering fire in front of Colonel Anderson as he came charging in with another platoon of B Company. There were quite a number of enemy dead mainly from the grenades that my platoon commander had thrown in. The Jap that had shot me was dead. I think we both must have fired at the same time because my bullet had penetrated the side of the rubber tree before hitting him in the face which was a mess. The Jap I had shot in the hip, together with several other wounded fanatics, were bayoneted where they lay. Colonel Anderson gave the order to gather up the automatic weapons and take an identification disc off our dead. Our wounds were covered with field dressings and our badly wounded were carried down to the road and placed in the trucks."

The Australian-led retreat began moving again at 1100 hours but by 1230 hrs had run into another, even stronger, Japanese roadblock. Here the enemy strength was estimated at more than two companies with at least six heavy machine-gun positions covering the road where it threaded across a section of low lying, tree covered swamp. Close quarters fighting with grenades, small arms and bayonets continued through the afternoon. So close were the Australians to the Japanese positions that it became impossible to use supporting artillery fire. At dusk Anderson decided to launch an all out assault on the Japanese positions backed by heavy smoke and mortar fire. The 2/19th war diarist saw the action this way:

"Every man was fighting mad. Mortar shells were directed onto targets by infantrymen, a few yards from the target (voice relayed back). Gunners were fighting with rifles and bayonets and axes. (Range too short for 25 pdrs except to Jap rear areas west.) A gun crew pushed its 25 pdr round a cutting and blew out the first roadblocks (vehicles) at 75 yards range. Carriers pushed within 5 yards of Jap machine guns and blew them out. Two carriers almost cut the 4-inch walls of a concrete house to pieces with Vickers. (House contained 3 Jap machine guns and about 60 men.) Men went forward under heavy machine gun fire and chopped roadblocks to pieces with axes. About 1830 hours the Japs had had enough and cleared out, leaving hundreds of casualties."

Australian troops once more collected the identification tags of their dead, disposed of the enemy wounded where they lay on the battlefield, loaded their own wounded into trucks and moved on. Darkness was now enveloping the convoy. Anderson was anxious to keep his column moving through the night in order to clear eight miles of open swampy terrain under cover of darkness. Past this was rubber plantation countryside leading to the village of Parit Sulong. Here the trees would at least give some protection from Japanese air attacks which were sure to resume at sun up. Every firefight and air attack had swollen the ranks of wounded. Anderson had been promised a relief force but there was no sign of it.

Chick Warden takes up the story:

"We walked all night and by dawn we were only a few miles from Parit Sulong village. We were told that the village was occupied by the enemy. The convoy had now stopped and we were ordered to leave the road and work our way towards the village. B Company on the right flank, A Company on the left and C Company advance-guard. We were not far from the village when C Company made contact with the enemy and were being attacked. With the support of A Company, our boys managed to halt the enemy charge and pin them down.

"B Company made a swing to the left and to the enemy's surprise we came in on a flank attack. A Company quickly made an encircling movement as we made our flank attack and this movement sandwiched the enemy and they died in this position. As we moved through where they lay the bayonet was extensively used otherwise we could have been shot in the back. About 15 feet in front of me one of the enemy was on his knees about to throw a grenade. My bullet hit him in the chest and he fell forward, the grenade exploding in his hand alongside his head.

"There were several encounters of hand-to-hand fighting and any of the enemy that moved or even did not move were either bayoneted or shot. None of the enemy survived to get away and my estimate was that about 300 Japanese died in this engagement.

"We also sustained casualties both dead and wounded. One of my section who had already been wounded twice during the previous days had now been killed and another had sustained a serious stomach wound. As following previous actions, an identification disc was taken from our dead and our seriously wounded were carried to the road and placed on the trucks. All enemy automatic weapons were gathered up for possible future use against them. We resumed our original intended advance towards the village.

By about 8. 00 am we were on the outskirts of the village and we were taking heavy machine-gun fire."

Warden describes the Australian attack against Japanese forces in Parit Sulong thus:

"It was evident the Japanese held the village in considerable strength and had turned the houses and buildings into strong posts. Our carriers were brought into this action and they raced forward peppering the buildings with machine-gun fire. They would then swing away and come in again making another run. It didn't take many such runs by the carriers on the building nearest to us before the enemy apparently decided they had had enough and as they ran out of the building we took care of them with our rifle fire.

"This procedure was repeated several times during the day as we slowly cleared the village of the enemy. About mid-afternoon we hurriedly helped refill the Vickers machine-gun belts in the carriers and it was getting on towards late afternoon before we reached the river and bridge and could say that we now occuped the village; that is, what was left of it. Some of the buildings were on fire and the others had been blown apart by grenades and mortar fire. Bodies of enemy dead lay everywhere and a conservative estimate would be that about 500 or 600 of the Imperial Guards Division had been killed in the village of Parit Sulong.

"Having occupied the village we immediately mounted an attack on the bridge but the enemy machine-gun fire was heavy in the confined space of the bridge and we were pinned down. We gradually managed to withdraw, taking care not to be silhouetted by the fires of the burning buildings in the village behind us.

"There were only four of us left now in 11 section out of the original ten; two of us had been wounded the day before. It was dark by the time we took up our night position with what was left of B Company on the western side of the perimeter and approach to the bridge. After a quick meal (bully beef and a biscuit washed down with a mouth full of water) we spread out about six feet apart and lay quietly in the rubber. We had walked a long way all night and had fought hard all day and it was good now to have a bit of a rest. We had been told to hold our fire during the night as it would disclose our position to the enemy and if possible use the bayonet and make the killing as quiet as possible.

"The night was so dark you couldn't see your hand in front of yourself. Through the night we received the occasional incoming mortar which really caused no concern or injury but in fact were actually to our advantage because they kept us awake and alert. It would have been so easy to go to sleep but we knew that sleep was not possible because we knew that our life depended on keeping awake and we depended on each other in the section. All night the enemy were probing and calling out "Hello Joe" and "Where are you, Joe" making out as if they were Indians but we just lay quietly and listened for any nearby movement which we knew for sure would not be one of ours. Late in the night there was an unearthly scream from somewhere to my right then all was quiet again."

The Parit Sulong battle raged throughout January 21. The rear of the convoy became target for intensified attacks by Japanese tanks and mechanised infantry. Daylight hours saw continuous air strikes on the Australian positions. Japanese mortar and artillery fire also took a fearful toll on the trapped forces. With the troops at the head of the column unable to break through the Japanese bridge defences, those in the rear sections found themselves being pressed inexorably inwards. The more the column compacted, the more vulnerable it became to Japanese strafing, bombing and artillery strikes. On the night of January 20 the Australian perimeter had been about 1,500 yards wide. Twenty-four hours later this distance had been reduced to less than 700 yards

In the afternoon of January 21, with less than a day's

supply of artillery and small arms ammunition, the Australians made further attempts to blast through Japanese defences around the concrete bridge spanning the muddy Simpang Kiri river. But the enemy refused to yield and the convoy's only escape route remained blocked. By now the condition of the convoy's wounded had become appalling. Virtually all medical supplies were exhausted, including desperately needed morphia. Casualty numbers had grown alarmingly. It became obvious to Anderson his men would be unable to sustain another day's combat unless the promised relief force arrived.

Later in the afternoon of the same day, Anderson, pressed by his two medical officers, attempted to get two ambulances packed with the worst wounded and flying white flags, past the enemy's bridge position. The Japanese commander refused the Australian request. Instead, he demanded the complete capitulation of Anderson's column after which, he said, medical attention would be provided. The Japanese officer retained the ambulances on the bridge's steep approach ramp, threatening to open fire with machine-guns should any attempt be made to move them. During the night the ambulance brakes were surreptitiously released and the two vehicles rolled silently back down the ramp and were able to return within the Australian perimeter.

A dawn airdrop on January 22 to the beleaguered Australians provided, among other things, morphia for the wounded. But in strict battlefield terms, the re-supply was far too little, far too late. The relief column had failed to materialise and the casualty situation could no longer be sustained. One last attempt was made to test the enemy's bridge defences. Elements of A Company of the 2/19th succeeded in advancing onto the bridge itself but were there confronted by six Japanese machine-gun positions on the far bank of the river.

By 9 am, Anderson had judged his position hopeless and

what remained of the convoy in danger of imminent annihilation. He issued orders for the destruction of all artillery pieces, carriers and transports. Following this there would be a withdrawal in small groups of all men capable of walking from the battlefield. A compass bearing of 340 degrees was provided to get the force away from Parit Sulong. The men were then instructed to swing east and head to Yong Peng via jungle and plantation tracks. It was a heartbreaking decision for Anderson. He had to abandon the wounded he had so desperately tried to protect and leave them to the mercy of the Japanese he had fought so savagely for five days.

Australia would bestow her highest military award for valour — the Victoria Cross — on Lt. Colonel Charles Groves Wright Anderson for his outstanding leadership throughout the Muar Front fighting. Japan, too, would recognise the bravery of her fighting forces in the same actions, conferring posthumously a special citation on all men of the Gotanda Tank Company, and another citation for the Imperial Guards' Ogaki Battalion which fought the Australians along the entire Bakri-Parit Sulong road.

It is not the purpose of this exercise to make moral judgements on either side's fighting tactics during the ferocious Muar Front action. Nor is it the intention to draw comparisons between the way the Australians, on the one hand, and the Japanese on the other, chose to deal with their respective enemy wounded. These are the sort of questions that will remain unresolved as long as men go to war. The object here is purely to examine those aspects of the Muar Front combat pertinent to Nishimura's arraignment before an Australian Military Court. They are vital points that court members on Los Negros never had a chance to consider due to the manipulated investigations of the case and the Army's careful structuring of the trial procedure.

One undeniable fact is that following four and a half days

of the Malayan Campaign's fiercest action the Australians emerged from the battlefield without a single prisoner. Close quarters combat resulted in the deaths of some 2,000 Japanese troops, the overwhelming majority being Imperial Guards. Another undeniable fact is that Australian troops, because of the circumstances of the fighting, killed (or executed — depending on your viewpoint) wounded Japanese where they lay. Furthermore, they followed at least a general understanding — if not an order — about taking no prisoners and leaving no wounded.

All this is directly relevant to the considerable emphasis placed by the Los Negros court on the Imperial Guards' divisional orders for handling prisoners. Nishimura never wavered from his original insistence, made in 1947, that he had only issued commands for prisoners to be removed to rear areas. The prosecution had single-mindedly worked to undermine this claim. Nishimura, for his part, had been unable to present any independent evidence to support his position. The trial system had ensured this.

But such evidence exists and it certainly existed at the time of the trial. No less an authority than the prosecution's star witness, Ben Hackney, knew many Australian soldiers had been captured by the Imperial Guards on the Muar Front. He knew the Japanese had moved these prisoners to rear areas as ordered by Nishimura. Hackney had personally met these men following his eventual capture and transportation to Kuala Lumpur's Pudu Jail, the Japanese main rear area holding point for prisoners of war.

Such details, significantly enough, were omitted from Hackney's documentary evidence. But in a subsequent 116-page manuscript entitled "Dark Evening," Hackney described a surprise reunion in Pudu with his own battalion's adjutant, Captain M. C. Morgan, a 26-year-old regular soldier from Seymour in Victoria. The two met on the Parit Sulong survivor's first night in the jail. "We talked for ages," Hackney wrote, "but firstly, of course, about members of our unit and what had happened to them, and I found that there were quite a few in Pudu." It must follow as a reasonable assumption that had Hackney appeared in the witness box on Los Negros, the defence would have verified, once and for all, Nishimura's long held position on the critical prisoners' order issue.

The question of Australian troops taking no prisoners and leaving no wounded has profound implications for the re-focusing of the Parit Sulong Massacre case. Anyone familiar with combat injuries and post-fighting battlefield conditions recognises it is generally easy to determine how killed-in-action (KIA) met their deaths and from what causes. Machine-gun fire, small arms fire, mortar bombs, artillery shells and air strikes all leave distinctive tell-tale signs. So do *coup de grace* bayonet thrusts or pistol and rifle shots.

In this context, the role played by self-confessed Parit Sulong executioner, Lt. Seizaburo Fujita, must be viewed as pivotal. It will be recalled that in the pre-trial legal spring cleaning the prosecution's first act was to withdraw the charge against Fujita. The court was then informed that no evidence would be given against the Japanese lieutenant, nor would there be any requirement for deliberations on the part he played. From that moment onwards the Fujita factor was pushed aside. It never became a trial issue. His unsworn, unsigned statement was considered relevant only in as much as it served to support the various affidavits indicating Nishimura had personally issued orders for the massacre.

Dismissed as unimportant by prosecution and court alike was the opening paragraph of Fujita's account. It read:

At about 0600 hours in the morning of the day following the capture of Bakri, 2 Battalion of 5 Infantry Regiment continued their advance along the road leading to Parit Sulong. On the orders of 2 Battalion

Commander, Lieutenant Colonel Kojima Yoshinori, I remained behind at Bakri with about 10 non-commissioned officers and other ranks for the main purpose of burying those soldiers of 2 Battalion who had been killed in the fighting there, and to locate any wounded and missing personnel of the battalion in that area. As a result of these duties I remained working in the vicinity of Bakri until the evening of the same day, following which I and the aforementioned non-commissioned officers and other ranks advanced along the road to Parit Sulong, stopping overnight in the jungle near a deserted village and from which place we could plainly hear the sounds of battle about 4,000 metres ahead of us.

In other words, Fujita and the ten Imperial Guardsmen in his charge spent from dawn to dusk on January 21, 1942, gathering up the corpses of their former comrades killed by the Australians. The dead they handled would have displayed all manner of frightful injuries. Among the bodies would have been a certain percentage readily identifiable — from the burial party's viewpoint — as executed wounded. On his arrival in Parit Sulong on the afternoon of January 22 Fujita verbally reported on his previous day's activities to Battalion Commander Kojima and Adjutant Sugihara. Both men happened to be standing together at the time. Fujita's "statement" failed to reveal the contents of his verbal report. But immediately thereafter the OC burial party found himself appointed OC Australian and Indian prisoners.

Mass murderer Fujita's activities, as far as the Los Negros trial was concerned, were incidental to the task at hand. It was therefore never contemplated that perhaps a front-line fighter, who had obviously made gruesome discoveries during battlefield burial duties, had infinitely more motivation to massacre than a divisional commander on a brief, routine post-battle inspection. Quite aside from the matter of motivation, Fujita's background was never considered in relation to that of Nishimura's whose Army history was steeped in matters of military law and who had sat in judgement on courts martial affecting the very destiny of his nation.

As far as Fujita and fellow front line soldiers were concerned, they needed no orders for what they saw as just retribution. Nishimura, for his part, had everything to lose and nothing to gain in terms of command control from capriciously inciting to slaughter at perhaps the most critical moment in Japan's Malayan Campaign. Could a man of Nishimura's proven calibre have been so irresponsible?

The Los Negros verdict would spur urgent rethinking of the whole process that had led to his conviction. However, by the time it became obvious a miscarriage of justice had occurred, an official cover-up would be deemed the better course of action.

Chapter 14

Questioning the documentary evidence

———— ◆ ————

Half an hour after their convictions, Lt. General Nishimura and Captain Nonaka, handcuffed together, were bundled into the rear of an Army lorry. Under armed guard they were driven back to Lombrum Point where Nonaka was unshackled and delivered into the custody of guards at the main prison compound. His admission forms noted that the convicted prisoner, was entitled to good behaviour remission of one third of his six-month sentence. Nonaka had been in custody for five months. In other words, he was due for release approximately a month before his trial began.

Nonaka's punishment, of course, demolished claims by Australian political and military leaders alike that the *Manus Trials* were only for suspected criminals whose convictions were likely to carry the death sentence. Even the most vindictive Australian investigator could never have envisaged the divisional commander's hapless personal aide being given the death penalty. Nonaka had been arrested and placed on trial simply because he was an essential element in the moves to convict Nishimura. Now that these had succeeded so spectacularly, the military looked to the controlled environment on Los Negros to ensure all questionable aspects of the convictions remained firmly under wraps. Taxing times lay ahead.

Nishimura was driven to the separate condemned section

at the western extremity of the prison complex. As the first inmate on death row, he was allotted cell A1. An RAN surgeon pronounced him medically fit to stand the rigours of solitary confinement and prison staff prepared for what they believed would be a short period of incarceration for the former general leading to his eventual execution.

Australian morning newspapers, reporting the sentences, highlighted Prosecutor Rooney's description of the former divisional commander — ". . . an evil man who cared nothing for human life or suffering. . . ." Editorials commented favourably on the outcome of the trial and a nation seemingly settled back satisfied that justice, thus far, had indeed been done. In reporting to Parliament on the Manus preparations four months earlier, Prime Minister Menzies had spoken nobly of his government's intentions. Australia's conduct in victory, he said, should be marked by an adherence to those great principles of clear allegation, prompt trial, and unswerving execution of judgment. These were the principles that had characterized the whole development "of what we call, in simple but proud terms, British justice." From the electorate's viewpoint, Canberra seemed to be right on track.

A separate set of legal provisions swung into force on the conclusion of the trials. Findings and sentences were subject to confirmation by Adjutant General Anderson. Nishimura and Nonaka each had the right to petition against findings and sentences, or both. Notice of any intention to petition had to be lodged within 48 hours of the termination of the trial. Petitions themselves were required to be submitted within 14 days.

As far as the military was concerned, transcripts of the court proceedings received at AHQ in Melbourne would have to be examined first by the Director of Legal Services (DLS), Colonel A. G. Allaway, of the Australian Army Legal Corps (AALC). He would advise whether the court had been legally convened and properly constituted and if the charge had been properly drawn and disclosed as an offence under the War Crimes Act. Allaway would also ultimately advise whether the sentences were valid and could legally be confirmed.

After the DLS review, the court proceedings were required to be submitted to the Judge Advocate General (JAG), Justice William Ballantyne Simpson, of the Supreme Court Bench, Canberra. Judge Simpson would advise and report on whether any petitions submitted should be upheld or dismissed and whether there was any reason why findings and sentences should not be confirmed. It was then up to the AG to make his final recommendations.

Choji Nakayama lodged his intention to petition within the specified 48-hour time frame. A week later he submitted the formal document signed by Nishimura. In this petition, Nishimura made it plain he was not pleading for mercy, nor was he afraid to die. He merely asked that his case be reviewed on the basis of the quality of evidence supplied by the prosecution. "Although I have spent all my life for my country as a member of the Japanese military, and was always glad to die for my country, I shall die in vain if I must submit my life according to the decision handed down by the Manus Island War Crimes Court," he wrote.

"What I wish to say here is that according to the system of trial by documentary evidence, irrespective of the evidence presented by the defence in court, the accused person will be found guilty of the charge. This is exactly the case with me."

Nishimura went on to argue that the affidavits of his three subordinate staff officers, produced by the prosecution, amounted to a conspiracy to place the blame for the massacre squarely on his shoulders. He repeated his claim that the only orders he ever issued concerning prisoners were for them to be removed to Yamashita's headquarters at the rear. It was a matter of common sense, he insisted, that a divisional commander would never give an order to execute prisoners by firing squad. But the court, he pointed out, had concluded he had done so.

"I cannot accept such a false charge, and I cannot die for such a false accusation," continued the Nishimura petition. "The fact that I had given an order for the evacuation of prisoners can be proved by my own sworn statement taken some three years ago at Singapore, at which time I had never thought such an atrocity had taken place. Without any thought whatever, I stated the situations as they were. This is the honest statement."

Nishimura maintained that had he been in Japan prior to the legal proceedings at Manus Island he would have been able to gather enough evidence to clear his name. But he had been incarcerated in Singapore since the end of hostilities and had been unable to make any outside contacts. "I came to know of this case for the first time when I boarded the ship for Manus Island at Hong Kong on May 21, 1950. It was then too late for me to do anything. In this respect I had to stand before the court without any statement for my cause."

His petition concluded: "I have often heard and read about people suffering from false accusation, but today I, too, am in the same circumstance. And reflecting on my trip to Europe many years ago I cannot help recalling the horrible impression I got at the Tower of London. They say history repeats. Today I feel as if I am tortured like those who had been thrown into the Tower of London. I know there is no re-examination in a war crimes court, but I trust the confirming officer will be fair to look once more into the truth of this case to see that I am charged on false accusations."

While the war crimes office on Los Negros handled the routine task of forwarding defence petitions to Melbourne, a serious complication presented itself demanding discretion and, above all, prompt covert action.

Brigadier Townley had become increasingly concerned

about the well being of one of the panel of military officers who had deliberated with him on the Parit Sulong case. Major Clarke, the Army intelligence officer and Japanese language expert, had developed symptoms of extreme distress. At times he appeared quite detached from from his surroundings and was urged by his colleagues to rest. Shortly after participating in sentencing Nishimura and Nonaka, Major Clarke was forced to seek medical advice from naval surgeons attached to *HMAS Tarangau*. Doctors diagnosed him as suffering from urticaria and acute auditory and visual hallucinations. The chief medical officer recommended the court member be returned to Australia forthwith. He also insisted a medical evacuation escort go along to assure the major's safety.

On July 6 a confidential signal was despatched from CRIMSEC MANUS to ARMY MELBOURNE setting out details of the medical officer's report. Its second paragraph read:

"BRIGADIER TOWNLEY URGENTLY RECOMMENDS THAT CLARKE BE RETURNED TO MAINLAND AS PRESENT MENTAL AND PHYSICAL CONDITION RENDERS HIM UNFIT TO BE A MEMBER OF A MILITARY COURT."

With journalists covering the trials still in residence at Nutt Point, the Australian Army OC, Lt. Colonel F. G. Pullen, moved quickly to ensure that Clarke's condition remained a closely guarded secret. Newspaper reports suggesting one of Nishimura's "judges" had, soon after the hearing, been deemed "unfit to be a member of a military court" would have constituted a devastating blow to Army prestige, especially at the beginning of the trials with public interest at its height.

Early in the morning of July 7, while reporters were still at breakfast and Nishimura was beginning his third week in solitary confinement, Clarke and his medical escort were driven to Momote airfield to board the 0845 hrs RAAF courier flight to Townsville. No more than a handful of officers at Los Negros would ever learn the truth behind the major's sudden departure. Clarke was admitted to Heidelberg Military Hospital near Melbourne where two weeks later doctors caring for him were unable to provide the AG's department any firm indication when their patient was likely to be discharged.

On the day it received this indefinite prognosis, AHQ also learned that RAN doctors were recommending a second medical evacuation from Los Negros. Now the OC War Crimes Section, Lt. Colonel Pullen, had been taken ill. Arrangements were quickly finalised for Pullen to depart Momote by RAAF courier flight for Melbourne on July 21. In the hasty personnel reshuffle that followed, Lt. Colonel Quinton, former investigator and more lately Military Court member, found himself transferred from his judicial role to the administrative one left vacant by Pullen's evacuation.

On the day Pullen departed, Quinton became OC 1 Australian War Crimes Section, with overall responsibility for ensuring the *Manus Trials* ran smoothly to their anticipated conclusions. This meant he was now directly responsible for the final executions.

Apparently unnoticed by the Army, Quinton was notching up an extraordinary war crimes history, particularly when it came to matters involving the former Imperial Guards commander. He had been directly associated with SEAC departments involved in tracking down and investigating Nishimura. He had sat in judgement at Nishimura's trial. He would soon be required to participate in the Army's post-trial legal review of the case. Should the petition on which he would deliberate be rejected and the sentence confirmed, Quinton would then personally promulgate confirmation of the death sentence and time of execution to Nishimura. Following that, he would organise Nishimura's hanging, supervise the ritual itself and the subsequent burial arrangements — a veritable one-man war crimes band.

In Melbourne the AG's office moved quickly to gather the required legal opinions necessary to confirm the sentences. By July 7 the Army's legal office had reported that the evidence fully justified both guilty verdicts.

In contrast to the brief opinion submitted by the Army lawyers, Judge Advocate General Simpson's August 7 report on the trial ran to five pages. Judge Simpson was proud of his military background. He had served in World War 1 with 11 Field Co., AIF, and had risen to the rank of brigadier in World War 11. From 1942-45 he had been Director General of the Commonwealth Security Service.

In his report the JAG quoted segments of the various prosecution affidavits. "From the above short quotations from the written evidence tendered by the prosecution it will be seen that there was ample evidence to justify a conviction if the court saw fit to accept such evidence as accurate," he said.

Judge Simpson flatly rejected the individual petitions of Nishimura and Nonaka and an accompanying letter from Defence Counsel Nakayama. He pronounced these documents as having "no points of law that need discussion." To underline the firmness of his views, the old soldier judge concluded:

"In my opinion the finding and sentence may legally be confirmed and if it is of any assistance to the confirming officer I desire to record the view that if the decision were mine, I would confirm both findings and sentences."

The Army now had all the legal opinions and reports necessary for the AG to announce his official confirmation of Nishimura's death sentence. However, information received from Los Negros indicated the Japanese were on the point of throwing an awkward spanner in the post-trial procedural works. Quinton, whose expanded responsibilities included handling the Defence Team's entire outgoing and incoming correspondence, had intercepted a private letter from Tokyo to Defence Counsel Nakayama. This had indicated moves were afoot to present new evidence supporting Nishimura's plea of innocence. The English language letter was in the form of professional advice from American lawyer, Mr Ben Bruce Blakeney, who had worked on behalf of Japanese defence counsel in numerous war criminal cases. Quinton copied the letter and sent the copy to AHQ together with a personal memo discussing the implications as he saw them.

Essentially, Blakeney was advising Nakayama to move fast as the Australians were likely to announce their confirmation of sentences very quickly. He instructed Nakayama to write a letter to the "reviewing authority" to the effect he had received advice from Japan that new evidence — not available at the time of the trial — might soon be found. Blakeney urged Nakayama to inform the Australians that should such evidence be unearthed he would be seeking a new trial for Nishimura. Nakayama should therefore request a delay of the formal review or confirmation for "a reasonable time to permit further correspondence with Japan and receipt of whatever evidence may be discovered."

Nakayama wrote a letter along the lines of Blakeney's advice and addressed it to Quinton who received it on July 31. It asked for a stay in proceedings for Nishimura.

Back at AHQ a brigadier despatched an urgent message on August 8 to the DLS. It read:

1. The proceedings of the trial of Nishimura and Nonaka have been received from the JAG who has advised that "if the decision were mine, I would confirm both findings and sentences." In the normal course of events, therefore, the proceedings would now be referred to the AG for his decision.

2. In view of the attached correspondence, and particularly the letter addressed to Nishimura's defence counsel by Blakeney (who, apparently, is the "rear link" in Tokyo for the Japanese defence team), I would be grateful for your advice as to the proper course of action.

3. It would be appreciated if this matter were treated as urgent.

Senior AHQ staff officers responsible for overseeing the *Manus Trials* realised they now had to tread very carefully. They were well aware of the vulnerabilty of the documentary evidence submitted by the prosecution during the hearing. They fully recognised that a sharp American lawyer, given the chance, could play havoc with the magically similar affidavits cranked out at the eleventh hour by Australia's war crimes office in Tokyo. There was also the danger of the defence discovering the prosecution's highly selective approach to presenting documentary evidence and its wilful suppression of other vital information during the trial.

Equally vulnerable was the personal position of Captain James Godwin. US lawyer Blakeney was well known to SCAP's Legal Department and obviously had direct links to its members. It would be simple for Blakeney to learn of the formal complaints lodged with the Australians about Godwin and the deep reservations the Americans held over the objectivity of the New Zealander's investigations.

The question was whether the Army, knowing the Japanese were on the point of making a possibly dramatic move, should push ahead with formal confirmation of Nishimura's conviction and sentence. If it did so — and thereafter faced thorny defence accusations on a whole range of issues — it might well be exposing itself to sharp criticism for attempting to steamroll the case.

In the third week of August, AHQ signalled Quinton that the Army had confirmed the convictions and sentences of both Nishimura and Nonaka. But there was a proviso. In view of the recent defence representations, said the signal, "the issue of further instructions regarding the disposal of the accused Nishimura will be deferred pending consideration of the new evidence providing it is received not later than 11 Sep 50."

Nishimura, in effect, was to be placed in a legal limbo. As far as the Army's internal organisation was concerned, his fate was sealed. He could be executed immediately the all-clear was given. But, just in case the Japanese had something up their sleeves, Nishimura would not be told of the confirmation of his sentence. Technically speaking, formal promulgation of the confirmation would be withheld. Without it there was no legal confirmation. Without confirmation there could be no hanging. Here was the perfect answer to any charge that the Army was steamrolling Nishimura's execution. The Army had placed a neat each-way bet in expectation of problems ahead and, meanwhile, Nishimura could languish in solitary confinement.

Chapter 15

Silencing a dissenting opinion

———— ◆ ————

The defence follow-up was fast. On August 18, Nakayama sought a meeting with Quinton and handed over a carefully prepared, well documented petition. This argued for a re-trial of Nishimura on grounds of newly discovered evidence. It was the realisation of the Army's worst fears. What was more, the petition contrasted starkly with the stumbling phraseology and poorly articulated arguments of the defence's previous paperwork. Its clear, concise English bore the unmistakeable stamp of the American lawyer back in Tokyo.

Suddenly, the Army became aware that it was no longer dealing with just a bunch of "surrendered personnel," struggling to provide legal services in a system they had yet to fathom and a language they hardly comprehended. Ben Bruce Blakeney now represented a very large fly in the Army ointment.

Formal charges and copies of prosecution evidence, the petition pointed out, were first received by defence counsel as late as February, 1950. There had thus been insufficient time to conduct interviews of prosecution witnesses prior to the defence team's departure for Manus. Since then, however, co-counsel remaining in Japan had interviewed the key witnesses — Inagaki, Sono and Hinokuma — and taken from them affidavits by way of cross-examination. These latest statements amounted to evidence of great importance to Nishimura's case, evidence which was not available at the time of the trial.

The petition declared that new affidavits by the three former staff officers showed that testimony recorded in their original statements had resulted from "leading questions, intimidation, suggestion and distortion" on the part of investigating officers. Serious doubts had therefore been raised about the truth and probative value of the affidavits presented in court.

No action short of a retrial of the case would serve the ends of justice, argued the petition. Furthermore, the requested re-trial should ensure Inagaki, Sono and Hinokuma, were all produced for cross-examination.

The new affidavits, in their original Japanese and translated English forms, were attached to the documentation. Very clearly, they covered the grounds stipulated in the petition; and much more. Unlike the petition itself with its first language clarity, the new affidavits exhibited all the clumsiness of colloquial Japanese indifferently transposed into English. But for all this, they were transparently independent of one another and reflected differing perspectives and assessments. The original affidavits of the three men had exhibited calculated similarities in observations, were couched in identical English legalese and clearly suggested a common instigator.

The following brief extracts are taken from the statements produced by the defence to support its demand for a re-trial.

Inagaki: (Providing examples of Godwin's interrogation technique.)

Godwin: You must have heard what Nishimura spoke.

Inagaki: Yes I heard it, may be, but I have no memory about it.

Godwin: You must have heard it clearly. Think it over again. I have fully investigated. I have certain statement in possession that certifies Nishimura issuing the order when, you say, he was just speaking.

Inagaki: It may be, but I can't recall it.

Godwin: You had best recall it, think it better, you must not forgot such an important thing like that.

(Prosecutor was excited very much. He went out the room instructing something to the interpreter. Later the interpreter begun to speak to me.)

Interpreter: Mr Prosecutor has a good knowledge about the case because a certain Fujita, officer in charge of prisoners of war at the time, have testified already in this room about the situation in which the order was issued.

Inagaki: Is that so. (I felt easy as the prosecutor was absent so I accosted him light-heartedly.) What was spoken by him in his statement?

Interpreter: Fujita said Nishimura ordered on the spot to kill all the prisoners of war by shooting, and it was reported by the personal adjutant.

Sono: "I had the following impressions of the interrogation. Some witnesses seemed to have been interrogated by Captain Godwin before I was interrogated, and Captain Godwin was apparently trying very hard to make my statement conform to those made by my forerunners and that he was in great haste to complete my interrogation. Such being the case, when I answered him that I could not recollect it, I made a misapprehended answer, or I said something seemingly different from those evidences given by my forerunners, Captain Godwin became so much excited that he seized me by the collar then thrusted me away or let me stand as a punishment, ranting and raving for a long time. He also said: "You shall be imprisoned at Sugamo Prison!" As he knew that I was then serving in the Australian barracks, he said to me: "If you would cooperate with me, you should be able to continue to work where you are now serving."

Hinokuma: "He gave me some questions about the incident near Parit Sulong, Malaya, in 1942, many of which I could not answer, because the incident had taken place more than seven years before so that I forgot most of its details. In spite of this fact Captain Godwin asked me and said: 'It was as such, wasn't it? So-and-so who came here before you told me as such and you were present there so that you cannot be unaware of the fact.' When I remained unable to answer him, having no memory of it, he said: 'If you will not answer me quickly, you shall not be permitted to go home for ever.' These words were given me while I could not clearly recall the fact and I gradually became to feel like thinking it had been just as he told me; so that I gave him such uncertain answers as 'It might have been so' or 'I suppose it was so.' These were my sworn statement on which I signed."

It took ten days for the package containing the petition and new affidavits to reach the AG's department. There it was immediately forwarded to the DLS with a memo requesting urgent advice be provided "as to an appropriate course of action." The implications were obviously very serious. If the combined weight of evidence originally supplied by Inagaki, Sono and Hinokuma was now to be rendered unacceptable, the entire case against Nishimura rested on the Hackney statement.

The court might have been left in the dark on Hackney's inability to identify Nishimura, but the Army certainly knew all about it. Furthermore, this was the sort of information that might be difficult to keep suppressed, particularly if the Japanese managed to draw public attention to the "new evidence" issue. Of special concern was the likely reaction of US lawyer Blakeney who had direct access to Tokyo's international press corps and had experience making use of its members in the past.

Serving as AHQ's Deputy Director of Legal Services

(DDLS) at the time was a 37-year-old Melbourne-born lawyer, Major Maxwell R. Ham. He was instructed to review and report on the latest Japanese petitions. Major Ham was one of the Army's most experienced legal advisors having worked in that capacity since joining the AALC as a captain seven years earlier. Within three days his requested report was sitting on the AG's desk.

In the first ten lines Major Ham had articulated the dilemma: The question facing the AG now was whether a substantial miscarriage of justice had actually occurred. The major clearly thought it had and set out to prove as much. The JAG "had stated in no uncertain terms" that if the decision were his he would confirm both finding and sentence. It therefore could be taken "as definite," said Major Ham, that there had been no substantial miscarriage of justice so far as the proceedings themselves were concerned. But, consideration must be given to whether the latest tendered documents "so alter the whole complexion of the original proceedings as to justify the confirming authority taking such further action as is considered necessary to secure justice."

Major Ham defined the affidavit supplied by massacre survivor Hackney as the principal evidence for the prosecution. This had, he said, given rise to the charges in the first place. The original statements by the three Japanese were, to some extent, merely corroborative of Hackney's story. In fact, they had been utilized by the prosecution "largely to fill in the gaps in detail." Major Ham singled out paragraphs 26, 27 and 28 of Hackney's statement noting that they were "very closely reflected" in the statements of Nonaka and the other Japanese.

"In this regard," he said, "attention is particularly directed to the similarity of the three statements and that of Nonaka both as to the method of expression and the chronological sequence". This similarity was susceptible of two explanations:

(1) That Captain Godwin, being thoroughly conversant with what Lt. Hackney had said, more or less put the words into the mouths of the three Japanese as suggested in the statements supporting the petition.

(2) That the facts deposed to in the statements had so imprinted themselves on the minds of the Japanese concerned that their recollections insofar as they were all together at the time were almost identical.

If the first explanation was true, there was some substance in the complaint of the Japanese and the corroborative value of the statements to Hackney's account became less. On the other hand, if the second explanation applied, the recent statements by the Japanese in support of the petition were merely "a manifestation of a tendency which has grown particularly during the Manus Island Trials of impeaching the motives and actions of the interrogators." Major Ham then went on to observe that as none of the Japanese gave oral evidence, it was necessary to look at the proceedings themselves in order to ascertain which of the two explanations was correct.

In this regard he saw the oral evidence given by Nonaka as "particularly important." Early in Nonaka's evidence from the witness box he had made a "very similar complaint" to those now being made by the three former junior staff officers. Namely, that his memory was vague when he gave his initial statement and that the interrogator used leading questions. If the three Japanese had given oral evidence, their original statements might have been queried and watered down in the same way as Nonaka's original affidavit had been. "In other words, possibly the court would have come to a different conclusion if it had had the additional evidence now contained in the statements in support of the petition before it." said Major Ham.

"The question what action should now be taken is one of some difficulty. If the original statements taken by Captain

Godwin had shown more individuality, I would be constrained to think that they were a true reflection of the recollection of the individual Japanese at the time and that the later statements were not bona fide.

"But the marked similarity does lend considerable weight to the allegation made that the words were largely put into their mouths by Captain Godwin. Furthermore, Nishimura himself has from the very outset denied his complicity in the crime and the principal evidence against him was in fact largely provided by Nonaka and the three other Japanese whose evidence is now queried."

Major Ham's report concluded: "This combination of facts gives me a reasonable doubt that there may have been a miscarriage of justice and as the life of a man depends on the matter being correctly evaluated I think that such action should now be taken in accordance with regulation 20 of SR164 of 1945 (Australia's Regulations for the Trial of War Criminals) as is best calculated to do justice. In this case I suggest that the proceedings and whole file be resubmitted to the Judge Advocate General for the benefit of his further advice."

The Ham report amounted to a devastating challenge to the nation's military rectitude at a time when the Army's hierarchy well appreciated they were under severe political pressure to finalise the *Manus Trials* as quickly as possible. No less than Prime Minister Menzies, in his address to parliament seven months earlier, had called for the termination of the long impeded war crimes process, describing it as "a wretched state of affairs in which justice is denied because it is delayed."

The Nishimura files were returned to the JAG. This time Simpson responded with a 12-page pronouncement. In it he stated unequivocally there could be no question of a new trial "for there is no power to order a new trial once the finding and sentence have been confirmed." This observation alone was highly questionable given the Army's tactic of withholding the formal promulgation of Nishimura's confirmed sentence.

Read in retrospect, Judge Simpson's review, dated September 12, 1950, is a most curious document. In summarizing his views he agrees with the Army's legal assessment that the most important evidence for the prosecution is that supplied by Hackney. Furthermore, he makes the point, correctly, that Hackney spoke without any knowledge of what orders were given by the general to his aide and by the aide to Fujita. But, in this context, what the judge apparently failed to grasp was the fact that Hackney's report, as Major Ham's assessment accurately pointed out, gave rise to the charges against Nishimura in the first place. Other evidence provided by Godwin had been utilized by the prosecution "largely to fill in the gaps in detail."

In other words, Hackney's statement about a conversation he, in a fearfully wounded state, supposedly observed being conducted in a language he didn't understand had spurred the charge against Nishimura. To a large extent, it had been baseless conjecture concerning the presence of a senior Japanese officer in Parit Sulong that had all along riveted the attention of investigators. Captain Godwin had used the three former staff officers to give substance to the conjecture and to fill in the details he required to make the charge stick.

Judge Simpson had to admit the "strong similarity" between the statements of Inagaki, Sono and Hinokuma when it came to describing events up to the time Nishimura "started to give his orders." This could be explained, he said, "by the fact that Captain Godwin, the interrogating officer, would unconsciously be apt to deal with the matters in a chronological order." If the judge's assessment here is to be taken at face value, it is tantamount to admitting that Godwin was leading the witnesses along the chronological path he required and was thereby placing words in their mouths.

The Simpson assessment continued: "It is not, as I understand the application, sought in a new trial to produce these three witnesses for cross examination, but to tender their statements as evidence." Here the judge had completely misread the defence's requests and intentions. It was indeed their requirement to have the three Japanese produced and placed in the witness box at the time of re-trial. The petition had made this point very clearly.

The main thrust of the petition was that the prosecution case in Los Negros had depended exclusively on documentary evidence and had, thus, deprived the defence of their basic right of cross examination. With the three witnesses in court the next time round, cross examination could then take place.

"If I am correct in this," said Judge Simpson, continuing from his erroneous premise, "then the reviewing officer or I would be in as good a position to judge of its effect as the court would be, and it is to be remembered that the court in arriving at its conclusion did not have the advantage of seeing these witnesses give evidence, although it did have the advantage of hearing and seeing the two accused give evidence."

We are now confronted with what appears to be an extraordinary lapse in logic on the part of the JAG. He argues that as long as all evidence is retained in documentary form and the three witnesses are not produced in person, then the reviewing officer and he himself remain in as good a position as the court to make judgements on the new testimony.

But with his very choice of words Simpson admits it would have been advantageous to the court in the first instance had the three men given evidence in person — ". . . . the court in arriving at its conclusion did not have the advantage of seeing these witnesses give evidence . . . ." The continuation of the judge's reasoning then seems predicated on the need to sustain the disadvantage of documentary evidence. This done, he, or the reviewing authority, was "in as good a position as any court" to be the final arbiter.

Having offered this particularly convoluted piece of legal opinion, Judge Simpson went on to make one statement on which there could be no confusion. "After a most careful consideration," he said, "I have arrived at the conclusion that the fresh evidence is not fresh in any sense." The JAG could not resist a swipe at the opinions expressed by Major Ham. "I do not place as much importance on the similarity of the statements as he appears to do. I note particularly the marked differences I have referred to in those parts of the statements where Nishimura and Imai's orders are quoted and these in my opinion are the most important part of the statements."

Judge Simpson's report finished with the words: "In all the circumstances of the case, I have arrived at the conclusion that there is nothing to suggest that there has been a miscarriage of justice such as would necessitate a new trial if a new trial were possible. It follows, therefore, in my opinion, that no action is called for on these present petitions."

From the Army's standpoint, Judge Simpson's legal opinon constituted full authority to move ahead with Nishimura's execution. As far as Major Ham's views were concerned, these could be filed and forgotten.

Chapter 16

Side-stepping the Solicitor General

———— ✦ ————

Adjutant General Anderson decided he was now in a
position to issue instructions for the death sentence
on Nishimura to be carried out. Still, a nagging doubt
at the back of his mind led him to seek one last opinion from
the nation's influential Solicitor General, Professor Kenneth H.
Bailey. It seemed an appropriate move as Professor Bailey
had been so instrumental in recruiting both Court President
and Chief Prosecutor for the *Manus Trials*. On October 3,
Anderson called on the Solicitor General in Canberra, sought
his comments on the case and handed across the Army's
Nishimura case file. Pointedly, all documentation on early
investigative efforts by 1 Australian War Crimes Section in
Singapore had been extracted from the file some time prior to
the hand-over.

If the AG was hoping for solid support for a decision to
push ahead with the execution, he was to be disappointed.
Professor Bailey, an expert on international law who had held
his Federal posting since 1946, was decidedly circumspect on
the issue. After reviewing the case, his opinions hardened.
At their next meeting Bailey urged Anderson to seek the
advice of both the Attorney General and the Army Minister,
Mr Josiah Francis.

The idea of thrusting the issue into the political arena at
this stage was not what Anderson had expected to hear. In
the meantime, Bailey personally prepared a study of the

Nishimura trial. Headed *"The Case of Nishimura,"* it is preserved among Professor Bailey's private papers at the Australian National Archives in Canberra. The document stands today as a solid rebuke of — and challenge to — the opinions and attitudes of Judge Advocate General Simpson. By inference, it also represents a damning indictment of the Army's entire handling of the Parit Sulong Massacre trial.

The Bailey study began by examining the various statements of the three controversial Japanese witnesses Inagaki, Sono and Hinokuma. "The general effect of the new statements," it observed, "is that the original statements were not voluntary as the law understands the term, and if believed they do seem to throw doubt on the evidence as to what orders were given."

It then turned to the JAG's rejection of the petition and went ahead, point by point, to dismantle all the judge's arguments.

The JAG believed, said Professor Bailey, that the new evidence would have been available for the defence. "But does this follow? If it be the fact that the allegations of pressure are true, it is reasonable to assume that the men were in some apprehension throughout the trial and did not feel free to speak out until some time afterwards. The opposite view, of course, is that they spoke the truth when the truth was forced out of them, and thought up denials and qualifications when they felt free to do so." The choice of the phrase "when the truth was forced out of them" seems to suggest an opinion on how the evidence might have been gathered in Tokyo.

The JAG had noted "marked differences" between the three witnesses' statements in the important parts where Nishimura and Imai's orders were quoted. "But Inagaki, Sono and Hinokuma all quote this much of the order in practically identical words — 'Instruct the officer in charge of the prisoners to execute all the prisoners.' The differences

Australia's Solicitor General, Professor Kenneth H. Bailey, clashed with the Army hierarchy over the trial procedure which had led to the death sentence imposed on General Nishimura. His dissenting view caused a major crisis at Army Headquarters.

are that Inagaki included the words 'by firing squad and cremate their bodies,' Sono only added 'by firing squad.' and Hinokuma said the order was to execute all 'in a suitable manner.' And, of course, the latter two men ascribed the instruction to cremate to Imai. This version seemed to have been accepted by the prosecution."

Professor Bailey's assessment continued: "If the men's allegations of pressure and dictation are believed, the essential order — to execute — could have been suggested to them, and the differences do not seem sufficient in themselves to rebut such allegations."

After challenging other aspects of Judge Simpson's views the Solicitor General's assessment then swung in support of Major Ham's report. "If the above comments are regarded as having any weight, more importance may be attached to the doubts expressed by Major Ham in his report on the file dated 8th September, paragraphs 3 to 8, than is accorded to it by the JAG."

The Bailey document's views verged on the caustic when it examined the rules under which evidence was presented during the Nishimura trial. "The trial was conducted on affidavit evidence. This course was sanctioned by Statute, and one would scarcely regard as relevant to this case the criterion applied (inter alia) by the Privy Council in deciding whether to grant leave to appeal in criminal cases, namely whether there was 'a disregard of the (ordinary) forms of legal process' ! (Ibrahim v The King 1914 A.C. at p. 615). At the same time, the method of trial precluded certain advantages normally vouchsafed to the accused, and this consideration invites special caution in accepting any conclusion upon which doubt may be thrown, particularly in a case where the sentence is death." The exclamation mark in the middle of this paragraph, pointedly enough, was Bailey's.

His document concluded: "It, therefore, seems to me that

the allegations now made justify further investigation as a first step, to be followed by further action if the results of the investigation warrant it, in pursuance of the wide powers given by Regulations 19 and 20."

At this point two highly authoritative legal opinions, entirely independent of each other, were casting formidable doubts on Nishimura's conviction. Of great significance is the fact that the two authors of these opinions had made their assessments based on very restricted overviews of what had transpired in the lead up to Los Negros. The Army had assured this.

Nonetheless, both the Army's legal advisor and the nation's internationally respected Solicitor General felt sufficiently compelled to argue that the new affidavits offered by the defence amounted to a serious enough indication of a miscarriage of justice. Further official deliberations were demanded, they both concluded.

Each had separately declared Hackney's statement the key document produced by the prosecution at the Los Negros trial. Part of their joint concern focused on the way all documentary evidence produced at the hearing appeared to have been inspired by the survivor's claims. But neither Major Ham nor Professor Bailey ever discovered the real degree to which Hackney's testimony had been undermined — a fact kept well concealed by the Army.

To what extent would their doubts have magnified had they known the background of Hackney's failure to identify Nishimura? What would have been their reactions had they discovered the Army had wilfully withheld from the proceedings all information on the identification issue? By the same token, how would they have interpreted a situation where a member of the trial bench and a member of the prosecution team, both knowing of this deficiency, had each remained silent on the matter?

The other focus of concern for Major Ham and Professor

Bailey was the questionable quality of affidavits produced by Godwin in Tokyo. Both were troubled by the astounding similarity in phraseology and content among documents supplied by supposedly independent witnesses, speaking during different interrogation sessions about an event that had occurred years earlier.

It is also appropriate to consider how the two reviewing experts might have judged Godwin's reliability in the light of his "clandestine cache." How would they have rated the fact that the cache contained interrogation reports directly clashing with prosecution evidence? In the same context, how would they have considered Godwin's diary confidences on the need to "paraphrase" conflicting statements of suspects under interrogation?

Similarly, what would have been their assessment of formal American complaints of Godwin's handling of investigations, specifically his remarks about Nishimura and the private opinions he repeatedly injected into related reports? Indeed, what would have been their evaluation of the New Zealander as a dispassionate war crimes investigator had they appreciated the extent to which his sufferings as a POW had obviously affected his approach to work? How would they have viewed the concept of his "privileged and sacred" mission to speak on behalf all those who perished at the hands of the Japanese? How would they have reacted to Godwin's vendetta against Nishimura, his personal views of Japanese suspects as "bastards", "mongrels", and "vermin", and his dismissal as "drongos" of all US Legal Department experts who disagreed with his ideas for the continuing prosecution of war criminals?

Finally, what would have been their appraisal of the situation involving an adjudicating panel member who, shortly after participating in sentencing Nishimura to death, had been proclaimed by the hearing's President himself as mentally and physically unfit to serve on a military court?

As Nishimura completed his fifth and sixth month in solitary confinement, discussions on his fate shunted back and forth between AHQ in Melbourne and the Solicitor General's office in Canberra. During these, Bailey forcefully expressed his deep reservations over the way the Army had brought Nishimura to trial and was now handling the aftermath. News of his views spread throughout the AG's department and beyond. In late December, a colonel at AHQ reported on them in a letter to Quinton.

Quinton responded by return mail:

"Personally I cannot understand what Prof. Bailey is 'not altogether happy' about the Nishimura case. It seems clear cut to me. I was also surprised at the death sentence on Sasaki being commuted. To my mind, he was one Nip who showed unbounded enthusiasm in his work of lopping the heads off the Aust Ps W at Ambon. While on the subject of hangings, could you advise me as to what fee should be paid the hangman. I have not mentioned any sum at all to the man as yet."

Quinton was just the sort of man the Army needed. Committed. But his written remarks to AHQ on this occasion bear special reflection in the light of events that were soon to unfold.

Australia lapsed into its traditionally lengthy Christmas and New Year holiday season. It wasn't until January 18, 1951, that the bureaucratic wheels resumed turning on the Nishimura case. On this occasion Bailey met Anderson at the Melbourne Barracks. The professor made it clear his interests now stretched beyond the formwork of legal arguments surrounding the trial. His office had begun reviewing the substance of investigations undertaken in Tokyo.

The Solicitor General was anxious to know whether the Army had researched the origins of the new statements. Had these been volunteered? How had Ben Bruce Blakeney come to hear that there "may be" fresh evidence? Had the latest allegations about the methods of interrogation used in

Tokyo been referred to Captain Godwin for comment? Above all, Professor Bailey wanted to know more about the confessed killer, Fujita. Later that same day, Anderson wrote to Bailey enclosing a requested copy of AHQ's latest information on the missing Japanese. It was a report by the Tokyo Police dated November 13, 1950. They had questioned Fujita's neighbours, waited in ambush for him and set up surveillance on his wife and brother-in-law. All to no avail. The search was continuing.

By this point, Anderson knew that the Solicitor General was not only deeply suspicious of the prosecution affidavits prepared in Tokyo but had now grasped the importance of Fujita to the events that had taken place at Parit Sulong. Furthermore, the AG recognised Bailey was greatly troubled by Fujita's strange disappearance.

As the weeks passed, numerous private petitions on behalf of Nishimura flowed onto files at AHQ. One in particular came from Colonel Takeo Iwakuro, former CO of the Imperial Guard's 5th Regiment. He was one of several senior Japanese officers (See Chapter 3, page 72) Australian investigators had plans of arresting when Hackney's identification of Nishimura fell through. Iwakuro's sworn statement made the intriguing claim that Fujita, after confessing his role in the massacre to Captain Godwin at the Meiji Building, had headed straight for his former CO's nearby Tokyo office to seek advice. Fujita had denied to Iwakuro that Nishimura issued any killing orders. All orders he received during the divisional commander's visit that day had come from Inagaki, Imai's personal aide.

It will be recalled that during testimony to the Los Negros court, Nonaka had explained the clear separation of duties between personal aides. He was Nishimura's conduit; Inagaki was Imai's. It would have been impossible for one officer's aide to issue the other officer's instructions. It was therefore impossible for Nonaka to have passed on Imai's orders to "cremate the bodies" as the prosecution suggested.

What credit should be given to reported remarks made by a confessed mass murderer on the run? Probably very little and the Australian Army chose to dismiss them outright. But Iwakuro's petition does raise the possibility that perhaps Hackney had seen Imai — not Nishimura — delivering instructions in Parit Sulong that day. All this, of course, is conjecture, but it is worth recording that Iwakuro's petition was supported with a similarly sworn document by former Major General Gunzo Morimoto who was with Iwakuro at the time of Fujita's visit.

Nishimura's wife, Setsuko, writing on behalf of herself, her son, Makoto and daughter, Tomoko, had despatched her first petition to the Los Negros Court President two days after her husband's conviction. "My husband Nishimura Takuma has a sincere and gentle character," she wrote. "When previously he was in the Army he was respected especially by his superiors and his subordinates. In the home, as my life's companion, and as the father of two children, he was affectionate and a good man, loved by relations, friends and acquaintances."

Seven months later, a now desperate Setsuko appealed directly to Sydney's Catholic Church leader, Norman Cardinal Gilroy, to intercede with the Australian military authorities. Like her husband, she did not plead for mercy. She requested Nishimura's case be investigated "more thoroughly, and if necessary to grant him a new trial and the chance to prove his innocence."

In her letter to Cardinal Gilroy, Setsuko wrote: "My own unshakeable belief in my husband and my refusal to credit his guilt of the charges against him have no value as evidence, perhaps, but they are my motivation in imploring your assistance. My husband is not — as I know Australian opinion has it — another 'Tiger of Malaya.' He is not a brutal committer of atrocities, but on the contrary is a man personally gentle, and of sufficiently high education and respected standing to have been picked as commander of the Imperial Guards Division, His Majesty the Emperor's own bodyguard."

At about the time these petitions were being filed, the AG's department was completing a number of studies of the Nishimura case to counter expected heightening objections from the Solicitor General. In one of these, a Lt. Colonel remarked: "It is also relevant to note that Japanese have no regard whatever for an oath — this has been made clear on numerous occasions." Perhaps, not surprisingly, the Army and other authorities paid little attention to the personal petitions received on behalf of Nishimura. Eventually, all were dismissed as irrelevant.

Faced with continuing strong verbal objections from Bailey in the new year, Anderson attempted to get the Solicitor General to articulate his position on the case in a formal written report. The professor, a Rhodes Scholar, was renowned throughout Australian and international legal circles for his intellectual prowess. Also widely recognised were the contributions made by the team of talented lawyers he had managed to attract to his department. Anderson knew the professor was no man to trifle with in a legal joust. But there was a downside to the functions of Bailey's office. Despite his recognised high standards of professionalism, the long delays experienced when dealing with him directly had become legendary. He was overloaded with work. He was also slow. The written report requested by Anderson failed to materialise although, clearly, the Solicitor General's personal assessment — *The Case of Nishimura* — had been intended as the basis for just such a submission.

By mid-February, with Nishimura completing his eighth month of solitary confinement — and the Army no nearer solving the impasse on his case — severe complications began arising in Los Negros. Three Japanese were already on the Lombrum Point death row awaiting execution. Several others were expected to join them shortly. Quinton had estimated trials could conclude five to six weeks hence. But no move could be made on executions until a decision had been taken on Nishimura. Unless this came quickly, Australia faced the very real prospect of seeing her Military Court packing up and returning home, leaving behind a stranded death row packed with condemned Japanese and no hanging decision in place.

When all this was measured against the backdrop of Prime Minister Menzies' assurances to the nation that the *Manus Trials* were all about "clear allegation, prompt trial and unswerving execution of judgement" it was obvious the Army now faced a major crisis of credibility.

Anderson decided the time had come to involve the politicians. At a meeting between the AG and Army Minister Francis, it was arranged that the minister would seek the involvement of his colleague, the nation's Attorney General, Mr John A. Spicer. In rapid succession, Spicer held discussions with Solicitor General Bailey and Prime Minister Menzies. On March 14, in a letter to the Army Minister, Spicer set down the procedure he recommended for breaking the deadlock on the Nishimura case. The controversial defence petition would be submitted to the Tribunal that had heard the case in Los Negros. The Tribunal would then supply its report on the merits of the application and, on the basis of this, the AG would make his decision. This would ultimately be sent to Cabinet for final confirmation. Most important of all, the Attorney General let it be known, in no uncertain terms, that his solution involved extracting the Nishimura case from the sphere of influence exercised by Professor Bailey. Spicer's letter informed the Army Minister that, once the suggested arrangements were approved, the Solicitor General "will return your files of papers to the Adjutant General in order that you may communicate with

Attorney General John Spicer was directly involved in formulating a deft political solution to the impasse caused when Solicitor General Bailey took strong objection to the way General Nishimura had been tried and sentenced to death for the Parit Sulong Massacre.

Army Minister Josiah Francis gave the official approval to Attorney General Spicer's recommendations for handling the Nishimura trial's aftermath. His ministerial nod enabled the Army to regain exclusive control of the case and thereby clear the path to the execution chamber.

the President of the Australian Military Court." It was a neat exercise in political intrigue and a powerplay unlikely to have been attempted without private prime ministerial endorsement. Army Minister Francis quickly gave his authority and the Attorney General's proposals were put into effect. The fate of Nishimura now rested exclusively back in the hands of the Army.

The format seemed straightforward enough. Except, of course, if consideration be given to the merits of a solution which called for a Military Tribunal to review its own findings. Surely, there would be a tendency for the reviewers to justify their original judgements? In this context, Quinton's correspondence with AHQ in late December and his remarks on Professor Bailey's reservations and Nishimura's guilt revealed a firmly committed bias.

There were other complications. Back in Los Negros, Major Clarke had not returned to the military court bench after his medical evacuation. Furthermore, a second Tribunal member involved in the Nishimura trial, Major Hayes, had also left the island. This meant that only three of the original five-man panel would be available for the review. The three men — Brigadier Townley, the Court President, Major Gerling, an infantry officer and, of course, the always available Lt. Colonel Quinton — duly considered the files sent from Melbourne. A report, submitted and signed by Townley, ran to one and a half typed pages. It concluded: ***"Having given the matter the consideration which its seriousness requires I find myself unable to recommend remissions. I have endeavoured to determine the question on a broad principle without confining my consideration to the question of whether the statements constitute "fresh evidence" or not.***

"Had majors Hayes and Clarke been available," *the* ***brigadier added, "I would, of course, have sought their views. Whether they should be now consulted or not is***

entirely a matter for the officer dealing with the petition. But it may not be irrelevant to point out that in a court of five members, as this was, a death sentence requires the concurrence of at least four. Lt. Colonel Quinton and Major Gerling have read this report and have authorised me to express their agreement therewith."

The point raised by Townley here is salient. An Australian military court of five members could only hand down a death sentence if it achieved a 4-1 concurrence among its members. If the same court was then asked to review the same death sentence in the light of new evidence, should the 4-1 vote remain mandatory if capital punishment is to be retained? Natural justice would seem to demand so. But the Army took a different view. On April 5, the AG's legal advisors submitted a two-paragraph opinion that it was not necessary to obtain the views of Majors Hayes and Clarke. The findings of the three-man review panel would suffice. This way, of course, any possible controversy over the mental condition of one of the judges at the trial would remain concealed and never become a contentious or public issue.

But there *was* an issue here. A very important issue. One of the five Tribunal members who handed down Nishimura's death sentence had shortly thereafter been evacuated from Los Negros suffering from acute auditory and visual hallucinations. His condition was so serious that he required a medical escort to move him back to Australia where he was immediately hospitalised for a lengthy period. What credence should be given to this man's vote, particularly in a life or death decision demanding a critical 4-1 majority? What would have been the status of Nishimura's death sentence if one of the four "fit" Tribunal members had dissented?

Over the months in Los Negros, a close bond of friendship had grown between Nishimura and his legal counsel.

Nakayama, for his part, had come to believe implicitly in his client's innocence and felt personally responsible for failing him in court. With Nishimura into his tenth month in solitary confinement and fast running out of time, Nakayama submitted an almost frantic final petition.

In it, he informed the confirming authority how his office in Tokyo had indicted the three Japanese prosecution witnesses on perjury charges. If the three witnesses had been called in court, argued Nakayama, the credibility of their statements would have been exposed. "It was due to my carelessness that they were not summoned," he lamented. "I, defence counsel, have to offer my humble apology to God for my incompetence."

Nakayama explained he had finished his war crimes work on Los Negros and was awaiting passage on a ship back to Japan. There he would pursue the perjury action and ask the authorities to arrest Fujita. "I, of course, know that the war crimes trials are not bound by Japanese laws or by a Japanese trial. But if the three persons indicted for perjuries are found guilty, the evidence which served for finding Nishimura guilty will become totally valueless. The trial of perjuries case is now underway as I have explained, so I beg you to listen to my submission for the postponement of the confirmation of his sentence." It was a hopeless move, doomed to failure.

At a Cabinet meeting in Canberra in the first week of May, Army Minister Francis formally submitted a summary of the *Manus Trials* noting they had begun on June 5, 1950, and concluded on April 9, 1951. The Tribunal had handed down 14 "death by hanging" verdicts — one individual, Ipachi Mayamoto, had been given two death sentences. There had been 56 terms of imprisonment imposed, including 15 life sentences. In addition, 43 suspected war criminals had been acquitted.

The Army Minister reported at length on the case of Lt. General Nishimura. The application by his defence counsel for a re-trial on the grounds of new evidence had been received after the termination of the Court proceedings. It had been referred to the Attorney General's department for advice after obtaining the views of the JAG as there was no precedent on which to determine the application's validity or otherwise. Pending the determination of Lt. General Nishimura's petition, action to effect other death sentences which had, by then, been confirmed, was deferred.

Absent from the ministerial report was any reference to the strong objections raised with the Army over the case by the Solicitor General. Neither was there any suggestion that one of the Army's own senior legal advisors had reported on the case in a similar light. And, of course, there was not the slightest hint that the Attorney General had been required to intervene personally with the Solicitor General to ensure the case was contained "in-house" by the Army. Further, the minister's submission to Cabinet made no mention that an ultimate military review of the case had been undertaken by only three of the original tribunal's five members. Finally, it made no reference to Townley's obvious preference for the full panel's views to be canvassed on a decision which had required a 4-1 majority vote. Minister Francis recommended to Cabinet that all petitions received on the *Manus Trials* be rejected. They were, and, with that, came the government's official sanction for the executions to proceed as per the Army's recommendations.

A month after the hangings, Quinton was still on Los Negros tidying up the aftermath. In a letter to Lt. Colonel R. Gilchrist at the AG's office, he expressed his gratitude for the AHQ signal that had cleared up confusion over payment to be made to the hangman. Quinton wrote:

As you know now, the payment of the fee was satisfactorily completed.
The amount not only astounded me but also the person

concerned. I had no idea that it would be as high as £100. Thought £30 or thereabouts would have been forthcoming. I am glad now that I did not recommend any fixed amount.

All matters concerning disposal of stores, handover of Nutt Point Camp etc, are nearing completion.

With the exception of one NCO, acting in capacity of caretaker, we are all now living at Lombrum at the War Criminals Compound.

There are myself, Capt Carter and four NCOs left now and only four native labourers and it is expected that all of us will be on our way back in a fortnight or so.

Personally, I would be interested in further service if a place could be found for me.

For personal and business reasons, I would be grateful if you could let me know when I arrive at AHQ whether there are any prospects in any sphere or locality. I do not mind where I would have to serve.

In one way, I shall be sorry to leave here and will miss the hot sunshine and healthy life. I have established excellent relations with the other services and made many good friends whom I shall also miss.

Looking forward to meeting you,

I am,

Yours sincerely,

signed: N. F. Quinton

❊ ❊ ❊ ❊

Four months after the Parit Sulong Massacre trial, the AG's office had prepared a confidential paper setting down staffing arrangements and duties for 2 Australian War Crimes Section in Tokyo and its PW & I department in Melbourne. The paper noted that during the period January 13 to October 2, 1950, staff engaged on war crimes in Tokyo had been reduced from 18 officers and 20 other ranks to four officers and six other ranks.

It went on to outline specific duties to be performed by the two sections from then on. Eight different functions were detailed for the PW & I office in Melbourne. These included receiving proceedings from Manus, advising next of kin of sentenced war criminals and preparing files in the AG's department. Fourth item on the list noted: "Sorting material received from 2 Australian War Crimes Section (Tokyo) and forwarding to Military History such information as is of value to them, filing information which should be retained *and destroying unwanted documents.*" (author's italics).

Large gaps in relevant Army files retained by the Australian National Archives offices in Canberra and Melbourne attest to the substantial extent of destruction that took place with "unwanted documents" on the Parit Sulong Massacre enquiries. They also attest to the extent of documentation stolen by Captain Godwin in Tokyo.

On July 17, 1951, with the executions over, staff officers in the AG's department gathered together all remaining legal papers concerning the case. On the cover of the file they wrote: PROCEEDINGS OF A MILITARY COURT — NISHIMURA TAKUMA AND NONAKA SHOICHI. Under regulations, the completed file was required to be submitted to the Central Army Records Office (CARO). The letter accompanying the file informed CARO officers:

IT IS ADVISED THAT, BY DIRECTION, THE INFORMATION CONTAINED IN THESE PROCEEDINGS WILL <u>NOT</u> BE DISCLOSED TO THE PRESS.

The Army's cover-up was complete. By the time anyone discovered how Australia succeeded in snaring the other Tiger, it wouldn't matter.

Epilogue

—————— ◆ ——————

Makoto Nishimura and his wife Ayako live in a quiet lane off a secondary road in Machida, approximately an hour by train west of Central Tokyo. There is a lush garden behind the two storey house where Setsuko Nishimura, widow of the former Imperial Guards divisional commander, once lived among the meagre collection of memorabilia that survived the 1949 fire in her native Akita prefecture. There are two albums, a bundle of letters and a few photographs. The widow Nishimura died in 1985. Her son's legacy includes this paltry assortment of mementos which sums up her husband's illustrious military career that spanned three decades, concluding ignominiously at an execution site on a remote island in the Bismarck Sea.

When the Australians hanged his father in Los Negros on June 11, 1951, Makoto Nishimura was studying for the entrance examinations to Tokyo University where he eventually majored in pedagogy. He was 19 years old and it had been eight years since he last saw his father. His sister Tomoko was 15; she was only seven when Lt. General Takuma Nishimura, then just retired from the regular army register, was appointed governor of military administration in occupied districts in 1943. He left Japan for Burma. He was never to return home.

Two framed photographs, one of his father in full military uniform, the other of his mother in a kimono, look on as the

64-year-old academic from Toyo University attempts to describe the absentee father he knew through erratic correspondence and the glowing testimonies of surviving peers. The incarceration, first in Singapore, then on Los Negros, and the eventual execution do not tally at all with the man he remembers: honest, cheerful, active but cautious.

The earlier memories are warm but they are so very few, limited to two distinct periods Makoto himself remembers. One lasted a year and a half beginning when Lt. General Nishimura returned from the battlefields of China in the spring of 1939 and ending when he got posted to French Indo-China in the autumn of 1940. The other was the year he spent home after returning from Sumatra and resigning from the army register. Some episodes return vividly to his son: his father leaving a new ball outside the home of a little girl whose toy he had run over accidentally in his car the previous afternoon; his father getting upset by the movie newsreels showing General Tomoyuki Yamashita proudly inspecting prisoners and captured weapons, the older Nishimura saying, "He should not take such a proud attitude in front of captives"; his father enjoying cigar and sake; his father saying once he was out of military life, he would want to be an elementary school principal.

"My father was away a lot," Makoto states. "I knew him when I was 7 and 8 years old. Then I knew him again when I was 10 and 11 years old. Then he was gone."

Respect was what he always had for his soldier-father. He heard his mother and older relatives speak admiringly of Takuma. Makoto understood early in life that he was the son of an important man. But that was all.

The next sharp memory is of a day in 1947. "When the sentence of the Singapore court was conveyed to us, I was 13 years old and my sister was 9. My mother was 44. I didn't know the details. Our father had been a sacrifice for the war. As children, that was our understanding. We were living in

Takuma Nishimura was a 33-year-old captain serving in the Tokyo War Office when he married 19-year-old Setsuko Oda in 1922. This is their wedding photograph.

Kokura but that had to change. We were in deep grief. We had nothing. Pensions had been stopped. My mother decided we should move to Akita, in Noshiro-shi, where her family was."

Setsuko Nishimura was 14 years younger than her husband. Her father was a doctor and so were her four brothers. Her photographs suggest grace and a quiet elegance. To her dying day, she believed she was the widow of a great man. She conveyed this sentiment to her children and her grandchildren.

Her pictures don't reflect the grit she displayed when, faced with a bleak future without her husband, she tackled the issue of survival in a country devastated by defeat. Back in Akita, Setsuko worked as an attendant in the hospital her

The Nishimura family portrait taken in Kokura shortly before Takuma (seated centre) left for Europe and military studies in 1934. Also shown are his brothers, their wives and children. Setsuko Nishimura is on her husband's right with son Makoto on her lap.

At age 48, Colonel Takuma Nishimura was appointed a regimental commander in Manchuria. His wife, Setsuko, son, Makoto, and daughter, Tomoko, accompanied him on this posting. The picture was taken in the regimental commander's official residence.

brother managed. She and her children were allowed to live in the hospital wing. She lived and worked thus for many years all the while hoping her husband would at least be moved from a Singapore prison to Sugamo where her children would get to see their father. She stayed in Akita until Japan resumed pensions in 1954. Then she moved to Tokyo.

Letters were the bridge that formed a semblance of connection. But Makoto was a teenager when his father was in prison and Lt. General Nishimura's correspondence was controlled by his captors. The Australians, for instance, had allowed him one letter every two months. There are nine letters from Los Negros in the Nishimura memory box, eight of them from death row, two written on the eve of his execution. The condemned man numbered his last letters; letter no. 5 is missing. His son thinks it was lost in transit. Or, perhaps, his father had addressed it to relatives; he must have asked them to please take care of his family.

The Los Negros correspondence does not refer to the trial at all. The only reference to it — and it was a passing one — is in the brief note he sent his family the day before the court passed its verdict. Even then he made no comments about the proceedings. My mind is calm, he told his wife and children.

The messages from death row bear no suggestions of rage or bitterness. Poetry accompanies most of the tranquil reflections. The famous haiku poet Kyoshi Takahama, for instance, is quoted in one letter: "Time will solve everything, I'm waiting for spring." A day before he was hanged, Lt. General Nishimura wrote his farewell poem. The tanka, roughly translated, said: "To live and to die with responsibility is the way of a leader. I blame no-one else."

His father's sense of responsibility is part of Makoto Nishimura's inheritance. "My grandfather was a pay officer of the 6th division in Kumamoto," Makoto begins. "After he retired from the army register, he became chamberlain of Kokura city. One of his subordinates cheated. My grandfather repaid the money and resigned his position. He felt responsible for what the man did. My father, Takuma, always remembered this story. When he was in Manus, he said that it was now his turn to face responsibility. He said responsibility is our family's fate."

Takuma Nishimura's last advice to his children echoed that belief. "When your time comes," he wrote hours before his execution, "do not turn your back on responsibility."

He also forbade them to blame others for what transpired in their lives.

His father would have been 107 years old had he lived, Makoto says wistfully. The things he had predicted for Japan are now happening all around his children. Lt. General Nishimura had foreseen a Japan dominated by business and technology.

"I didn't write my father often," Makoto says. "I was very young. It was difficult to express myself. But I remember sending him a letter when he was in Singapore, when he was in Outram Road Prison. I needed advice about my future. My father wrote back and said I should concentrate on the practical sciences and become a technologist. He also said I should keep up with my sports. He did not think an academic life would suit me."

Makoto had once entertained the thought of becoming another soldier like his father. Every boy whose childhood was spent against the background of imperialist Japan had nursed dreams of a military career. The wish was understandable. In the late 1930s when Makoto was a child, the leaders of Japan were military men. But history put paid to his early ambition. By the time Makoto could qualify to sit for entrance examinations, Hiroshima and Nagasaki had been bombed, the Emperor had called for the cessation of hostilities, Japan had unconditionally surrendered and

Photographs for an incarcerated father. These two family photographs were taken specifically to reassure General Nishimura — then incarcerated in Singapore's Outram Road Jail — that his wife and children had not been injured in the big fire at Noshiro-shi in February 1949. He took both pictures with him to Los Negros and they were his only company during his agonizing 354 days in solitary confinement on Lombrum Point's death row.

Makoto was seventeen years old when this picture was taken. His sister Tomoko was thirteen.

military schools had disappeared.

"I have to be a different man from my father," Makoto explains. "Our backgrounds determine this. He was born in 1889. The military life was his only life. I was born in 1932. My generation knows both imperialism and democracy. I was a boy when Japan was militarist and imperialist; then the war came and when it ended the democratization began. As an academic, my politics are slightly left of centre. I value freedom and democracy."

He looks amused when it is suggested that he had deliberately gone against the advice his father gave from a Singapore prison. Makoto is a teacher and he plays no sports, not even golf. No, he shakes his head, it was not intentional: "It's just the way life turned out for me." He thinks he probably made the right choice; otherwise he could be shuffling paper in a dull office, stuck in a boring job.

Daily, he takes the commuter train from his home in Machida to his classes in Toyo University, a trip that takes more than an hour each way. He conducts teacher training courses: principles of teaching, history of education, methods of teaching. He claims his students have lively and progressive minds. They want to know more about the Pacific conflict; they ask why very little of it is found in their textbooks. They write provocative essays and Makoto says he sometimes wonders how he would feel if they ever got around to mentioning his father's name. The possibility does not daunt him.

"We have to live with history," Lt. General Nishimura's son stresses. "We have to accept historical facts. My father played a role in the period of militarist and imperialist Japan. I must accept that reality."

Makoto Nishimura appears to be incredibly stable and amiable for someone who lost his father to the gallows.

"I was protected by my mother and other relatives," he ponders. "I was 19 and had not seen him for a long time.

A small family survives. Setsuko, then aged 52, her son Makoto, 23, and daughter Tomoko, 19, move back to Tokyo and celebrate the return of peace in their lives with this photograph taken four years after the Los Negros executions.

We learned about his execution first from news despatches. We received the official announcement of his death from the governor of Fukuoka a month after. It was very sad but the pain was not so severe because he had been away for many years."

There was also the extenuating factor of his father's position. "He was an important officer known for his upright attitude. His conduct always courted respect," Makoto pursues. "When he was executed, we did not feel discriminated against. There were many people who expressed their sympathy. We were not made to suffer. Nobody made me feel I was the son of a war criminal."

The philosophical outlook that prevailed in Lt. General Nishimura's prison letters finds parallel tones in his son's reasoning. "There were people in Japan who were worse off than we were," Makoto declares. "There were people who were bombed, who had lost their homes and their entire families, who had nothing. So when my father was hanged, I thought it was better to concentrate on my studies and go on with the rest of my life rather than dwell on the circumstances of his death."

There were, anyway, very few items a grieving family could cling to. Forty five years on, the thin file has yellowed and faded: the document of accusation, 28 handwritten pages in Japanese of Defence Counsel Choji Nakayama's closing address to the Los Negros court, petitions filed by Lt. General Nishimura and Nakayama. A copy of the appeal Setsuko Nishimura sent to Norman Cardinal Gilroy, then head of the Roman Catholic Church in Sydney, Australia, is neatly folded and tucked among the family photographs. Setsuko salvaged this from the Akita fire. The pages are crisp with age.

A few frames have not found themselves into this cache of remembrances. They are imprinted in Makoto Nishimura's memory and he summons them with an objectivity so remarkable he might as well have been talking about the heat outside, or the humidity.

"My mother did everything possible to save my father's life," he recalls. "She travelled from Akita to Tokyo frequently to meet anyone who seemed available. Sometimes, I accompanied her. When I could not go, other relatives in Tokyo went with her. My mother wanted to talk about my father's case. She wanted to hear what other people had to say.

"She went to see Hinokuma Fukashi at his home in Tokyo during the period of the appeal. But his wife said he was out. So my mother returned home. She was very sad. She said she had the very strong feeling that Hinokuma was just hiding in the backroom."

The men who had been interrogated by Captain James Godwin and made to sign startlingly similar affidavits against

The close bond of friendship that developed between Defence Counsel Choji Nakayama and General Nishimura on Los Negros Island ultimately passes on to the executed officer's son, Makoto. In this 1960 photograph taken of the reception for Makoto and his bride, Ayako, lawyer Choji Nakayama sits (fourth from left) at a place of honour with the wedding party.

Lt. General Takuma Nishimura appeared unable to face the family of the man they had helped send to the gallows.

"When they were at Manus," Makoto says, " Nonaka Shoichi promised my father he would visit the Nishimura family on his return to Japan. He never came. He did not honour his promise."

Over the years, Captain Nonaka was the one person Makoto Nishimura had wanted to meet. But Lt. General Nishimura's former personal aide proved a difficult prey. He made appointments he did not keep, offering no excuses for the breaches.

"In 1985, 35 years after the war," Makoto continues, "I thought I would finally get to talk to Nonaka. There was a gathering of the Rabaul-Manus Friendship Society at Sangane in Aichi prefecture, between Tokyo and Osaka. I found out that the room next to mine was reserved for Nonaka. I thought, at last! But, again he didn't show up. Shortly after that, I heard he died in Nagoya."

Strangers had proved kinder. There was the unnamed Japanese prisoner who was tasked with cleaning the cells of the executed men on Los Negros and burning their things. "He saved my father's glasses, his seal and the last photographs my mother had sent. He gave them to Hiroshi Itsui and Mr. Itsui returned them to us when he came back to Japan," Makoto remembers.

Defence Counsel Choji Nakayama's kindness is likewise treasured. "Mr. Nakayama came back to Japan just in time to hear that my father had been hanged," Makoto discloses. "He was very upset and angry. He very much wanted to pursue the perjury charges against Inagaki, Sono and Hinokuma. But he needed my family's support to do it. My mother sought her brothers' advice. They said there was no point blaming others for my father's death. They said it would all be pointless because nothing would ever return Takuma to us. So we did not press charges and Mr. Nakayama had to forget about Inagaki, Sono and Hinokuma."

Choji Nakayama remained a close family friend of Setsuko Nishimura and her children until his death in 1967. The Los Negros experience affected the Japanese barrister deeply and he became a surrogate father to the young Makoto. When the general's son and Ayako got married in 1960, Choji Nakayama sat in a place of honour at the wedding table.

It may be remembered that Nakayama had openly blamed himself for Lt. General Nishimura's conviction, calling his handling of the Los Negros defence ineffectual and incompetent. This public acceptance of failure is known to Nishimura's son. But no matter. "He tried his best to save my father. Nakayama was a good man," Makoto pronounces. "He was a big help to my family. Mentally, he guided us through the crisis following the execution."

Brother and sister. Forty-five years on from their father's execution, brother and sister, Makoto and Tomoko, both married with grown-up families, remain close. This recent photograph was taken at a party in Yokohama celebrating the marriage of one of Tomoko's children.

As a young man, Makoto says he kept to himself. He did not become part of societies formed by war criminals and their families. He adds, "I did not feel I was the son of a war criminal. I did not seek stories about my father. The stories came to me. But as I grew older I became interested in his life and I came to know him."

Makoto has been to Singapore twice and on both occasions called in at Changi Prison. The first visit was with a group of war veterans in May 1972, 25 years after a British-convened military court sentenced his father to life for alleged involvement in the infamous Chinese Massacre. He was 38 years old. On this trip he heard stories about his father from the former soldiers who had known the Imperial Guards divisional commander as a fellow prisoner in Changi.

On his second Singapore trip in early 1996, Makoto went to see the Surrender Chambers on Sentosa island.

Slowly, he is learning more and more about the father he

Makoto Nishimura at 64 is an academic and lecturer at Tokyo's Toyo University. He pours over the Imperial Guards' war diary in the living room of his home in Machida.

last saw when he was 11 years old. Among the keepsakes handed down by his mother is the original, and, probably, the only extant copy of the Imperial Guards' war diary. He pores through its pages as if he were preparing for one of his lectures. He searches for entries centred on the Bakri action and the Parit Sulong massacre. January 17 to January 22, 1942. Furious fighting, Makoto reads, many Japanese and Australians dead.

He takes off his reading glasses, closes the journal and hands it across for one to scan.

Perhaps, he says, it has been a blessing that he started to be interested in what happened to his father when he was nearly forty years old. His interest has not been marred by blame or anger or bitterness. Or shame. There is also the fact that there are documents one can turn to these days.

"One day," he says," perhaps I'll be able to talk about it with my children."

He has three sons: a mathematics teacher, a chemist and an architect. He has not discussed Lt. General Nishimura's story with them. "I am still learning about him myself," Makoto reasons. "I did not know many details about my father. So when they were children I did not know what to say. It is not right to urge children to make up their minds about something that is not very clear."

Historical documents that have been declassified bring encouraging tidings. There are files to prove that what Lt. General Nishimura tried to tell the Singapore court in 1947 was the truth: he was not part of any conspiracy that led to the Chinese Massacre. There are papers and papers to prove that the Los Negros trial in 1950 had been a travesty and that, from day one, Lt. General Nishimura was doomed.

"But what good does it do?" his son asks. "He will not come back. My father said time solves everything. A long time has passed and it went by so rapidly."

An hour away by train from Machida is the Ikegami-

Hommonji, a Buddhist temple founded in 1274 during the Kamakura era. The 85-year-old head priest of the temple was once the chaplain in Singapore's Changi and Outram Road Prisons. Yearly, veterans and their families come from all over Japan to Hommonji for a memorial service.

Early in 1996, for the first time, Makoto Nishimura attended the Hommonji spring remembrance day service. Afterwards, he mingled with the aged warriors and heard a few stories about his father.

"The old men knew a little French," Makoto smiles. "They said my father taught them French in jail. So he was teaching others while he was learning English."

He took a further step in confronting the past in late August this year. After years and years of indecision, Makoto thought it was time to go to Manus and visit the scene of his father's last months.

"We must stick to historical facts," he repeats. "There were massacres and people died. On both sides. Everyone suffered. I accept the role that my father had in the war. But there are things I do not think my father did. I don't think he should have been punished for these things."

He looks out and surveys the garden he personally tends. Pots of aloe vera line the length of the living room window. It's green everywhere and Lt. General Nishimura's son looks pleased with his handiwork.

"I believe," Makoto confides, "that there is a time to speak and a time to be silent. I am now like the old soldiers. I pray for the soul of every war dead. The source of every unhappiness lies in war. I believe that my father was hoping for eternal peace for all the world at the time of his death — more than the recovery of his personal honour.

"That," Makoto Nishimura asserts quietly, "is my belief."

Where it all ended. Ghosts of war haunt the still standing Quonset hut remnants of the Lombrum Prison compound on Los Negros Island.

For years, local authorities have been talking about demolishing the rusting reminders of the Pacific conflict's last war crimes trials. But the huts that were once part of the Lombrum Point Prison somehow defy the inroads of progress.

Glossary of abbreviations

AALC	Australian Army Legal Corps
AG	Adjutant General
AHQ	Army Headquarters
AIF	Australian Imperial Force
BCOF	British Commonwealth Occupation Force
CARO	Central Army Records Office
CRIMSEC MANUS	Army signal address for 1 Australian War Crimes Section, Manus.
DLS	Director, Legal Services (Department)
DPW & I	Director, Prisoners of War & Internees (Department)
HQ	Headquarters
IMTFE	International Military Tribunal for the Far East
JAG	Judge Advocate General
LHQ	Land Headquarters
Lt.	Lieutenant
MMBW	Melbourne Metropolital Board of Works
OC	Officer in Charge
PNG	Papua New Guinea
POW	Prisoner of war
PW & I	Prisoners of War and Internees
QMG	Quarter Master General
RAN	Royal Australian Navy
RSSAILA	The organisation known throughout Australia as the RSL has undegone numerous changes of name since it was first established in 1916. From 1940 to 1965 it was officially called the Returned Sailors' Soldiers' and Airmen's Imperial League of Austrialia.
SACSEA	Supreme Allied Commander, South East Asia
SCAP	Supreme Commander Allied Powers
SEAC	South East Asia Command
Sgt.	Sergeant
SIB	Special Investigations Branch

Research notes

Research for this book involved, in part, reference to the following file sources:

Australian Archives

A416/7	BF 337/1/4
A462/1/2	446/1/2
A472/1	81942, W18153, W18153 Part 3.
A518	C16/2/6
A1067/1	P46/10/49/1 Part 3
A1068/7	P147/12/16
A1838/1	481/6/1/1
A1838/278	3101/10/13/1 Part 3
A4639 XMI	Vols 1, 3, 4, 5, 6, 8.
A4940/1	C2
A5953/1	48/4
A6006/3	1919/2/24
A6456/3	R084/001
A15954/1	264/3
CRS/M1505	Box 77 (916)
M1511	Item 1
MP 375/11	
MP 375/15	
MP 729/7	35/421/65
MP 729/8	66/431/13
MP 742/1	262/1/5130, 336/1/434, 336/1/716, 336/1/1591, 336/1/1962, 336/1/1965, 336/1/2036, 336/1/2116, 336/1/2136, 336/1/2137, 336/1/2148, 336/1/2187, 336/1/2194
MP 927	A336/1/19
MP 1185/8	1932/2/4
MP 1395/2	
MP 1395/3	Box 4
MP 1395/3	Box 9
MT 885/1	W/3/5309
SP 109/3	323/20
B 4156, B 5562, B 5563, B 5569	

Australian War Memorial

AWM 51	125
AWM 53	8/3/19
AWM 54	553/5/25, 553/5/26, 1010/1/9, 1010/1/26, 1010/2/34, 1010/9/76
AWM 73	45
AWM 76	B220
AWM 93	50/2/23/391, 50/2/23/428
AWM 166	AG Co-ord 218, 219, 220 (3), 221 (47) 222 (5).

Public Record Office, UK

WO 203/6319	
WO 311/541	
WO 311/587	
WO 325/1	8C 189277
WO 325/30	XC 189369
WO 325/88	189115
WO 325/108	XC 10427

Bibliography

The Tall Man Who Never Slept, by James Bradley, Woodfield Publishing, 1991.

Singapore 1941-1942, by Masanobu Tsuji, Oxford University Press, 1988.

Massacre at Parit Sulong, by Gilbert Mant, Kangaroo Press, 1996

MacArthur, by S. L. Mayer, Bison Books, 1984.

Betrayal in High Places, by James MacKay, Tasman Archives, 1996.

The killer they called a god, by Ian Ward, Media Masters Publishers, 1992.

Luck's a Fortune, by David MacNicoll, Wildcat Press, 1979

The Grim Glory, 2/19 Battalion AIF Association, Sydney, 1975.

A History Of The 2/29 Battalion - 8th Australian Division AIF, The 2/29 Battalion AIF Association, Melbourne, 1983.

The Japanese Thrust, by Lionel Wigmore, Australia in the War of 1939-45 series, Australian War Memorial, Canberra, 1957.

Appendix A

The papers in this section comprise the complete case against Lt. General Takuma Nishimura and Captain Shoichi Nonaka. The case rested entirely on this documentary evidence. Both men were found guilty. Not a single witness was called for the prosecution.

Evidence taken at Sydney on 12 November 1945 before Mr.
Justice Mansfield.

NX71148 Lieut. Ben Charles HACKNEY, 2/29 Battalion, being duly
sworn, gives the following evidence:

My full number, name, rank and unit are NX71148 Lieut.Ben
Charles Hackney, 2/29 Battalion. My home address is 12
Benelong Crescent, Bellevue Hill, Sydney.

On the evening of 17 January 1942, 2/29 Battalion made contact
with the enemy at Bankri and from the morning of 18 January the
battle was at its height. On 19 January 1942 we joined up with
2/19 Battalion some little distance south of Bakri. From Bakri
we withdrew to Parit Sulong, where we were held up by a bridge
and strong Japanese forces defending the bridge. We made a
stand there from the morning of 21 January until we were
captured the following day, and we had very heavy casualties.

The following is a summary of the happenings between 22 January
1942 and 21 March 1942 inclusive. I do not know the names of
the Japanese responsible and I do not know of my own knowledge
what unit it was that captured us at Parit Sulong, but I have
heard subsequently from Col. Kappe that it was the Japanese
Imperial Guards Division; these soldiers were bigger than the
usual Japanese soldiers.

1.   Many men comprising A.I.F. and Indian Army soldiers - the
majority severely wounded, some of whom had been lying in
trucks, vans etc. up to four days with necessarily limited
medical attention and were subjected to the treatment briefly
outlined below at PURIT SULONG by I.J.A. soldiers.

2.   Prior to the closing in of IJA soldiers I myself had been
wounded in four places making me incapable of walking and
greatly restricting any movement.

      (a) a bullet through the left leg below the knee causing a
           fracture
      (b) shell splinter in back,
      (c) shell splinter in outside of right calf,
      (d) Shell splinter in rear of right knee.

3.   These soldiers made up some of the casualties of the 65
Fd Bty (2/15 Fd Regt.); 4 A Tk Regt.; 2/19 Inf Bn; 2/29 Inf
Bn, and other units of the 45 Indian Bde, under which command
these A.I.F. forces had been placed. These soldiers had been
gathered together during the days prior to and including the
22 January 1942, and were by 1200 hrs 22 January 1942 assembled-
some in trucks, others lying about in various positions (many
of whom because of wounds had been unable to gain the shelter of
a vehicle) - on or about the roadway immediately NORTH of the
PARIT SULONG Bridge.

4.   Enemy fire of all types continued for some time to pour in
from all directions upon the vehicles and personnel who had
gathered along a short section of the road after an order had
been given for all troops who were able to do so to vacate the
position. Because of lack of unwounded soldiers and scarcity
of arms and ammunition very little retaliation fire went out
from this group in return for that of the enemy. Another
officer and I operated for as long as ammunition was available
a Bren gun from beneath a utility truck in order to in some way
add to the comparitive lack of fire from our position and to per
perhaps lengthen by at least a short period the time when the
enemy would inevitably close in on our position, and thereby
enable those who had been able to get away to have a better
opportunity of travelling a fair distance before the Japs had use

of the road and were able to push forward and perhaps prevent our men from gaining contact with our forces from whom we had been cut off for several days.

5.   About 1430 hrs all fire from the convoy ceased and shortly afterwards from all directions especially WEST Japanese soldiers closed in on our position. Indications amidst much unintelligable yelling, were made for our personnel to assemble at a point WEST of the road and over a parit which ran by the side of the road.

6.   Some of the fit men - of whom there were very few - were allowed to assist the more unfortunate; others were compelled to move immediately to the assembly point and remain. This assembling was a slow process as many were incapable of movement. Men were lying about in all directions. Some dead, many seriously wounded who had been unable to gain any shelter whatever being incapable of any movement. Others unable to made much progress, had managed to crawl or drag themselves to one of the many vehicles and there lie exhausted.

7.   The following are some of the acts committed by the Japanese during the process of assembling the men.

          (a) On many occasions a Jap approaching a wounded man, would indicate for him to move along with the rest; however, sometimes the soldier would be incapable perhaps of any movement whatever. Upon failing to do as the Jap indicated the latter would immediately begin yelling and making signs- still no movement by the wounded soldier whereupon he would be bashed about with the rifle, kicked, and on some occasions eventually either run through many times with the bayonet, or with the rifle close to his head - shot. This was the fate of a good many wounded men.
          (b) Sometimes men hobbling towards the little bridge over the parit which led to the assembly place, and others who were crawling, would have a Jap come up to them and be dealt a terrible blow sometimes to the body but most always to the head, with the but of the rifle. Some were knocked down, whereupon they would be kicked.
          (c) The fate of others was to be hurried when they were already moving as fast their wound would allow by some Japs using a variety of methods - some kicking, some often striking with their rifles and other times many prodding the men with their bayonets.
          (d) One man badly wounded in the chest and thigh was making to the bridge very slowly by crawling and dragging himself along the ground. He was hit several times by Japs but was incapable of moving faster. A Jap drove his bayonet into the man and made as if to push him along the edge of the road. The man fell full length face downwards, whereupon the Jap thrust in his bayonet several times and then left him, moving off to some other unfortunate who would also be brutally treated to make him move faster.
          (e) A Jap came to my position. He pushed another officer, who was with me and standing, away, then indicated for me to move also. I pointed out that I was unable to do so, where upon he began kicking me; but even knowing what was wanted and with the urge to avoid this foul treatment, I was unable to move when required to stand. He then struck me several time with his rifle, then prodded me with his bayonet. Finally, he let the officer come back but even with his help I was unable to walk, my left leg being useless and my right altogether too painful. The Japs started screaming again and began belting us both with his rifle butt. Eventually, with the aid of another, I managed to get along by swinging myself on their shoulders. When crossing the small bridge the three of us were struck many times by the Japs on both sides.

(f) By these various means all the prisoners were either herded into the area or killed by shooting or bayoneting, or left dying on the road.

(g) Upon approaching the bridge over the parit all personnel had to take off any equipment and throw on the road watches, pens, pencils - anything visible to the Japs except clothing.

(h) After crossing the bridge, almost everyone being hit as he did so with a rifle by one or all of the Japs who were on both sides, all prisoners had to remove their clothing except their boots and socks and putties, which was thrown into a heap. The clothes were thrown amongst the prisoners after a considerable time had elapsed, during which they had been searched.

(i) One wounded man who had been placed by our own people upon a table form and put inside an office truck, was seen by a Jap. The table form was dragged out and left leaning against the back of the truck. The fellow had been dead for some time and become stiff. The body was then propped up in an upright position on the tabletop. Situated in this position, it created enormous amusement to the Jap concerned and was an object of ridicule to many Japs afterwards.

8. When all had assembled the prisoners were made to sit in the nude in a circle within a ring of Jap guards. There were approximately 110 A.I.F. soldiers and 35 to 40 Indian Army soldiers.

9. Many Japanese troops were by this time moving along the road, some on foot, others on bycicles and many in lorries (both Jap and civilians). They were halted often and on these occasions many would come over to have a look at the prisoners - about 150 nude bodies, unshaven, dirty, mostly wounded, some wounds being bandaged and others gaping, dirty and blood clotted, some fresh and many reopened by movement and still bleeding freely. To the Japs the prisoners were of great interest, some showing mirth, other ill temper and wickedness; many hit or kicked (or both) and punched and prodded men with bayonets, often if possible kicking where a wound lay open, and so great was their satisfaction upon any visible evidence of pain that the dose was often repeated.

10. One Jap tormented prisoners by drawing his sword and wiping the blood off it be repeatedly dipping it in the water in the parit and drawing it over an officer's throat. Others he tormented by making as though to run them through or cutting their throats.

11. All those on the outside of the group, and particularly those closest to the road were treated worst. I was one of those near the road, having been amongst the last to arrive at the assembly point, and was, like others, kicked, struck and battered many times, most always with rifles and on some occasions with sword stabbers. The Japs most always used their rifle butts. The wound in my back attracted the attention of many who whenever possible took delight in kicking and belting the place where the wound was exposed.

12. Many prisoners were knocked unconscious when dealt terrific blows on the head with rifle butts.

13. The Jap in charge of the prisoners was dressed quite differently from the personnel of the guard, with dark coloured tunic, breeches, knee high boots, armed with pistol and sword with some braid at the hilt, and carrying a large map case. He gave orders to the guard.

14. The prisoners were forced into a little shed or garage which was altogether too small in view of the following circumstances and actions, as given below:

(a)   The Japs ~~grunted, yelled, kicked,~~ hit and prodded with
bayonets until most of the prisoners had scrambled
into the shed.

(b)   Some were knocked unconscious and others killed during
the process.

(c)   Some walked on top of the more helpless, wounded men
were pushed and fell upon others and terrific yells of pain
were practically continuous.

(d)   Those closest to the opening were first to be put into
the shed which soon became a stinking, scrambling hell hole
full of tortured, groaning, delirious wounded soldiers.

(e)   Those still fit were unable to do anything except for
those immediately around them.

(f)   The shed was much too small, fellows near the doorway
being hit, kicked and prodded scrambled in, endeavoured in
vain to avoid hurting their comrades. There was not room
even to put a foot down without stepping on some part of
some body already with bodies above and below.

(g)   ~~Again and again fellows were forced in on top of others.~~

15. Many men were groaning most of the time and there were yells,
repeated time and time again, by many for water. It was hours
and hours and with some a day or more since they had had a drink,
for water and those to issue it had been scarce during the four
days of the progress along five miles of road. Water was not
given to the prisoners.

16. Six officers were taken from the group and put together
about six or seven yards away.

17. Requests we~~re made at first and when these were ignored~~
demands were made of the Jap in charge to provide medical attention
and water for the prisoners and also smoking materials (of which
much of the prisoner's own was lying in a heap nearby), but
these were ignored. This Jap could read but refused to speak
~~English.~~

18. A little later another move was made ~~and agin the prisoners
were subjected to violence and terrific brutalities by the
guards.~~ This time all the ORs were put into two rooms off some
coolie quarters. This was a long process; many had to be carried
and, although not far, steps had to be climbed; the dead were
not allowed to be left; their bodies too had to be taken into
these rooms. The ~~worst wounded were again treated wickedly~~;
they were expected to move as fit and ~~when failing~~ to do so were
struck, kicked and punched. ~~Many~~ incapable of any movement
without assistance ~~were bashed~~ on the head and some were killed
by bayonetting ~~and~~ few were shot. Altogether, a large number
~~were wounded further by the Japs.~~

19. When all the ORs were in the rooms the doors were closed.
The six officers were made to sit on the steps in front of one
of these rooms.

20. Reque~~sts and demands for medical aid, water and sm~~okes were
again agnored and although these were made time ~~and~~ time again
throughout the whole period, they were ignored by the Jap in
charge.

21. Shortly afterwards an Indian soldier who had been hiding
in one of the many vehicles (which were being inspected and
searched by the Japs) was brought to the building. He had a bad
wound on one hand, the top part of which had been blown away,
and one leg ~~of~~ his trousers was saturated with blood as though he
were bleeding from some wound in his thigh. He was immediately
str~~uck to the ground by a Jap and his pockets cleaned~~ out.

22. The ORs who had been jammed into the small rooms were scrambling to the windows groaning all the time, and yelling time and time again for water and to be let out.

23. The noise of battle was long gone; nowhere xcept in the far distance could be heard even a gun. Occasionally, an enemy plane flew overhead.

24. Still going down the road were lorry after lorry of Japanese soldiers and much artillery equipment. Very seldom now was there a halt but each time the convoy did stop Jap soldiers invariably came across to the building to see the prisoners.

25. Later, many staff cars came along, two of which were preceeded by tanks and motor cyclists and followed similarly. They halted in front of the place where the prisoners were and many Japs came over. They were met by the Jap in charge of the prisoners amidst much shouting, saluting, and bowing by this Jap and the personnel of the guard. Other Jap soldiers in the area also gave their attention to the party which consisted of officers and some very senior ones.

26. One of these new arrivals was outstanding and presumably the Commander of the Japanese forces in the area - a short, stocky fellow. A body guard kept close with him always. He was well dressed, his sword hanging low and with a great amount of brown cord at the hilt, knee high boots and spurs all glistening. The attitude of the Japs to this officer was as though he was something far and above any of them as though to them he was a God.

27. He looked at the officer prisoners, who were made to move off the steps and stand; then mounted the steps, the body guard keeping very close, and looked through the window at the mass inside of one of the rooms.

28. Upon leaving the building he spoke to one of the officers accompanying him who in turn passed on what were apparently orders to the Jap in charge of the prisoners.

29. Leaving a couple behind this party then departed. Again came the yelling, bowing, and saluting. At first the tanks, then the cycles then the cars moved off, and after them were more cycles and tanks. Along the road wherever Japanese were to be seen, they paid their compliments to these two cars very reverently.

30. One of those remaining was asked to allow water to be given to the prisoners, many of whom were all the time yelling for it. A little Malay boy who had been with the convoy for some time was told by him to get some. On returning, however, the Jap in charge noticed the container and immediately hit it out of his hands and then kicked the kiddy.

31. He was asked about medical attention but said that Japanese medical men were too busy. Later asked for water, he said that if the Jap in charge said, "No," there was nothing he could do about the matter. When asked could the cigarettes be got from theheap of prisoners' belongings he replied, "Not yet".

32. Another group of Japs arrived and took many photographs and made notes. After this was completed, the cigarettes and water which had been held out by the personnel of the guard to the prisoners, some of whom had been let out of the rooms for the purpose of being photographed, but held just beyond their reach, were retained by the Japs and thrown away respectively, which made worse the feelings of the already near despairing men.

33. The ORs were again forced into the room.

34. The Indian soldier, who had been knocked down in front
of the building was showing signs of regaining consciousness.
He began to sit up but the Jap in charge kicked him over again.
He sat up again and this time was viciously kicked many times.
For a while the Indian lay still groaning and jabbering. The
Jap yelled at him and took a rifle from one of the guards and
bashed the Indian, then thrust the bayonet into him time and time
again. Then he was heaved into the parit by the Jap thrusting
the bayonet into his body and heaving. A few seconds and the
terribly blood stained, horrible face emerged above the water
and the Jap levelled the rifle and fired. The head jerked but
remained above water; there was another shot and this time the
head disappeared.

35. The traffic going south was not so thick now and moving
more freely, occasionally a motor cyclist or a car going north.
There were still a few who left the road to see the prisoners
or to poke about the vehicles inquisitively, some occasionally
kicking a body to see if any life was left in it.

36. About sunset the guards began to move about the house.
Machine guns were brought from where they had been resting
between tours of duty and placed in front of the building.

37. The officers were then tied together by the following methods.
Two guards approached the officers undoing as they came a small
coil of rope which they took from their belts. The officers
were then made to stand, two of them unable to do so without
assistance and both incapable of walking. Both hands of each
officer were tightly tied behine his back. After this, another
length of rope was tied to the wrists, passed up under the chin
and around the neck and then down again to the wrists, where it
was pulled tight, thus forcing the hands well up the back and
making the rope terribly tight against the throat. The secong
rope was not cut but was passed on to the wrists of the next
officer, where a similar procedure was carried out; then again
on to the next and so on, so that as well as making more
secure the tying of each, they were all linked together. During
this process, the two Japs treated the officers unmercifully,
jerking the ropes this way and that and many time lashing them
severely about the head and body with loose lengths, often
kicking ferociously at some part of the body that was swaying or
stumbling - through the Japs' own treatment - in the wrong
direction for them to do whatever they wished, During this
procedure I was kicked in the legs and lashed about the body and
head, particularly the latter, many times, this being mainly
because I was unable to stand properly and each time a rope was
pulled I swayed this way or that, thus continually hindering these
Japs in their work.

38. This done, the ORs were brought out from the rooms. One by
one as they came down the steps they were tied brutally with
their hand behind their backs; the first was then connected to
the second but only from wrist to wrist, not over or around the
neck as with the officers, then from the second to the third
and so on, the first then being tied to the nearest of the small
line of officers.

39. The supply of rope ran out and some Japs were bringing pieces
of wire and with these were tying up many of the prisoners.

40. Complaints were made to the Japs in charge regarding this ill
treatment. Nearly every man was lashed, mostly about the head,
and kicked by the Japs. Often a soldier who was more difficult to
tie because of his wounds preventing his movement, was subjected
to lashings (sometimes now with wire) and kicking. Occasionally,
another guard seeing his fellow soldier beating a prisoner, would
rush up and add to that prisoner's misery by striking him with his

rifle butt.

41. This habit of one Jap coming to another when that other was illtreating a prisoner, so as to add to his efforts also, occurred very often.

42. The Jap in charge took no notice of the complaints.

43. It was necessary to move the first lot well away from the steps of the building to allow the others to come down from the rooms and be tied. They were shifted back towards the shed which before had been filled with prisoners. When the line of officers moved, one of them fell immediately. After being kicked in all parts of the body and being struck man time with rifle butts, he was cut free from the chain. I fell after very little movement. The Japs became more annoyed apparently because I was the second one to fall and I suffered similar ill treatment, but to a greater extent. I was kicked in all parts of the body and struck many times on the head and body with rifles. One kick split my right eyebrow which then hung down over the eye, the blood pouring over my face. After some kicks and hits the Japs would force the others along. In this way I was dragged a short distance. Then would commence again another reign of blows and then I would be dragged a few more feet. Eventually, the Japs cut me loose and left me lying upon the ground in a much worse, painful and aching condition than before. The wound in my back and been kicked many times, which kept it bleeding freely, as were all the other wounds and cuts I had received.

44. Towards the end, either the supply of rope and wire was exhausted or the Japs grew tired of tying the prisoners as a few, numbering about 20, were left untied. The remainder were tied in groups of 20 to 25 each. The dead were left in the room.

45. The prisoners were then made to move along the front of the building towards, and then around the south end. There were many who were unable to move at all, and others because of being tied, could not get the necessary assistance, so that many stumbled, some fell, causing others also to fall. These were then kicked and struck, and bayoneted, until as many as could do so were again standing, and then the line proceeded slowly, some still being dragged, of which a few occasionally raised themselves to their knees only to be again thrown off balance. Many of these were then freed from the line and left lying. The Japs grasped others and dragged them along, some were kicked, some struck other deeply prodded with bayonets.

46. The prisoners were then herded into a group and the massacre which followed was to say the least most violent and wicked.

47. Rifles and machine guns belched forth a storm of death - a few fell, a group fell. After the first while a few remained standing - these were either struck by rifle fire or hit by a burst from a machine gun. Rifle and machine gun fire went toward any person who yelled. Firing was indiscriminate and many men had fallen not because of death but because they had either been pulled down by others falling or because the indiscriminate firing had only added to the number of their wounds and the pain they suffered.

48. Some Jap soldiers then returned to the front of the building and began taking away the bodies of those who had been cut free from the chains. These they dragged round the corner in the same direction as the others had been taken.

49. They left behind only one body; this being the furthest away and of the bodies of the two officers who had previously been cut free from the chain. This was I. To me the fate of the prisoners was quite evident, and my only hope of escape was to endeavour to make the Japs believe that I was dead, and perhaps

stand a chance of being left lying there. I knew that I should
have appeared dead enough provided that I remained quite still.
Blood had been running over my face from the wound in my eyebrow
and also from a few cuts in my head which ahd bled freely. I
was hat-less; had not done my hair for ages; I was unshaven
for more than five days; my hair was matted with blood and
dirt; my neck and shirt top were very bloody; the wound in my
back still bleeding and small pool of blood on the ground; my
shirt torn to ribbons and saturated with blood below the wound
and all along the side; 'my shorts also very bloodstained. My
right leg from the knee down was also bloody; the old bandage on
my left leg was long since dirty and discoloured; one bayonet
had gone through the bandage and entered the calf above the
exit hole of the bullet; also above the back of my left boot
another bayonet wound bled freely.

I lay quite still, very uncomfortable and aching as I was
still bound securely and painfully tight; the rope still being
around my neck prevented me from stretching my arms, my hands
still being in the vicinity of my shoulder blades. Some Japs
came, stood over me for a while, and as if to make sure one
pushed me several times with his boot. I allowed my body to
move quite freely in whatever direction it was forced. One or
more of them then kicked me in several places. With this they
left. ~~{Inxxinxxxifanxbehindxtexfix~~

50. Many Japs went to the road,leaving a few behind to fire in
the direction of any sound or whenever anyone moved, and returned
bringing many of the tims of petrol which ere carried on our
vehicles.

51. They proceeded to pour this over the prisoners, many of
whom were still conscious.

52. The prisoners were then set alight, and amid screams and
yells of pain, fright, nervousness and delirium, burnt to death.

53. I lay outside the building unable move even justa little to
a less aching position. Whilst there the outburst of curses and
yells that had accompanied the beginning of the firing and had
since somewhat subsided was not very long after revived again.

54. I could see the flickers of a fire which occasionally would
burst out very brightly. The prisoners were being burnt, and
many were screaming and yelling terribley. There came to me the
smell of burning rag and then what was just as distinguishable
the odour of burnt flesh.

55. I had managed to be'dead' as far as some of the Japs were
concerned and now was determined even more than ever before that,
no matter what pain I was suffering, how my body ached, or how
uncomfortable, or what cramps I had to endure, I would remain
'dead' until such time as the Japs departed.

56. Throughout the whole period Japs came from the road to see
what was going on. In passing me sometimes I would only be
pushed, other times completely ignored, and on other occasions
individuals acted unmercifully. How many time I was kicked,
battered with rifles by those Japs passing, I know not, but all
the time I had to maintain that lifeless attitude.

57. Jap personnel for ages maintained a patrol about the area.
Occasionally a shot or shots would be fired. Many time one or
more of them in their wanderings came across my body; some just
passed by, others would satisfy themselves by previously used
methods - kicking and hitting mostly on the head. Some
unfortunately used their bayonets, most just pricking me in the
back. On two occasions they were more than pricks; once the

Jap jumped and grunted as he lunged forward but fortunately he
was too far away and the bayonet entered my side between the
ribs and apparently did no harm; the other when a bayonet
point struck my right elbow making it useless for many days;
one Jap decided he would have my boots and caused me much pain
whilst he roughly pulled them off my feet.

58. As time went on activity in the area became less and less,
until eventually there was no sign or sound of any Jap about. I
waited long after this before being certain that no one was
patrolling I knew that to be seen moving would be the end.

59 Much later, after I had forced myself from my bonds, which
was a very painful and long and tedious task - and got some
water, I was met by a sergeant and another soldier, both smelt
very strongly of petrol - they had been with the group when
fired upon and set alight.

60. Sgt. Croft told me that they were amongst the few who had
not been tied, and had been together when the prisoners were
fired upon, they had fallen with the first burst of firing - neither of them hit - and lay with the remainder. When the petrol
was brought from the road they had both had some thrown on them.
Then the group had been set alight. The fellow with Croft had ,
yelled out and was immediately fired on. Sgt. Croft then got
this fellow and himself free from the heap of men, had lain still
and quiet close by until the Japs left the area.

61. The soldier, whose name I do not know, died when in the
jungle a short distance west of Parit Sulong, on the following
afternoon the 23 Jan 42.

62. Sgt Croft left me at first light on the morning of the
24 Jan 42 accompanied by an English soldier who had come to our
position in the jungle in the early hours of 23 Jan 42 and who
had been cut off from our forces when north of Parit Sulong.

63. Pte. O.H.Robertson of 2/19 Inf Bn is reported to have seen
Sgt Croft about two days later (approx 26 Jan 42). But as far
as is know Sgt Croft has not been seen since that date.

64. After spending 36 days lying in and crawling about the
jungle and rubber plantation area between Parit Sulong and Batu
Pahat, I was captured by Malay policemen and taken to Parit
Sulong police station on the 27 Feb 42. I was still unable to
walk had suffered a great deal from my wounds, exposure,
starvation and filth, and had become very weak and dirty and lost
a tremendous amount of weight.

65. The following day 28 Feb 42 I was handed over to Jap
soldiers by the Malay Police and taken by some of these Japs to
Batu Pahat where I was left for some time outside a building
approx south of the town which was a Japanese HQ, convalescent
Depot and hospital combined.

66. About sunset of that day a Jap came to me carrying a piece
of rope, this he put round my neck with a slipknot. Calling for
two Indians to help me, I was taken about 150 yards to a guard
room. On the way, if I at any time lagged back, the Jap gave
the rope a severe pull which jerked my neck considerably and I
was many times prevented from breathing as the rope pulled too
tight on my throat.

67. Upon arrival at the guard room - which had an open front,
the Japs came out and watched as I was being lashed to a post.
With my back against it, rope was first wound around my throat
and the post, then over my chest. More rope was brought, my
hands tied behind my back, and the rope then wound round and
round, until I was securely and tightly tied to the post from

~~my neck to my feet.~~

68. ~~The personnel of the guard then went past in single file,~~ each either hitting, punching or kicking me as they passed on their way back into the guard room.

69. So I remained until well into the night. Several times the guard commander came out and looked at me. My beard greatly amused him and he would stand laughing as he plucked hairs out of it one by one. Each time a relief came out of the room I was punished in some way or other, and again when the relieved ones returned. Generally by being smacked or punched on the face and chest or kicked.

70. On the afternoon of the next day, the 1 March 1942 I was taken by a Jap guard to a hospital. Here a Jap doctor refused to admit me and refused also medical attention and said he would have to send me elsewhere as the hospital was too full.

71. I was taken to the Batu Pahat police Station and there put into a cell where there were 8 English soldiers who had been brought there a few days before, when captured a few miles out of that town.

72. One of these men was very ill and suffering greatly from bad wounds in shoulder and head.

73. During the following 15 days the numbers were increased to 22, some of whom were wounded. The following conditions existed.

  (a) Medical attention was refused each time requests for some were made.
  (b) Although asking many times for soap, only on one occasion was a very small piece provided. Everybody was very filthy and clothes dirty.
  (c) Food very inadequate - amounting to two small meals each day of about one third of a pint of rice.
  (d) One Jap often walked into the section of the gaol and calling on a man, punch him on the face and chest and finally with one terrific blow, mostly always to the face, knock the fellow back into the cell.
  (e) On two occasions a man was taken into a corridor and made to fight the Jap - receiving all the blows and not being allowed (under the penalty of much more severe treatment) to hit back.
  (f) Two Indian Army soldiers were sometimes put in front of some of these men and made strike them on the face.
  (g) Chinese who were locked in the gaol were often severely ill-treated. One was put into a straight jacket after being beaten about the head and body by a pair of crutches (both of which were smashed into small pieces during these beatings), and starved until he died.

74. On 17 March 1942 the 22 prisoners commenced a journey to Kuala Lumpur.

75. Upon arrival at KLUANG railway after spending the night of 17/18 March at AYER HITAM we were taken across the rails and made to clean out a filthy dirty cattle truck. After this all were put inside and the door closed. After some time during which the truck was shunted back and forth several times, it was attached to a goods train and set off northward.

76. On arrival at GEMAS, we walked to the police barracks. Everyone was weak and myself still unable to walk without assistance.

77. ~~The following morning 19 March 1943 we were taken early~~ to

the railway ~~atation~~ and put into an open coal ~~truck~~ ~~the~~ ~~bottom~~ of
which was covered thickly with coal dust and refuse.

78. It was unbearably hot in the open truck during the day, and
some of the men became very ill and bilious.

79. From KUALA LUMPUR railway station we were taken to PUDU Gaol
in that town arriving about 0130 hrs 20 March 1942. An untidy,
unshaven, filthy dirty, partly clothed, unrecognisably group in
tattered garments and mostly barefooted (some suffering a good
deal from wounds and illness, and all very weak from starvation
and exposure.

80. Soon after my arrival there I weighed myself and found that
I was 8 stone 7 pounds having lost 5 stone 3 pounds (or 73 pounds)
since ~~going~~ ~~into~~ ~~action~~ ~~63~~ ~~days~~ ~~previously.~~

This is the tenth and last page of the evidence of
NX71148 Lieut. Ben Charles HACKNEY, 2/29 Battalion.

I certify that the above evidence is true and correct.

Sd. B.C. Hackney, Lieut.
NX71148, 2/29 Bn.AIF.

Taken and sworn before me at)
)
Sydney on 12 November 1945.)
)
    Sd. Illegible.   )
       Commissioner.   )

Certified true copy of the original which is in my possession.

signature
1 Aust War Crimes Section

Singapore: 10th June 1947.

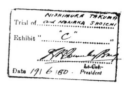

On this *eighth* day of *May* One thousand nine hundred and
forty-six, Ben Charles HACKNEY of Buckburraga, Burraga, in
the State of New South Wales, Grazier , makes oath
and says as follows:-

1. Attached hereto and marked with the letter "A" is sketch of
   the Parit-Sulong Bridge Area referred to in evidence given
   by me at Sydney on 12 Nov 45 before Mr. Justice Mansfield.

   > The figure "1" on this sketch indicates the assembly point
   > referred to in paras 5, 7(f) and 8 of evidence previously
   > given by me on 12 Nov 45 before Mr. Justice Mansfield.

   > The figure "2" on this sketch indicates the building into
   > which all captured were forced as mentioned in para. 14 of
   > previous evidence above referred to.

   > The figure "3" on this sketch indicates the building
   > mentioned in para.18 of previous evidence above referred to.

2. Distances indicated on attached sketch, "A", are only approximate,
   being stated to the best of my ability at this date.

3. Attached hereto and marked with the letter "B" is map of the around
   Singapore Area. Enclosed thereon with thick blue pencil line *a cross*
   is the Parit-Sulong Bridge Area referred to in evidence
   given by me at Sydney on 12 Nov 45 before Mr. Justice Mansfield.

SWORN by the abovenamed deponent,)
Ben Charles Hackney at *Bathurst*)
this *eighth* day of *May* One)
thousand nine hundred and forty-six.)

BEFORE ME *Leslie Williams*
A Justice of the Peace.

292

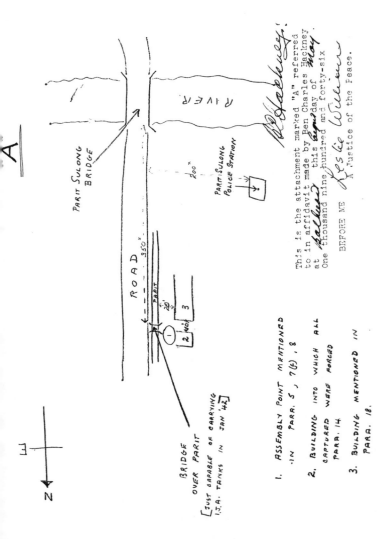

A

N

E

ROAD ← - - - 350ˣ →

PARIT SULONG BRIDGE

RIVER

PARIT SULONG POLICE STATION → ☐

200ˣ

20ˢ

PARIT

2 HDQ⟁ 1

3

BRIDGE OVER PARIT
[JUST CAPABLE OF CARRYING
I.J.A. TANKS IN JAN '42]

1. ASSEMBLY POINT MENTIONED
   IN PARR. 5, 7(b), 8

2. BUILDING INTO WHICH ALL
   CAPTURED WERE FORCED
   PARR. 14.

3. BUILDING MENTIONED IN
   PARR. 18.

This is the attachment marked "A" referred
to in affidavit made by Ben Charles Hackney
at _Kalura_ this _second_ day of _May_
One thousand nine hundred and forty-six.

BEFORE ME _Leslie Williams_
A Justice of the Peace.

Trial of NISHIMURA, TAKUMA
     NONAKA, SHOICHI
        "   "

Exhibit "........D........"

Date 19/6/50   President
Lt.-Col.

JGG/bej

SWORN STATEMENT

I, INAGAKI Tadahiro, of TOKYO-to, NAKANO-ku, KAMITAKADA ICHOME, 19 Banchi, proprietor of a Dye Works, swear I shall tell the truth according to the dictates of my conscience, and that I shall conceal nothing nor will I add to the facts.

1.   The following is a brief summary of my military history over the period December 1941 until February 1942:-

1941	December	Stationed at SAIGON, French Indo China, as a member of Headquarters KONOYE Division; rank Reserve 2nd Lieutenant.
	About 10 December	Arrived at BANGKOK, SIAM, with Headquarters KONOYE Division.
	Latter part December	Entrained for MALAYA, and after detrainment proceeded by motor vehicle arriving at MUAR River on 14 or 15 January.
1942	About 22 or 23 January	Passed through BAKRI and PARITSULONG areas, arriving at BATU PAHAT on the same day.
	About 31 January	Arrived at JOHORE BAHRU with Headquarters KONOYE Division, and was confined in hospital there until the termination of the battle for SINGAPORE on about 16 February 1942.

2.   I was attached to Headquarters KONOYE Division in about November 1941, and from that date until May 1942 I acted as a liaison and administrative officer, working under the staff officers on that Headquarters. I also acted as adjutant to the Chief of Staff, Colonel IMAI Kamejiro, and I usually accompanied him wherever he went, especially during the Malayan campaign. In about late May 1942 and whilst stationed in SUMATRA I was appointed to the position of personal aide to Lieutenant-General MUTO Akira, the General Officer Commanding KONOYE Division at that particular time. During the Malayan campaign the KONOYE Division was commanded by Lieutenant-General NISHIMURA Takuma, this officer being replaced by Lieutenant-General MUTO in April 1942. As I can now recall, the following two officers were attached to Headquarters KONOYE Division as adjutants to Lieutenant-General NISHIMURA during the aforementioned campaign:

       Major TODA Takeshi - senior adjutant

       Captain SONO Yoko

During the said campaign Lieutenant-General NISHIMURA's Personal Aide was Lieutenant (later Captain) NONAKA Shoichi who was transferred back to his parent unit, namely the Transport Regiment of KONOYE Division, in about late

          J. G. G. Godwin
          3-10-49. Captain   稲垣忠弘

February 1942. Lieutenant NONAKA was replaced by Lieutenant YOSHIDA from the
Field Artillery Regiment of the same division, the latter remaining as such
until his return to Japan in May 1942.

3.   The following is briefly what I recall of my movement and events
pertaining thereto from the BAKRI area to BATU PAHAT:

(a) In the late afternoon of either 22 or 23 January 1942 Headquarters
KONOYE Division, including myself, departed in convoy (cars and trucks) from the
BAKRI area, and headed along the main road leading to PARITSULONG. This convoy
was composed of about 8 cars and about 3 or 4 trucks, my car (Austin) being near
the head of this transport column and followed by, I believe, two staff officers'
cars, Colonel IMAI's car, Lieutenant-General NISHIMURA's car, and Major TODA's
car in that order. I seem to recall that Captain SONO was travelling at the
head of this convoy, as it was his duty to direct same to its destination.

(b) That same afternoon and whilst nearing the approach to the bridge over
PARITSULONG River, Captain SONO directed the convoy to stop. As soon as the
convoy stopped I looked back and noticed that Lieutenant-General NISHIMURA,
Colonel IMAI and other staff officers were getting out of their respective
vehicles and were then walking towards a building approximately 10 to 15 metres
away from the right-hand side of the road: this building was rectangular in
shape and stood on pillars about $3\frac{1}{2}$ feet above the ground. Prior to Captain SONO
directing the convoy to stop I had noticed what appeared to be about 20 - 30
Australian prisoners of war sitting in various postures on the porch of the said
building. I was not surprised when I saw the prisoners of war as I had learned
previously at Headquarters KONOYE Division in the BAKRI area that many (number
stated but not remembered) prisoners of war and their equipment had been taken
as a result of the battle for PARITSULONG.

(c) When I saw Lieutenant-General NISHIMURA and others approaching the said
building I ran over to join them, arriving there as Lieutenant-General NISHIMURA
was in the process of talking to a Japanese officer. I do not know the name of
this officer but I think his rank was either that of a 2nd Lieutenant or 1st
Lieutenant, and he appeared to be the officer in charge of the prisoners of war.

J. G. Godwin
3-10-49 Captain.   稲 垣 忠 弘

After Lieutenant–General NISHIMURA had finished conversing with this officer he, Lieutenant NONAKA and Colonel IMAI mounted the porch and looked through either the door or a window of one of the building's two rooms. From where I was standing I could not see into either of these two rooms, but I reached the conclusion from the stench and noise that they contained many badly wounded prisoners of war. Moreover, those prisoners of war on the porch appeared to be wounded and there were at least three prisoners of war lying dead at different places, in front of the building. I now do not recall whether any or all of the Australian prisoners of war I saw were naked. I do not recall having seen any Indian prisoners of war amongst the prisoners of war in question.

(d) As Lieutenant–General NISHIMURA and others turned and started to retrace their steps, several of the Australian prisoners of war, whom I presumed were of officer rank, commenced (or appeared so) to ply the former with questions in a loud voice, but their remarks were ignored. After Lieutenant–General NISHIMURA had stepped down off the porch and rejoined us other officers, he turned to Lieutenant NONAKA who was standing beside him and gave him, as far as I can now recall, the following oral order:

"Instruct the officer in charge of the prisoners of war" (rank and name was stated but I now cannot remember same) "to execute all the prisoners of war by firing squad, and then cremate their dead bodies."

I was standing about 3 metres away from Lieutenant–General NISHIMURA when he gave Lieutenant NONAKA the above order, and I feel sure that those other officers who were present also overheard same. After Lieutenant NONAKA had acknowledged this instruction he turned to where the officer in charge of the prisoners of war was standing nearby, and in my hearing repeated Lieutenant–General NISHIMURA's order to him. I do not remember this officer passing any comments after receiving the above order. Immediately after this had been done, Lieutenant–General NISHIMURA then directly ordered Staff Officer Supply Major MORIOKA Eisaku to remain behind and supervise everything. I do not think that Major MORIOKA made any comments after he had acknowledged Lieutenant–General NISHIMURA's order.

J. G. Godwin
3-10-49. Captain   稲 垣 史 34

(e) After the above orders had been given to those concerned, Lieutenant-General NISHIMURA and staff, including myself, returned to our respective vehicles. Major MORIOKA and the officer in charge of the prisoners of war accompanied us to the roadway and remained there to salute Lieutenant-General NISHIMURA as he and the rest of the convoy moved off over PARITSULONG bridge towards BATU PAHAT. We stopped at a river to the north of BATU PAHAT at about 1900 hours that same night, and because of the difficulty of crossing same in the dark we stayed there overnight. Early the following morning Colonel IMAI, Signal Officer Captain SARUTA Shigeo, and myself crossed the river and continued our advance to BATU PAHAT ahead of Lieutenant-General NISHIMURA and other staff officers. We arrived at the northern outskirts of BATU PAHAT at about 1400 hours that same afternoon, Lieutenant-General NISHIMURA and others arriving at about an hour or so later. Headquarters KONOYE Division was immediately established amongst some deserted native style houses, about 4 or 5 kilometres to the north of the aforementioned town.

4.   At about 1800 or 1900 hours that same day and whilst reporting on official business to Colonel IMAI in his office, Major MORIOKA entered, whereupon I excused myself and waited outside the open entrance. As I can now recall, I overheard Major MORIOKA report to Colonel IMAI that all the dead bodies of the prisoners of war at PARIT SULONG had been cremated with the aid of gasoline. I am now unable to recall those parts of Major MORIOKA's report that pertained to the actual carrying out of the execution of the prisoners of war at PARITSULONG. I do remember, however, that when Major MORIOKA finished making his report Colonel IMAI said, "Well done."

5.   I recall that Major MORIOKA Eisaku was killed in an aircraft accident at SINGAPORE some time in about the middle of 1943.

J. G. Godwin
3-10-49 Captain   稲垣忠弘

In making this statement I acknowledge that it was made freely and voluntarily and that no threats were used nor promises made to influence my statement.

Signature of Deponent.. 稲 垣 忠 弘 ....

I, 19291433 Sergeant Dix ASAI of T.I.S., hereby certify that I duly translated the above statement to the deponent, in his own language, prior to his signature which appears above, and he then appeared to fully understand the same.

Signature of Interpreter.......................

SWORN before me, 819576 Captain James Gowing GODWIN, an officer of the New Zealand Military Forces and now attached 2 Australian War Crimes Section SCAP at TOKYO this Third day of October One thousand nine hundred and forty nine.

Signature of Interrogator... J. G. Godwin ...

JGG/bej   SWORN STATEMENT

I, SONO Harumitsu (Yoko), of TOKYO-to, SHIBUYA-ku, HACHIMAN DORI, 2 Chome,
25 Banchi, employee of British Commonwealth Occupation Force (EBISU Camp,
TOKYO), swear I shall tell the truth according to the dictates of my
conscience, and that I shall conceal nothing nor will I add to the facts.

1.   The following is a brief summary of my military history over the
period from December 1941 to February 1942 :-

1941	December	Stationed at SAIGON, INDO CHINA, as a member of Head-quarters KONOYE Division; rank Captain (Regular Army).
	11 or 12 December	Arrived at BANGKOK, SIAM, with Headquarters KONOYE Division.
	Latter part of December	Entrained for MALAYA, and after detrainment proceeded by both motor vehicle and bicycle, arriving at MUAR River on about 15 January 1942.
1942	About 22 January	Passed through BAKRI and PARITSULONG areas, arriving at the outskirts of BATU PAHAT on the following day.
	31 January	Arrived at JOHORE BAHRU with Headquarters KONOYE Division, remaining there until about 13 February 1942.

2.   I was attached to Headquarters KONOYE Division in about the early

part of November 1941, and from that date until late October 1942 I acted as

second senior adjutant to the General Officer Commanding KONOYE Division.

During this said period there were only two adjutants working under the G.O.C.

of KONOYE Division, namely the senior adjutant, Major TODA Takeshi, and myself.

In addition, the G.O.C. of KONOYE Division had a personal aide; however, such

an appointment was held by three different junior officers at different

periods during the time I held the aforementioned position. During the Malayan

Campaign the G.O.C. of KONOYE Division was Lieutenant-General NISHIMURA Takuma,

this officer being replaced by Lieutenant-General MUTO Akira in about April 1942.

The Chief of Staff of KONOYE Division during the above campaign was a Colonel

IMAI Kamejiro, who was replaced by Colonel OBATA Shinbo in late February 1942.

At a date prior to my attachment to Headquarters KONOYE Division until about

20 February 1942 the Personal Aide to Lieutenant-General NISHIMURA Takuma was a

Lieutenant (later Captain) NONAKA Shoichi, who was transferred back to his

parent unit, namely the Transport Regiment of KONOYE Division, after being

replaced by a Lieutenant YOSHIDA (FNU) of the Field Artillery Regiment.

3.   The following is briefly what I recall of my movement and events pertaining thereto from BAKRI area to BATU PAHAT area :

(a) Some time in the afternoon of about 22 January 1942, Headquarters KONOYE Division, including myself, departed in convoy from the BAKRI area, and headed along the main road leading to PARITSULONG. The day of our departure from there was the day during which the battle for PARITSULONG ended. I recall that this battle had been fought by units of the 5 Infantry Regiment against Australian and Indian forces. The aforementioned convoy was composed of about 6 cars and about 3 or 4 trucks, my car being at the head of this column of vehicles, followed by liaison officer Lieutenant INAGAKI Tadahiro's car, two cars containing the Chief of Staff Colonel IMAI Kamejiro, and staff officers Lieutenant-Colonel SUZUKI Kimitsugu, Major MORIOKA Eisaku, and Captain HINOKUMA (FNU), Lieutenant-General NISHIMURA's car (accompanied by his Personal Aide, Lieutenant NONAKA Shoichi), and Major TODA's car, in that order. I was at the head of this convoy for the reason that as an adjutant to Lieutenant-General NISHIMURA it was one of my duties to direct the movement of his Headquarters to its destination.

(b) Later that same afternoon and whilst nearing the approach to the bridge over the river at PARITSULONG, an order to stop the convoy was passed to me (by means of hand signals) from behind. I do not know who ordered the convoy to stop there but I presume it was either Lieutenant-General NISHIMURA or Colonel IMAI. As soon as my car stopped I stepped out, checked the road in front for security reasons, and then ran back towards Lieutenant-General NISHIMURA's car. As I was running towards his car I noticed that he, Lieutenant NONAKA, Colonel IMAI, Major TODA and staff officers had got out of their respective vehicles and were in the process of walking towards a wooden building approximately 25 metres in from the right-hand side of the main road. I recall that there was a narrow stream with a small bridge over it near the right-hand side of this road. On crossing this bridge I noticed that Lieutenant-General NISHIMURA and others were standing in a group in front of the above building, and on joining them I saw about 3 or 4 wounded prisoners of war, who appeared to be Australians, in various postures near a flight of steps leading up to the

entrance of one of the rooms of this building. At the same time as I saw the
above I also noticed that Lieutenant-General NISHIMURA was in conversation with
some junior officer (a 2nd or 1st Lieutenant) whose name I do not know. This
officer was not a member of Headquarters KONOYE Division and I therefore presumed
that he was the officer in charge of the prisoners of war at this place and of
the 3 or 4 guards on duty there. I do not recall what Lieutenant-General
NISHIMURA and this officer were discussing.

(c) After the said conversation had ended, Lieutenant-General
NISHIMURA, Colonel IMAI, Lieutenant NONAKA, and I believe the abovementioned
junior officer, mounted the said steps of the building and looked through the
doorway for a few seconds. From where I was standing I could not see inside this
building, but by the amount of noise coming from it I judged that there were many
prisoners of war confined therein. I do not remember seeing any of the prisoners
of war attempting to speak to Lieutenant-General NISHIMURA or other officers, nor
do I recall seeing the bodies of any dead prisoners of war lying on the ground
outside the building.

(d) Almost immediately after Lieutenant-General NISHIMURA and others
had descended the steps and rejoined us other officers, he turned to his
Personal Aide Lieutenant NONAKA Shoichi who was standing near him, and in the
hearing of all those officers present, including myself, gave him, as far as I
can now recall, the following oral order:

> "Instruct the officer in charge of the prisoners of war" (rank and
> name was stated but I now cannot remember same) "to execute all the
> prisoners of war by firing squad."

Before Lieutenant NONAKA could turn to relay Lieutenant-General NISHIMURA's
order to the officer concerned, Colonel IMAI Kamejiro gave him the following
additional order:

> "The bodies of the prisoners of war will be cremated on completion
> of the execution."

On receipt of both of the abovementioned orders, Lieutenant NONAKA turned and in
the hearing of those present, including myself, repeated them to the officer in
charge of the prisoners of war. I do not remember whether this officer passed
any comments after receiving the above orders.

(e) Almost immediately after the above orders had been given to the officer concerned, I left the scene and ran back towards my car so that I would be ready to direct the convoy on its way. About two or three minutes later I received an order from behind to start the convoy rolling. We passed over PARITSULONG Bridge and headed along the main road leading to the south; however, before reaching the road that branched off in the direction of BATU PAHAT we stopped and rested overnight as scattered enemy resistance in that area blocked any further advance. During our overnight stay at this place I happened to hear during a conversation with Lieutenant NONAKA Shoichi, that the prisoners of war at PARITSULONG had been captured by soldiers of 5 Infantry Regiment and that these prisoners of war were a mixture of Australian and Indian soldiers, the latter belonging to the 45 Indian Brigade. I recall that when we stopped at this place to rest overnight, I discovered that Staff Officer Supply Major MORIOKA Eisaku was absent and I am almost positive that he did not rejoin Division Headquarters until some time the following day. Other than what I have already stated, I know nothing more concerning the prisoners of war at PARITSULONG.

4. Before and during the Malayan Campaign it was obvious to me and other Headquarters officers that Lieutenant-General NISHIMURA Takuma and Colonel IMAI Kamejiro were not on friendly terms with one another. On most occasions, Colonel IMAI added to or varied Lieutenant-General NISHIMURA's orders. His action, therefore, to Lieutenant-General NISHIMURA's order in regard to the disposal of the prisoners of war at PARITSULONG, was not unusual.

In making this statement I acknowledge that it was made freely and voluntarily and that no threats were used nor promises made to influence my statement.

Signature of Deponent...﹚̅秀﹚.........陽　光.........

I, Sergeant Fred K. OSHIMA of T.I.S., hereby certify that I duly translated the above statement to the deponent, in his own language, prior to his signature which appears above, and he then appeared to fully understand the same.

Signature of Interpreter....................................

SWORN before me, 819576 Captain James Gowing GODWIN, an officer of the New Zealand Military Forces and now attached 2 Australian War Crimes Section SCAP at TOKYO this Fourteenth day of October One thousand nine hundred and forty nine.

Signature of Interrogator...J. G. Godwin.....

JGG/bej   SWORN STATEMENT

I, HINOKUMA Fukashi, of TOKYO-to, SUGINAMI-ku, ASAGAYA 3 Chome, 474 Banchi,
company employee, swear I shall tell the truth according to the dictates of
my conscience, and that I shall conceal nothing nor will I add to the facts.

1.   The following is a brief summary of my military history over the
period from December 1941 until February 1942 :

1941	December	Stationed at SAIGON, FRENCH INDO CHINA, as a member of Headquarters KONOE Division; rank Captain (Regular Army).
	About 11 December	Arrived at BANGKOK, SIAM, with Headquarters KONOE Division.
	Latter part of December	Entrained for MALAYA, and after detrainment proceeded by motor vehicle arriving at MUAR River on about 15 January 1942.
1942	About 22 January	Passed through BAKRI and PARITSULONG areas, arriving at the outskirts of BATU PAHAT in the evening of the following day.
	About 31 January	Arrived at JOHORE BAHRU with Headquarters KONOE Division; landing on SINGAPORE Island on 9 February 1942.

2.   I was attached to Headquarters KONOE Division in August 1941, and from
that date until July 1942 I held the position of Staff Officer Intelligence on
that Headquarters. However, during the Malayan Campaign I was mainly performing
the duties of the Staff Officer Operations, Lieutenant-Colonel SUZUKI Kimitsugu,
as this officer was directing battle operations at the front. Nevertheless,
Lieutenant-Colonel SUZUKI maintained constant liaison with Headquarters KONOE
Division whilst he was absent in the field. During the said campaign the
General Officer Commanding KONOE Division was Lieutenant-General NISHIMURA Takuma,
this officer being replaced by Lieutenant-General MUTO Akira in SUMATRA in
early May 1942. The following is a list of those officers, and their appointments,
who were attached to Lieutenant-General NISHIMURA's Headquarters during the
Malayan Campaign :

          Colonel   IMAI Kamejiro   -   Chief of Staff.
          Lieutenant-Colonel SUZUKI Kimitsugu - Staff Officer Operations.
          Major   MORIOKA Eisaku   -   Staff Officer Supply.

Sgt. Fred K. Oakman   J. G. Godwin
                      18-10-49 Captain

303

Captain	HINOKUMA Fukashi	-	Staff Officer Intelligence.
Major	TODA Takeshi	-	Senior Adjutant.
Captain	SONO Harumitsu	-	Adjutant.
Captain	SARUTA (FNU)	-	Communications Officer.
Lieutenant	NONAKA (FNU)	-	Personal Aide to G.O.C.
Lieutenant	INAGAKI Tadahiro	-	Liaison Officer.

3.   The following is briefly what I recall of my movements and events pertaining thereto from the BAKRI area to BATU PAHAT area :

(a) Some time in the afternoon of about 22 January 1942, Headquarters KONOE Division, including myself, departed in convoy (cars and trucks) from the BAKRI area, and headed along the main road leading to PARITSULONG. This convoy was composed of about 6 or 7 cars and about 4 or 5 trucks, the car in which I was travelling being the third one back from the leading vehicle. As I can now recall, this convoy was being directed to its destination by Adjutant Captain SONO Harumitsu as it was one of his duties to act as a convoy leader when Headquarters KONOE Division was on the move. The car in which I was travelling was followed by Major MORIOKA's car, Colonel IMAI's car, Lieutenant-General NISHIMURA's car (accompanied by his Personal Aide Lieutenant NONAKA), and Major TODA's car, in that order. I am now unable to recall whether Lieutenant-Colonel SUZUKI was a member of this convoy.

(b) That same afternoon and whilst nearing the approach to PARITSULONG Bridge, Captain SONO directed the convoy to stop. As soon as the convoy stopped, Captain SONO ran back to the G.O.C's car and began to converse with Lieutenant-General NISHIMURA. Colonel IMAI Kamejiro then got out of his car and went over to listen to their conversation. About two or three minutes later Lieutenant-General NISHIMURA and Lieutenant NONAKA alighted from their car and on seeing this Major MORIOKA, myself and other Headquarters officers got out of our respective vehicles. We then walked towards Lieutenant-General NISHIMURA, who, accompanied by Lieutenant NONAKA and Colonel IMAI, was moving towards a small bridge that spanned a narrow creek on the right-hand side of the road. I recall that just before I got out of my car I happened to notice about 4 or 5 Caucasian prisoners of war in various postures near the steps of a one-storied wooden building located

Sgd. Sied X. Oulung J. G. Godwin
18-10-49 Captain

い 阪 k

about 20 - 30 metres in from the right side of the road: this building stood about
3 or 4 feet from the ground. When I saw these Caucasian prisoners of war I took
it for granted that they were Australian soldiers, as I knew previously that enemy
troops of that nationality had been engaged in battle operations against
Lieutenant-Colonel KOJIMA's battalion (5 Infantry Regiment) in the PARITSULONG
area.

(c) After Lieutenant-General NISHIMURA, Colonel IMAI, Lieutenant NONAKA
and other Headquarters officers, including myself, had crossed the aforementioned
bridge we were met by a junior officer (rank 2nd or 1st Lieutenant, but name not
remembered) of Lieutenant-Colonel KOJIMA's battalion and who then made a report
to Lieutenant-General NISHIMURA concerning prisoners of war, full details of which
I now cannot remember. However, I do remember him reporting that more than 100
Australian prisoners of war had been taken during the fighting for PARITSULONG and
that the majority of them were wounded. I do not recall whether this junior
officer reported the capture of any Indian soldiers. From what this junior officer
said I learned that he was the officer in charge of the above prisoners of war and
the Japanese guards who were on duty outside the aforementioned wooden building.
After this said officer had made his report he led Lieutenant-General NISHIMURA
and we other officers over to the said wooden building, following which he,
Lieutenant-General NISHIMURA, Colonel IMAI and Lieutenant NONAKA climbed the steps
onto the porch and looked through either the doorway or a window of one of the
building's two rooms. As Lieutenant-General NISHIMURA and the other said officers
were in the process of doing this I noticed that the 4 or 5 Australian prisoners of
war resting near the steps were badly wounded and seemed to be in great pain.
Even though I could not see into any of this building's rooms from where I was
standing, I gathered by the groans of pain, screams and stench that many badly
wounded Australian prisoners of war were confined therein. I do not recall having
seen or heard of any Indian prisoners of war being held in custody thereat.

(d) After Lieutenant-General NISHIMURA and others had stepped down from
the porch and rejoined the other officers, he turned to his Personal Aide, Lieutenant
NONAKA, and in the hearing of all those officers present, including myself, gave
him, as far as I can now recall, the following oral order :

J. G. Godwin
Sgt 2nd X. Salaam   18-10-49. Captain   川 陽 夜

> "Instruct the officer in charge of the prisoners of war" (rank and
> name was stated, but I now cannot remember same) "to execute all
> the prisoners of war in a suitable manner."

At that time I interpreted the words "in a suitable manner" as meaning by firing
squad, as there would be no other appropriate method of killing such a large
number of prisoners of war. Before Lieutenant NONAKA could turn to repeat
Lieutenant—General NISHIMURA's order to the officer concerned, the Chief of Staff,
Colonel IMAI Kamejiro, gave him the following additional order:

> "The bodies of the prisoners of war are to be cremated on
> completion of the execution."

On receipt of both the abovementioned orders Lieutenant NONAKA turned, and in
the hearing of those officers present, including myself, repeated the context of
them to the officer in charge of the prisoners of war. This officer simply
acknowledged these said orders. Immediately after the above orders had been
passed to the officer concerned, Lieutenant—General NISHIMURA directly ordered
Staff Officer Supply Major MORIOKA Eisaku to remain behind and supervise everything.

(e) After the above orders had been given to those concerned,
Lieutenant—General NISHIMURA, Colonel IMAI and other officers, including myself,
returned to our respective vehicles, following which Colonel IMAI gave Captain SONO
the signal to start the convoy rolling. After we had passed over PARITSULONG
Bridge I left the convoy and, in accordance with orders issued previously by
Colonel IMAI, made a brief reconnaissance in an effort to ascertain whether the
Japanese 5 Infantry Division had captured YONG PENG. I rejoined Headquarters
KONOE Division later that same evening; however, due to scattered enemy
resistance and difficult river crossings, Division Headquarters did not reach the
outskirts of BATU PAHAT until the evening of the following day. At about 1900
hours that same evening Major MORIOKA rejoined Division Headquarters, where on his
arrival he told me that he was about to make his report to both the G.O.C.
Lieutenant—General NISHIMURA and Chief of Staff Colonel IMAI. I was not present
when he made his report to the G.O.C. and the Chief of Staff; however, when he
returned to the staff officers' sleeping quarters he told me that the order he had
received at PARITSULONG had been carried out. That same evening, whilst eating

Sgt. Fred X. Ashmun   J. G. Godwin
                        18-10-49 Captain

dinner, Major MORIOKA also told me that the prisoners of war at PARITSULONG had
been shot to death and that their bodies had been then cremated with the aid of
gasoline. He added that this whole incident was pitiful to see.

4.　　　　Before and during the Malayan Campaign it was obvious to me and all
other Headquarters officers that Lieutenant-General NISHIMURA Takuma and Colonel
IMAI Kamejiro were not on friendly terms with one another. On most occasions
Colonel IMAI's opinions differed from those of Lieutenant-General NISHIMURA, and
because of this he invariably added to or varied the latter's orders. Because of
this unusual situation, I believe that Lieutenant-General NISHIMURA did not discuss
the matter of the disposition of the prisoners of war at PARITSULONG with Colonel
IMAI before or after his arrival there, and that the order for their execution
was given arbitrarily by him.

5.　　　　I recall that the Infantry Group Commander of KONOE Division, Major-
General KOBAYASHI Takashi, remained behind at SAIGON with 3 Infantry Regiment
until after the capture of JOHORE BAHRU. Major-General KOBAYASHI and 3 Infantry
Regiment then left SAIGON and rejoined the rest of KONOE Division in time for the
assault on SINGAPORE Island in early February 1942.

In making this statement I acknowledge that it was made freely and voluntarily
and that no threats were used nor promises made to influence my statement.

Signature of Deponent...囗......阪......𡈽...

I, Sergeant Fred K. OSHIMA of T.I.S., hereby certify that I duly translated the
above statement to the deponent, in his own language, prior to his signature
which appears above, and he then appeared to fully understand the same.

Signature of Interpreter............................

SWORN before me, 819576 Captain James Gowing GODWIN, an officer of the New
Zealand Military Forces and now attached 2 Australian War Crimes Section SCAP
at TOKYO this Eighteenth day of October One thousand nine hundred and forty nine.

Signature of Interrogator...........................

A F F I D A V I T

We, James Gowing GODWIN, a Captain in the New Zealand Military Forces at present serving with 2 Australian War Crimes Section SCAP in TOKYO, Japan, and Dix ASAI, a Sergeant in the United States Army serving as an interpreter and translator in Japan, severally make oath and say as follows :-

1.   That on 6 and 7 September 1949 at 2 Australian War Crimes Section SCAP we interrogated FUJITA Seizaburo.

2.   That the document now produced and shown to us and marked "A" is a true record of the statements made by the witness in response to questions put to him by us on those days.

3.   That the said witness was ordered to return for further questioning on the following day but did not do so and has not since been located.

4.   That the photograph now produced and shown to us and marked "B" is a photograph of the said FUJITA Seizaburo.

SWORN by the said James Gowing GODWIN)

at TOKYO this .....30........ day of   )

October 1949   )

   J. G. Godwin.........

  Before me

     ....Major
      (H. F. DICK)
  An officer of the Australian Military Forces.

SWORN by the said Dix ASAI   )

at TOKYO this ....30......... day of)

October 1949   )

  Before me

     ....Major
      (H. F. DICK)
  An officer of the Australian Military Forces.

This is the document marked "A" produced and shown to James Gowing GODWIN and Dix ASAI at the time of swearing their affidavit this 20ᵗʰ day of October 1949,

Before me   ....Major
(H. F. DICK)
An officer of the Australian Military Forces.

I, FUJITA Seizaburo, of KANAGAWA-ken, YOKOSUKA-ZUSHI, SAKURAYAMA, 2260 Banchi, company clerk, swear I shall tell the truth according to the dictates of my conscience, and that I shall conceal nothing nor will I add to the facts.

1.   The following is a brief summary of my military history over the period from December 1941 to 1 February 1942:-

1941	December	Attached as general duties officer to Number 2 Battalion Headquarters of 5 Infantry Regiment of KONOE Division at BANGKOK, SIAM, with the rank of Reserve 1st Lieutenant.
1942	11 or 13 January	Left Southern SIAM by motor vehicle for MALAYA in company with 5 Infantry Regiment, arriving at MUAR in the evening of either 15 or 16 January.
	16 or 17 January	Proceeded on foot and arrived in the vicinity of BAKRI, which is located between MUAR and PARITSULONG, in the morning of the following day.
	18 or 19 January until 20 January	Engaged in battle operations against enemy forces in the BAKRI area.
	21 to 22 January	Stationed in the rear of the battle for the northern approach to the bridge over the river at PARITSULONG.
	23 January	Advanced along the road from the hills south of PARITSULONG to YONG PENG, but before reaching there turned off towards the coast, arriving in the vicinity of BATU PAHAT about 26 January, with 5 Infantry Regiment.
	1 February	Arrived at JOHORE BAHRU with 5 Infantry Regiment.

2.   At about 0600 hours in the morning of the day following the capture of BAKRI, 2 Battalion of 5 Infantry Regiment continued their advance along the road leading to PARITSULONG. On the orders of 2 Battalion Commander, Lieutenant-Colonel KOJIMA Yoshinori, I remained behind at BAKRI with about 10 non-commissioned officers and other ranks for the main purpose of burying those soldiers of 2 Battalion who had been killed in the fighting there, and to locate any wounded and missing personnel of the battalion in that area. As a result of these duties, I remained working in the vicinity of BAKRI until the evening of that same day, following which I and the aforementioned non-commissioned officers and other ranks advanced along the road to PARITSULONG, stopping overnight in the jungle near a deserted village and from which place we could plainly hear the sounds of battle about 4,000 metres ahead of us. Early the following morning (22 January 1942) we

continued to advance along the road to PARITSULONG, arriving at 2 Battalion
Headquarters at about 0700 hours that same morning. On arrival at this
temporary Headquarters, I discovered that units of 2 Battalion were engaged in
battle with enemy forces about 1,500 to 2,000 metres ahead and towards PARITSULONG.
In the early part of that afternoon, when the sound of this battle could no longer
be heard, I and the rest of Battalion Headquarters proceeded along the road in the
direction of PARITSULONG. After we had walked a distance of about 1,000 to 1,500
metres I saw units of 2 Battalion resting in open places about 30 to 40 metres in
and to the right of the road. At about the same time I saw what looked like a
large number of naked Indian and Caucasian prisoners of war grouped in a circle
in front of two buildings located about 20 metres in from the right-hand side of
the road and about 80 metres away from where we turned off to join up with the
Battalion. I only glanced at these prisoners of war for about a minute, and
during this period I noticed that some of them were standing up whilst many
others were sitting down, the whole group being guarded by Japanese soldiers.

3.   On reaching the area where 2 Battalion was resting, I reported directly
to the Battalion Adjutant, Lieutenant SUGIHARA (FNU), who was standing in company
with Lieutenant-Colonel KOJIMA Yoshinori. After I had finished making my report
about the work I had completed at BAKRI, the Officer Commanding Number 7 Company,
Lieutenant KURABAYASHI (FNU) who was standing nearby told me that, as a result of
the fighting, his company had captured many Australian and Indian prisoners of war.
In addition, he told me that these Australian and Indian prisoners of war had been
assembled and made to undress at the place above mentioned. At Lieutenant
KURABAYASHI's request I accompanied him to this place, and on our arrival I noticed
that there were about 30 Australian prisoners of war in various postures outside
the larger of the two buildings. I also noticed that there was a continuous movement of Australian prisoners of war in and out of this building; however, as I
did not look inside I am unable to state how many prisoners of war were confined
therein at that particular time. Except for seeing one Indian officer I did not
see any other Indian prisoners of war on that occasion. I believe I only
remained at this place for about 3 minutes before returning to where units of
2 Battalion were still resting. During this short space of time I did not witness
any of the Japanese guards illtreating any of the prisoners of war. Furthermore,
I did not see any wounded prisoners of war, and those whom I did see appeared to
be strong and healthy. Lieutenant KURABAYASHI did not return with me but remained
behind with the prisoners of war and guards, whom I believe were members of his
company.

4.   At about 1630 hours that same afternoon, whilst units of 2 Battalion
were in the process of completing preparations to continue their advance over
PARITSULONG Bridge to YONG PENG, I was ordered orally by Adjutant Lieutenant
SUGIHARA to remain behind as officer in charge of the Australian and Indian
prisoners of war, and that members of the Battalion Artillery Platoon would
relieve those members of 7 Company who were presently guarding the prisoners of
war. In addition, Lieutenant SUGIHARA directed me to contact Division Headquarters
and make necessary arrangements for the removal of the prisoners of war to
echelons in the rear. As I can now recall, the Officer Commanding the Battalion
Artillery Platoon, 2nd Lieutenant SAKANAKURA, was present with most other 2
Battalion officers, including Lieutenant-Colonel KOJIMA Yoshinori, at the time I
received the above instructions; this was a meeting of Battalion officers held
normally for the issuing of battle orders etcetera, prior to any operation.

5.   Some little time later, before I was able to contact Division Headquarters,
Lieutenant-General NISHIMURA Takuma and some of his staff officers arrived on the
scene. After NISHIMURA had inspected the prisoners he spoke to his Personal
Aide, whose name I have forgotten. The Aide then came over to me and said, "It
is the General's order that you execute all the prisoners of war" or words to that
effect.

6.   After the General and his staff officers had left I caused the prisoners
of war to be executed by machine gun and rifle fire.

JGG/bej   SWORN STATEMENT

I, NONAKA Shoichi, of AICHI-ken, Nishi KASUGAI-gun, SHINKAWA-cho, AZA DOKINO SHINDEN
432 Banchi, employee of an export company, swear I shall tell the truth according
to the dictates of my conscience, and that I shall conceal nothing nor will I add
to the facts.

1.   The following is a brief summary of my military history over the
period from December 1941 until February 1942:-

1941	December	Stationed at SAIGON, FRENCH INDO CHINA, as a member of Headquarters KONOE Division. Rank 1st Lieutenant (Regular Army).
	About 11 December	Arrived at BANGKOK, SIAM, with Headquarters KONOE Division.
	Latter part of December	Entrained for MALAYA, and after detrainment proceeded by motor vehicle, arriving at MUAR River on about 15-16 January 1942.
1942	About 22 January	Passed through BAKRI and PARITSULONG areas, arriving at the outskirts of BATU PAHAT in the evening of the following day.
	About 31 January	Arrived at JOHORE BAHRU with Headquarters KONOE Division, landing on SINGAPORE Island on about 9 February 1942.

2.   I was attached to Headquarters KONOE Division on 7 July 1941 and from
that date until about 27 February 1942 I held the position of Personal Aide to
Lieutenant-General NISHIMURA Takuma, the General Officer Commanding KONOE
Division during that period. On about 27 February 1942 I was transferred back to
my parent unit, namely the Transport Regiment of KONOE Division, my successor as
Personal Aide to Lieutenant-General NISHIMURA being Lieutenant YOSHIDA (FNU) of
the Artillery Regiment of the abovementioned Division. The following is a list
of officers, and their appointments, who were attached to KONOE Division Headquarters during the Malayan Campaign:-

Lieutenant-General NISHIMURA Takuma	- G.O.C. KONOE Division.
Colonel IMAI Kamejiro	- Chief of Staff.
Lieutenant-Colonel SUZUKI Kimitsugu	- Staff Officer Operations.
Major MORIOKA Eisaku	- Staff Officer Supply.
Major TODA Takeshi	- Senior Adjutant.
Captain SONO Harumitsu	- Adjutant.
Captain HINOKUMA Ryo (Fukashi)	- Staff Officer Intelligence.

J. G. Godwin
28-10-49 Captain   野中正府

311

Captain   SARUTA   (FNU)   — Communications Officer.

Lieutenant NONAKA Shoichi   — Personal Aide to G.O.C. (myself).

2nd Lieutenant INAGAKI Tadahiro — Liaison Officer.

3.   The following is briefly what I recall of my movements and events pertaining thereto from the BAKRI area to BATU PAHAT area:

(a)   Some time in the afternoon of 22 January 1942, Headquarters KONOE Division, including myself, departed in convoy (cars and trucks) from the BAKRI area, and proceeded along the main road leading to PARITSULONG. This convoy was composed of about 7 cars and about 3 or 4 trucks, the car in which I was travelling being also occupied by the G.O.C. Lieutenant-General NISHIKURA, and was about the sixth one back from the leading vehicle. As I can now recall, this convoy was being directed to its destination by Adjutant Captain SONO, his vehicle being followed by Lieutenant INAGAKI's car, Major MORIOKA's car, Captain HINOKUMA's car, Chief of Staff Colonel IMAI's car, Lieutenant-General NISHIMURA's car (accompanied by myself), and Major TODA's car in that order. I do not remember whether Lieutenant-Colonel SUZUKI was a member of this particular convoy.

(b)   That same afternoon and whilst nearing the approach to the bridge over the river at PARITSULONG, Captain SONO directed the convoy to stop. Before our departure from BAKRI I overheard Lieutenant-General NISHIMURA instruct Captain SONO to stop the convoy at the above place in order that a short inspection of this area in which troops of 5 Infantry Regiment of KONOE Division had been recently engaged in battle operations against Australian and Indian forces, could be made. About one or two minutes after the convoy had stopped, Captain SONO appeared and reported to Lieutenant-General NISHIMURA that we had arrived in the area where the battle for PARITSULONG had taken place. As soon as Captain SONO had finished making the above report Lieutenant-General NISHIMURA and myself alighted from our vehicle, following which Colonel IMAI got out of his car and joined us. When Colonel IMAI joined us Lieutenant-General NISHIMURA instructed him, firstly to inform the rest of Division Headquarters officers to accompany him (NISHIMURA), and secondly to have the non-commissioned officers and guards remain on the road with the convoy. On receipt of these instructions Colonel IMAI shouted them out aloud, whereupon the rest of Headquarters officers alighted from their respective vehicles and commenced to run towards us. As soon as this happened, Lieutenant-

J. G. Godwin
28-10-49. Captain   野 中 正 帝

General NISHIMURA, Colonel IMAI, Captain SONO and myself moved towards a small bridge that spanned a narrow creek on the right-hand side of the road. Just after we had crossed this bridge Lieutenant-General NISHIMURA was reported to by a junior officer (2nd Lieutenant, but name not remembered) of 5 Infantry Regiment of KONOE Division. I am now unable to recall the full details of this junior officer's report, but I do remember that he informed Lieutenant-General NISHIMURA about matters pertaining to the fighting in the PARITSULONG area, including the capture of over 100 prisoners of war by his battalion, whom he stated were confined in a wooden building which he pointed out. This building was a single-storied one and was located about 60 metres in from the right side of the main road. From what this said officer reported I gathered that he was the officer who had been left behind in charge of the said prisoners of war and the 7 or 8 guards who were stationed outside this building on duty. After this junior officer had finished making his report he led us towards the aforementioned building where, on arrival, I noticed 4 or 5 wounded Australian prisoners of war in various postures near the steps leading up to the verandah. I also noticed about 6 or 7 Australian soldiers lying dead at different places, a short distance away from the front of the building.

(c) After reaching the above building Lieutenant-General NISHIMURA, accompanied by Colonel IMAI, the said junior officer, and myself, climbed the verandah steps, walked over to the nearest of the building's two doors, and peered through the lattice work of same. As I only took a quick look inside I am now unable to recall fully what I saw; however, I do remember seeing many Australian prisoners of war in various postures, most of whom appeared to be wounded. There was a nauseating stench of blood emanating from the prisoners of war confined in this room. In addition, these prisoners of war were making a considerable amount of noise, but I do not remember whether I heard any particularly loud groans or screams of pain. I did not look into the other room of this building; however, from the noise I gathered that it also contained many prisoners of war. I do not remember seeing any Indian prisoners of war outside of or confined in this building. After we had looked inside the aforementioned room, Lieutenant-General NISHIMURA, Colonel IMAI, the said junior officer, and myself turned around and retraced our

J. G. Godwin
28-10-49. Captain.

野 中 正 帝

313

steps, joining the rest of Headquarters officers at a place a few metres away in front of the building.

(d) On joining these other officers Lieutenant-General NISHIMURA turned to me and in the hearing of all those officers present, gave me the following oral order:

"Instruct the said junior officer" (rank and name was stated but I now cannot remember same) "to execute (SHOBUN SEYO) all the prisoners of war by firing squad."

No sooner had I acknowledged Lieutenant-General NISHIMURA's order by saying "Yes, I will repeat" than the Chief of Staff, Colonel IMAI Kamejiro, gave me the following additional order:

"The bodies of the prisoners of war are to be cremated on completion of the execution."

After similarly acknowledging Colonel IMAI's order, I turned towards the junior officer and walked over to where he was standing, about 5 or 6 metres away from Lieutenant-General NISHIMURA. I then repeated to him the aforementioned orders I had received from both Lieutenant-General NISHIMURA Takuma and Colonel IMAI Kamejiro. The officer concerned simply acknowledged these two orders by saying that he would so do. After I had relayed the said orders to him, I rejoined Lieutenant-General NISHIMURA just as he and others began to walk back towards the roadway. Almost immediately after I had rejoined him, he stopped, turned around and directly ordered Staff Officer Supply Major MORIOKA Eisaku to remain behind and supervise everything. Major MORIOKA simply acknowledged this order by saying he would so do. Both Major MORIOKA and the said junior officer accompanied us to the roadway to pay their respects to Lieutenant-General NISHIMURA as the convoy moved off.

(e) We passed over PARITSULONG Bridge and headed along the main road leading south; however, before reaching the road that branched off in the direction of BATU PAHAT we stopped and rested overnight as the fighting in that area had not yet ended. At about 1000 hours the following morning we continued on our way, arriving eventually in the northern outskirts of BATU PAHAT township at about 1800 hours that same day. Some of the other members of the convoy arrived

J. G. Godwin
28-10-49. Captain   野 中 正 帝

there before Lieutenant-General NISHIMURA and myself. I recall that shortly after the convoy stopped at this place Major MORIOKA arrived, following which I believe he reported to the Chief of Staff Colonel IMAI; however, I am unable to remember whether he also reported to Lieutenant-General NISHIMURA. I do not know what the text of his report was to Colonel IMAI, but I imagine that it concerned the carrying out of the execution of the prisoners of war at PARITSULONG. However, I do recollect hearing from someone (name and rank not remembered) that same evening that the dead bodies of the prisoners of war at PARITSULONG had been cremated with the aid of gasoline. Other than what I have stated already I know nothing more concerning the prisoners of war at PARITSULONG.

4. I recognise the photograph hereto attached marked "No. 1" as a photograph of the junior officer (2nd Lieutenant) referred to in this my sworn statement and to whom I passed the orders of Lieutenant-General NISHIMURA Takuma and Colonel IMAI Kamejiro for the execution and cremation of the prisoners of war at PARITSULONG as set out above.

In making this statement I acknowledge that it was made freely and voluntarily and that no threats were used nor promises made to influence my statement.

Signature of Deponent.....野 中 正 市...........

I, Sergeant Dix ASAI of T.I.S., hereby certify that I duly translated the above statement to the deponent, in his own language, prior to his signature which appears above, and he then appeared to fully understand the same.

Signature of Interpreter................

SWORN before me, 819576 Captain James Gowing GODWIN, an officer of the New Zealand Military Forces and now attached 2 Australian War Crimes Section SCAP at TOKYO this Twenty-eighth day of October One thousand nine hundred and forty nine.

Signature of Interrogator................

STATEMENT.

Lt.Gen. NISHIMURA Takuma having been duly sworn states:-

      I am NISHIMURA Takuma, a Lieutenant General, General Officer Commanding Imperial Guards Division. I was the Commanding Officer of the above Division during the Malayan campaign and arrived at PARIT SULONG about the 22 January 1942. At the time of my passing through this town, I was accompanied by a few tanks.

      The north side of the bridge was at that time held by Col. IWAGURO 岩畔 雄,   the south side being held by Major YOSHIDA Masaru. *Maj. Yoshida took the bridge before Col. Iwaguro's arrival.*
      I noticed on the north side several trucks of prisoners of war, and I had issued instructions that all prisoners of war were to be sent back to Headquarters. *There were some distance away.*
      Col. IWAGURO was Commanding Officer of the 5th Regiment.

      I do not know of any prisoners being shot, and if such things did happen, they were without my knowledge as I had given definite instructions that all prisoners of war were to be sent back to Headquarters.

      There was no anti-Tank Regiment under my command.

      It was a long time ago that this battle was fought, and I have forgotten the names of any of the junior officers. I do not know Capt. NAKAMURA, ~~but he may possibly have been one of the Company Commanders~~, *but these two
I gave the orders to take the bridge,
Regiments fought independently.* T. NISHIMURA 西村琢磨

NISHIMURA Takuma.

Interpreter.

I, OKUDA Naotake certify that I have translated the above statement to the witness in his own language, prior to his signature, which appears above, and he has stated the same to be true and correct in every particular.

奥田直威 Okuda
Naotake

Sworn before me, Alwyn Alfred SHERLOCK, Captain of the Australian Imperial Forces, this 27th day of August 1947

A.A.Sherlock.
1 Aust War Crimes Sec.

Detailed to examine the above by the Commander-in-Chief, Far East Land Forces.

(Authority: ALFSEA War Crimes Instruction No.1., para 7)

Appendix B

The following documents have been selected from archive files to support various aspects of the Nishimura story outlined in this book. By cross referencing files it can be readily established that the Army undertook extensive destruction of relevant papers – particularly relating to investigations – throughout the period 1950-51.

GENERAL HEADQUARTERS
SUPREME COMMANDER FOR THE ALLIED POWERS
LEGAL SECTION

AUSTRALIAN DIVISION
(Requesting Agency)

DATE: 9 Sep 49

SUBJECT: Apprehension of Suspected War Criminals

TO: Criminal Registry Division, Apprehension Branch, Legal Section

1. Request that the following named person be apprehended and interned in prison for trial as a Suspected War Criminal.

    a. Name: **FUJITA, Seisaburo.**
    b. Rank or Title: **Lieutenant.**
    c. Units to which attached: **1 Battalion, 5 Infantry Regiment of KONOIE Division.**
    d. Dates and places of service: **MALAYA & SUMATRA. 1942/1943.**
    e. Home Address (if known): **KANAGAWA-ken, YOKOSUKA-ZUSHI, SAKURAYAMA, 2,260 Banchi.**
    f. Synopsis of Charges presently prepared, subject to amendment, against subject Suspected War Criminal:

        Murder of about 150 Australian and Indian prisoners of war in Jan 42

    g. Synopsis of Evidence to support charges:

        Sworn Statements held by this Division.

    h. Anticipated place of trial:
    i. Other information that might assist in apprehension of desired person:

        Attended for interrogation at MEIJI Bldg. on 6/7 Sep, failing to report back on 8 Sep 49.

    j. This Division presently has ~~insufficient supporting evidence~~ ~~xxxxxxxxxxxxxx~~ sufficient supporting evidence to constitute a prima facie case against this man.

_____ Lt Col
Chief of Division.

318

AWM 166 [218]

A.A.E. C121 (Small)
(To 9ads of 100)
(Rev. 2d June, 1944)

AUSTRALIAN MILITARY FORCES

SERIAL No. ....

ECK **CIPHER MESSAGE** X9.3137

*This message will not be distributed outside British or U.S. Government Departments
or Headquarters or retransmitted, even in cipher, without being paraphrased.*
(Messages marked O.T.P. need not be paraphrased)

FROM	2 AUST WAR CRIMES SCAP WARNING	DATE—Time of Origin 16 1157 I
TO	FOR ACTION ARMY MELBOURNE	Reference to this message will NOT be made in any unclassified message
	FOR INFORMATION	(This warning will appear on all reproductions of this message.)

A 237. CONFD FOR DPW & I FROM GOSLETT. YOUR 2649AG UNDATED. US
AUTHORITIES NOW REFUSE TO SANCTION APPREHENSION OF ANY MORE JAP
WAR CRIMES SUSPECTS UNTIL SUCH TIME AS WE GIVE THEM A DEFINITE
UNDERSTANDING THAT SUSPECTS WILL BE MOVED FROM JAPAN FOR TRIAL
BY AUST COURTS

ACTION
19 SEP 1949

DISTRIBUTION
A(DPW & I) ACTION (2)

19 SEP 49

319

SECRET
SECRET

X9.3150

CIPHER MESSAGE

FROM: 2 AUST WAR CRIMES SEC SCAP   19 1619 I

TO: ARMY MELBOURNE

PRIORITY   A 240.   SECRET.   FOR DPW& I FROM GOSLETT.
FURTHER TO MY SIG MESSAGE A237 AND MEMO WC 910 BOTH OF 16 SEP.
FIRST.   HAVE BEEN INFORMED VERBALLY BY CHIEF LEGAL SEC GHQ TO
EFFECT THAT A FAILING RECEIPT OF NOTIFICATION BEFORE 1 NOV 49
THAT AUST GOVT READY AND ABLE ACCEPT DELIVERY AND B OWING TO
PERIOD THAT SUSPECTS HAVE BEEN IN SUGAMO SCAP CONTEMPLATES
RELEASING ON 1 NOV 49 ALL SUSPECTS HELD ON BEHALF AUST
AUTHORITIES.   SECOND.   RELEASE WOULD BE WITHOUT PREJUDICE
TO REAPPREHENSION SHOULD AUST GOVT BE PREPARED PROCEED AT
LATER DATE IN ACCORDANCE FEC POLICY DECISION OF 3 APR 1946.
THIRD.   MEMO TO ABOVE EFFECT HAS BEEN PASSED BY DIPLOMATIC
SEC GHQ TO AUST MISSION

WARNING
Reference to this message will NOT
be made in any unclassified
message (This warning will appear
on all reproductions of this
message.)

DISTRIBUTION
A(DPW& I) ACTION

20 SEP 49

SECRET

ACTION
20 SEP 1949
COPY

I Certify that I have this day examined
NISHIMURA TAKUMA 1647/M.312
....
He is fit to undertake the journey to..JAPAN..
He has been vaccinated and innoculated
against Cholera.
Vaccination reaction. of burning ...

To :
The Officer in Charge *R.A.N. War Criminals Compound.*
or any other Prison to which the prisoner may here-
after be lawfully transferred.

WHEREAS one *NISHIMURA, TAKUMA*

was this day convicted of a War Crime by a Military Court
held at *MANUS ISLAND*

he will be held in custody at the order of the Court
until such time as, the sentence having been confirmed
and promulgated, you are required on the order of the
competent authority to release him or to hand him over
in order that sentence may be put into effect.

For which this shall be sufficient Warrant thereunto.

Signed this *twenty-second* day of *June*   1950

...................Brigadier,
                   PRESIDENT.

Note : He has been sentenced to *suffer death by hanging.*

...................Brigadier,
                   PRESIDENT.

Confined in Cellcom A1.
Sentence confirmed
HANGED at Manus 11-6-51   *22-6*

84 4539

Royal Australian Navy

IN REPLY PLEASE QUOTE

No._____

H.M.A.S. "Tarangau",
MANUS ISLAND.

30th June, 1950.

This is to certify that NISHIMURA, Takuma,

is fit for confinement in the solitary cells at

the War Criminals Compound, Manus.

Jam P Caw

SURGEON LIEUTENANT R.A.N.

3-1

To be attached to
NISHIMURA's papers.

O.C. War Criminals Compound
Manus Island

PERSONAL AND
CONFIDENTIAL

AUSTRALIAN MILITARY FORCES

XA.2527

MILITARY BOARD

(ADJUTANT-GENERAL)

Quote In

Reply..................

ARMY HEAD-QUARTERS
VICTORIA BARRACKS

Melbourne, S.C.I,

3rd October 1950

My dear Solicitor General

By sentence of a War Crimes Court on 22nd June 1950,
one Nishimura Takuma, a former Japanese Lieut-General was sentenced
to death by hanging on being found guilty on the charge of

"Committing a war crime, that is to say murder in
that (he) at Parit Seelong in Malaya on the
22nd January 1942 murdered a number of Australian
and Allied prisoners of war."

A petition by the accused against the finding and
sentence was dismissed and on the advice of the Judge Advocate
General, as there was ample evidence before the Court to support
the finding, I confirmed the finding and sentence.

Subsequently, representations were made on behalf
of Nishimura Takuma that there had been a miscarriage of justice.
There was submitted in support affidavits by three Japanese
refuting material parts of their statements which had been used
by the prosecution at the trial.

Although these representations did not come within
the ambit of regulation 17 of Statutory Rules 164/195, the whole
matter was carefully considered by the Judge Advocate General who
concluded that there was nothing to suggest that there had been a
miscarriage of justice.

Accordingly I propose to issue instructions for the
sentence of the Court, as confirmed, to be carried out but before
doing so, submit the file herewith for any comments you may wish
to make.

Yours sincerely —

W.M. Anderson
adjutant and general

Professor K.H. Bailey,
Solicitor-General,
CANBERRA. A.C.T.

Discussed with Chifley & Welblemen
on 3 Oct and in subsequent discussion should seek
minuter for attorney general. K.H.B.

Suggested advice that ...

AUSTRALIAN MILITARY FORCES

....

MILITARY BOARD

(ADJUTANT-GENERAL)

XA.2591

Quote In

Reply...................

ARMY HEAD-QUARTERS
VICTORIA BARRACKS.

Melbourne, S.C.I,
10ᵗʰ November, 1950.

My dear Solicitor General,

      You will remember that, early in October, I discussed with you in Canberra the action which might appropriately be taken in the case of one Nishimura Takuma, a former Japanese Lieutenant-General who was sentenced to death by the Military Court at Manus.

      I appreciate that you are extremely busy with other urgent matters, but I would be most grateful if you could let me have your opinion on Nishimura's case as early as practicable.

Yours sincerely

Wm Anderson

Discussed with Adjt-Genl
by phone 13/11/50

KHB.

Professor K.H. Bailey,
Solicitor-General,
CANBERRA.   A.C.T.

AUSTRALIAN MILITARY FORCES

....

MILITARY BOARD

(ADJUTANT-GENERAL)

PERSONAL

Quote In   XA.2693.
Reply

ARMY HEAD-QUARTERS
VICTORIA BARRACKS.

Melbourne, S.C.I,

18. Jan 51.

My dear Solicitor General.

   With reference to our conversation on
18th January, 1951, regarding the case of ex-Lt-Gen Nishimura,
I am attaching, as requested, the latest Japanese police
report in our possession as to the whereabouts of Fujita,
who was also to have been tried with Nishimura.

   The report was made on 13th November, 1950,
and no information has been received since that date.

Yours sincerely,

WMAnderson

Professor K.H. Bailey,
Solicitor General,
CANBERRA. A.C.T.

KHB

Author's note: The documents on this and the two
previous pages are letters from Adjutant General Anderson to
Solicitor General Bailey. The handwritten notations were
made by Professor Bailey.

EXTRACT OF JAPANESE POLICE REPORT

L.	Permanent domicile	:	Tokyo-To, Bunkyo-Ku, Kago-Cho, 220 Younfer brother of Family Head Saichiro.
2.	Former address	:	Kangawa-Ken, Yokoshka-Shi, Zushi-Machi, Sakurayama 2260.
3.	Former place of employment	:	ASAHI KASEI Kabushiki-Kaisha/ASAHI Chemical and Synthetic Industry Company/, 4th floor, Konishiroku Building, Tokyo-To, Chuo-Ku, Nipponbashi, Muromachi, 3 Chome, 1.

Name : Ex-1st Lieutenant FUJITA, Seizaburo

Born : on February 1, 1910

Former position: Chief of the General Affairs Branch of the
above-stated company.

On September 4, 1949, we were ordered, through your Chief
of Search Division, to have the above stated person report himself to the legal section, GHQ, SCAP, as an important war crime
witness, and we immediately conveyed this order to him through
Chief of Police Station at Zushi. On the following day he
presented himself to the said Section, but as every office of the
Allied Forces was closed for holiday on that day, he left there
and attended the company as usual. On the 6th, he reported
himself to the same Section, and on the 7th he left his home
telling the family that he was visiting the Legal Section, GHQ,
SCAP. However, he did not report to the same Section on that
day and since then he is in hiding somewhere. Later, on
January 27, 1950, he was named as a war criminal. We already
reported to you about the course of search we made. Since
then we continued thorough search, lay in ambush for him, and
listened to the hearsays of his neighbours. But so far we have
not obtained any such information as to contribute to new search.
On July 2 this year hiw wife aiko removed to the house of
MINAMI Eiichi who is her elder brother-in-law and now resides
at TOKYO-To, NAKANO-Ku, UCHIKOE-CHO, 1. FUJITA's former house
is now used as a dormitory of the company, but his elder brother-
in-law WAKIMURA Yoshitaro lives in its nieghbourhood. So, we
are paying keen attention to communications between them keeping
close contact with the Mteropolitan Police Board. But so far
we have not succeeded to get any material contributory to our
search. Careful search is being continued.

----------oOo-----------

WARRANT OF EXECUTION

WHEREAS former Lt-Gen NISHIMURA Takuma on the 22nd day of June 1950 was sentenced to death by military court held at MANUS. And whereas the finding and sentence of the said military court have been duly confirmed in accordance with the War Crimes Act 1945, and whereas I have reviewed the said sentence, now therefore I, Warren Melville ANDERSON, Adjutant-General of the Australian Military Forces, hereby approve of the carrying out of the sentence confirmed as aforesaid.

Dated this *Seventh* day of *August.*
One thousand nine hundred and fifty.

WMAnderson

Major-General,
Adjutant-General.
AUSTRALIAN MILITARY FORCES.

(ii)

CERTIFICATE BY OFFICER SUPERVISING THE EXECUTION

I, *Norman Y. Quinton* certify that I was present at and supervised the execution of the abovenamed *NISHIMURA TAKUMA* at *Manus Island* at *0600* hrs on the *eleventh* day of *June* 19 *56*

Dated this *eleventh* day of *June* 195 *7.*

N Y Quinton Lt Col
Signature

(iii)

CERTIFICATE BY MEDICAL OFFICER PRESENT AT THE EXECUTION

I, *Mand Chambers* a legally qualified medical practitioner certify that I examined the body of the person executed in accordance with the above certificate and pronounced life extinct.

Dated this *11th* day of *June* 195 *7*

Maud Chambers
Signature

AUSTRALIAN MILITARY FORCES

336 · 1 · 23 37
Folio No. 1.

In reply
please quote: /72 /51

1 Aust War Crimes Section (MANUS)

R.A.N. Post Office No. 3,

CONFIDENTIAL

C/- G.P.O.

12 Jun '51

Army Headquarters,
Victoria Barracks,
MELBOURNE.

TRIAL BY MILITARY COURT - NISHIMURA Takuma

1.   Reference your XA 2867 of 30 May '51, it is advised that the
Finding and Sentence as confirmed was promulgated to NISHIMURA
Takuma by myself on 10 June '51.

2.   The sentence of death was executed on 11 June '51.

3.   Certificate of Promulgation and Warrant of Execution
returned herewith.

......................Lt-Col.
(N.F. QUINTON)
O.C., 1 Aust War Crimes Sec., (MANUS)

RECEIVED
20 JUN 1951
A. G.. BRANCH

Registry, 18/6/6

S. G. Off 21/6/51.

A7 19/6/51

19/6

Author's note: The above document establishes that
General Nishimura, consigned to a legal limbo for almost a
year so that he could be held in solitary confinement, received
the official promulgation of the court's Finding and Sentence
on June 10, 1951 and was executed the following day.

12731

17 Jul 51.

CARO.

PROCEEDINGS OF A MILITARY COURT - NISHIMURA Takuma
AND NONAKA Shoichi

1.   Forwarded herewith for information and perusal with
a view to noting any casualty information, are the proceedings
of a Military Court held at Manus from 19 Jun 50 to 22 Jun 50
at which the abovenamed Japanese were tried.

2.   It is advised that, by direction, the information
contained in these proceedings will NOT be disclosed to the
Press.

3.   Please return proceedings to this Directorate as
early as practicable.

Colonel,
AG Co-ordination.

Author's note: Paragraph 2 of the above document orders
the Central Army Records Office (CARO) not to disclose to the
Press any of the information contained in the attached file.
Similar orders were issued to other Army departments as part
of the overall measures undertaken by the AG's office to
cover-up what had occurred during the process of trying and
eventually executing General Nishimura.

329

The next three documents were among a huge collection removed from the 2 Australian War Crimes Section in Tokyo by Captain James Gowing Godwin.

- 1 -

File 151G
File 151H
File 168

Weekly Investigation Report: Week ending 21 Sept, 1949.
Operation Parit Sulong.

(1) Completed the interrogation of former Captain Shoichi Nonaka who held the position of personal aide to the GOC Konoe Division, Lieutenant General Takuma Nishimura at the time of the Malayan Campaign. Nonaka admitted to having been a member of the convoy (HQ Konoe Division) that stopped at Parit Sulong in the late afternoon of 22 January, 1942. According to Nonaka he and Lt-Gen Nishimura were travelling in the same vehicle and upon stopping at Parit Sulong he, Nishimura and the Chief of Staff, Colonel Imai, and other HQ Officers alighted from their respective vehicles and walked over towards some buildings on the right-hand side of the main road. About half-way there the said party was met by a junior officer (a 2nd Lieutenant - name not remembered) who reported directly to Lt-Gen Nishimura. Nonaka states he is unable to recall the full details of this officer's report; however, he does remember him saying that a great number of prisoners had been taken during the battle for Parit Sulong and that most of them were confined in a large wooden building which he pointed out. After finishing his report this said officer led the GOC and accompanying officers towards the building identified. On arrival at the building Nonaka noticed about six or seven wounded Australian soldiers in various postures near the steps leading up to a wide verandah. He also recalls seeing the bodies of many dead Australian soldiers scattered about at different places in front of this building. Among the dead were some Indian soldiers.

(2) Nonaka then recounted how he, Lt-Gen Nishimura, Colonel Imai and the officer in charge of the prisoners climbed onto the verandah and peered through one of the building's two open doors at the mass of wounded POWs confined therein. After this short inspection had been made, the said party retraced their steps and rejoined the other HQ officers in front of the building. Nonaka stated that Lt-Gen Nishimura turned and gave him the following oral order.

(3) "Instruct the officer in charge of the prisoners to exterminate (Shobun Seyo) all the prisoners by firing squad. Execute them all." No sooner had Nonaka acknowledged this order than the Chief of Staff, Colonel Imai gave him the following additional order.

(4) "The bodies of the prisoners are to be cremated on completion of the execution and all traces of their disposal obliterated." Nonaka confesses to having relayed these two orders to the officer concerned, following which and whilst walking back towards the parked vehicles, Lt-Gen Nishimura directly ordered Staff Officer-Supply Major Eisaku Morioka to remain behind and supervise every-thing. Former Colonel Kamejiro Imai has previously been requested for interrogation; however, the Japanese authorities have officially reported this former senior officer as having died from sickness in Siberia on 22 March, 1947. Thus and despite our request for official Soviet verification, of which none has been forthcoming, further inquiries to the Soviet authorities reveal the following.

(5) Colonel Kamejiro Imai had never been listed as a prisoner-of-war of the Soviet Union. His alleged captivity and death by sickness is completely unknown. This investigation officer quite frankly discounts the truthfulness or veracity of the notification received from 'Japanese Army Records' and is more inclined to believe the Soviet authorities as an impartial source of honest information.

[Observation]: At most times and whenever a class A war criminal is finally identified, particularly if formerly a powerful and influential senior officer, we invariably encounter subtle obstruction to their apprehension by means of deviousness and duplicity. For a variety of dubious circumstances too numerous to mention, the usual obstructive coincidences of major war criminals effectively vanishing is no accident, but when such disappearing acts are unaccountably but officially confirmed without investigation by Japanese authorities, one is tempted to suggest the word 'collusion'. It is hard to avoid being cynical. This charade happens too often with regard to many officially sanctioned Japanese fabrications. The second part of this priority investigation should shortly be concluded and entered into Official Weekly Reports as quickly as possible. I have only to add my disappointment that the powers that be (Legal & Prosecution Div') do not propose to proceed with a fresh prosecution against Lt-General Nishimura, a most evil man. Perhaps the sheer horror of what he ordered against defenceless and wounded Australian POWs, particularly the large number, would shock the world.

J. G. Godwin. (Capt)
J. G. Godwin
Investigating Officer
2nd Aust' War Crimes Sec.
21-September, 1949.

JGG:BEJ   Weekly Investigation Report: October 1949. Capt J. G. Godwin
File.151G   MASSACRE OF PRISONERS OF WAR, PARIT SULONG 1942.

(1) Interrogated former Major Fukashi Hinokuma who had a grim story to tell and which was recounted to him in full detail over a meal by Staff Officer, Supply, Major Eisaku Morioka. It was Morioka who was detailed by the GOC (Nishimura) to remain at Parit Sulong and supervise the mass execution. This is the horror that was revealed.

(2) 'One hour before dark, the wounded prisoners were ordered to make their way to an assembly point at the rear of a short row of damaged shops. Those who were unable to walk were carried by the walking wounded, while others, also walking wounded, were made to carry the bodies of their dead comrades who lay scattered about on the ground. The pretext used to entice the Indian and Australian prisoners to drag themselves to what was in effect, the designated execution site, was medical treatment, water and food. Concealed within the rear rooms of damaged and unoccupied shops (their owners had been killed) three squads of executioners waited behind tripod mounted heavy machine-guns. When all of the prisoners had arrived at the assembly point and were either sitting or laying prone, depending upon the seriousness of their wounds, the three machine-guns began their wicked thumping chatter of death. Such concentrated machine-gun fire cut swathes of carnage from three different points, enfilading the closely grouped prisoners, chopping flesh and limbs to pieces. When cries of pain and shock were silenced so were the machine-guns.

(3) Morioka mentioned to Hinokuma that seven prisoners had to be bayoneted despite the concentrated gun-fire. They had still showed signs of life. Funeral pyres were quickly expedited by collapsing the shop structures with hand grenades and mortars, following which 161 bodies were carried in an endless stream to the timber-dry debris and placed in piles where the engulfing flames would consume most efficiently. A considerable amount of paraffin obtained from captured forty-four gallon drums and some sixty gallons of gasoline were then splashed and spilled over and around the piled corpses.

To ensure total incineration, tyres and demolition material
from the collapsed shop buildings were also heaped onto the
quite large pyres. At 8-00pm, according to Major Hinokuma
and as related by Major Morioka, he, Morioka, gave the signal
for everyone to stand clear. Then a flaming torch was flung.
The demolished buildings erupted with a whooshing catatclysmic
roar. In the event four adjacent dwellings and nine shops
burned to the ground before midnight. As told to Hinokuma by
Morioka, the stench of roasting flesh permeated the warm night
air until the small hours of the morning when the fierce
flames had reduced to mere flickers above piles of grey-white
ash. But even then, radiated heat from concealed red-hot
embers could be felt twenty yards away. Without any doubt
the mass cremation, like the preceding massacre, was an outstanding example of efficiency. Morioka told Hinokuma it was
4-00am before he snatched a few hours sleep. He awoke a little
after 10-00am and stepping outside and under the hot morning
sunlight he stared across at where the shops had stood. Nothing
remained except scattered mounds of pale-grey ash little more
than two feet high. Clearly, incineration had been total.
After enjoying a good breakfast and self-satisfied at the
report he would be able to give to the Chief-of-Staff of H.Q.
Konoe Division, now temporarily quartered at Batu Pahat, he
left Parit Sulong at about midday and was driven south to rejoin
H.Q. Konoe Division.

COMMENT: This interrogation will continue as a high priority
to get to the bottom of this evil and murderous affair. I have
to admit my absolute astonishment at the apparent absence of
humanity in many of the Japanese atrocities being investigated.
Without exception inherent and sadistic cruelty by the Japanese
is the experience most often encountered, heightened by their
total lack of remorse. A grim but true reflection indeed.

J. G. Godwin (Capt)
J. G. Godwin
Investigating Officer
2nd Aust' War Crimes Sec.
7,14,21,28, October, 1949.

Masanobu Tsuji

The following secret Military Intelligence summary on the activities of Imperial Japanese Army Colonel Masanobu Tsuji was supplied to 2 Australian War Crimes Section in Tokyo by its equivalent British office in the Japanese capital. War crimes officer, Captain James Godwin, a New Zealander attached to the Australian investigating team, had the document copied. The copy became part of the "clandestine cache" he eventually stole from the Australian files in the Meiji Building. The document substantiates a suspicion long held by historians that Britain had full knowledge of Tsuji's key role in the Singapore Chinese Massacre at the time seven Japanese officers — including General Nishimura — went on trial for the mass killing in 1947. As such, it presents as firm evidence that the prosecution's case in the Chinese Massacre Trial was based on false accusations.

❊ ❊ ❊ ❊

Colonel Tsuji was attached to Japan's Department of Strategic Planning at the War Ministry. He was a man with a complete lack of conscience. Among the many war crimes attributable to him was the Alexandra Hospital massacre at Singapore, as well as the Singapore Chinese massacres. The following is a resume of Tsuji's war criminality as obtained by Colonel C.H.D. Wild.

Following his posting to Manila where American and Filipino forces were collapsing under the sheer weight of numbers of Japanese troops, he was responsible for the following: Beleaguered and surrounded in an exposed valley and woefully short of ammunition, three hundred American marines were on the verge of surrender when once more waves of Japanese troops hurled themselves onto precariously defended positions. But this was no ordinary attack. Colonel

Tsuji, who was observing the unequal contest and well aware that the Americans must be getting desperately short of ammunition, gave an order that would seal their doom. 'When the Americans surrender,' he said, 'take them prisoner then execute them.'

To the horror of concealed eye-witnesses — indigenous rural peasants who watched from vantage points high in the surrounding hills — the surviving American marines who surrendered after their ammunition was exhausted were bound and formed in lines, all 280 of them, by their exultant Japanese captors. Imploring with prayers and tears, the peasant womenfold called upon their faith to stop the carnage that followed. Bayoneted, shot or beheaded, every prisoner was dead within two hours.

After the fall of Bataan and Corregidor, 80,000 American and Filipino servicemen were herded into columns and forced to drag their weary, exhausted and some wounded selves towards captivity. This was known as the Bataan Death March. It was Colonel Tsuji who ordered this inhuman march while expressing the wish that for any pretext, as many prisoners as possible should be killed. In furtherance of this notorious death-wish he announced: 'Japan is fighting a racial war and for the Emperor to triumph and to release our victorious soldiers to fight on other battle-fronts, prisoners must be executed.'

Tsuji partly got his evil wish. During the shuffling march that was to last for sixty-seven miles, the prisoners were subjected to appalling brutality. They were clubbed with rifle-butts, bayoneted and shot if they collapsed or fell behind the main column of prisoners. At the end of the forced march, 10,000 prisoners had been murdered. This left 70,000 to dispose of.

Fortunately, Tsuji was recalled to Tokyo before being sent south again, but this time to the Netherlands East Indies and Guadalcanal to impose a further reign of terror on more hapless prisoners. With his departure from the conquered Philippines, the survivors of the Bataan Death March were confined in harsh prisoner of war camps and though genocide was no longer the order of the day, they were nonetheless treated with vindictive and cruel treatment. In countless instances, intentionally starved to death, denied life-saving medical attention and forced to endure all the vicissitudes and miseries their Japanese captors imposed.

Colonel Wild had amassed a considerable dossier on Colonel Tsuji that if successfully prosecuted would most certainly have guaranteed his execution as a war criminal. All of this vital information and documentation was destroyed in the plane crash. Tsuji already had a head start as a fugitive from justice when Colonel Wild was tragically killed. By the time further documentation and re-investigations were gathered and concluded, at least another valuable year would pass. Such a time-span had given Tsuji the opportunity to go underground somewhere in Asia, probably with the help of Siam's considerable gold bullion that he had ordered seized and which like him vanished.

On one singularly bloody occasion and following a desperate break-through on the Bataan Peninsula, close on 400 exhausted American soldiers without supplies of any kind, including ammunition, were compelled to surrender to overwhelming numbers of the enemy. Unknown to the Americans and only a day previously, a large number of American soldiers had surrendered to the Japanese, but only to be promptly butchered. Had this fact been known, it is doubtful whether this second surrender would have occurred. More probably the exhausted Americans would have preferred *death in hand-to-hand combat.*

After being taken prisoner and under heavy guard, a platoon of Takasago volunteers from Formosa was detailed to execute all the captured Americans. Such a large number of prisoners to suffer the death penalty must have pleased Colonel Tsuji who had arrived on the scene. 'Kill them all' he ordered, adding, 'chop their heads off.' There followed a most gory and bloody massacre of close on 400 white troops that is probably best left to one's imagination. These atrocities along with the subsequent Bataan Death March are now quite well-known but unlike ourselves, Washington is not pursuing the matter with the same vigour as our office.

We are aware that there were many evil Japanese but clearly, Colonel Tsuji was the most evil of all. We have learned that Tsuji, besotted by arrogance and fanaticism, brewed his own disgusting medicine from the livers of executed British, American and Australian airmen to drink for power and invincibility. During our interrogations of Japanese war crimes suspects, Tsuji's name keep recurring. It has been recalled by other Japanese officers that at the South Pacific Hotel on the Island of Palau in 1942, Tsuji boasted about his special medicine and often with a request for further supplies of livers from beheaded airmen.

One more example of Tsuji's criminality should suffice. On 26 September 1944, Lieutenant Benjamin A. Parker of the 14th Airforce, 25th Fighter Squadron, 51st Fighter Group flying mission F1027 and escorting Allied bombers, had his fighter aircraft hit by anti-aircraft fire. At the time Northern Burmese Japanese positions were being counter-attacked by Allied forces. Parker was noticed bailing out of his stricken aircraft by other pilots but was neither seen nor heard from again.

Parker was quickly captured by a Japanese patrol and force-marched to the area HQ of a Japanese forward command post. It was his unenviable fate that the officer in command was none other than Colonel Masanobu Tsuji. There followed intensive interrogation with Tsuji playing a leading inquisitorial role. Despite dire threats and thuggery, Parker would only give his name, rank and serial number.

We have learned what followed from Japanese suspects being interrogated at Singapore. Enraged and with patience exhausted, Tsuji struck the defenceless airman with a slashing blow across the face with a steel bomb fragment. As blood welled from the deep wound, he ordered Parker's immediate beheading with a blunt Burmese sword. At the first blow Parket slumped forward, his head only partially severed. With blood welling from a deep neck wound his arms were gripped by watching Japanese soldiers before being raised back to his knees. It required two further strokes from the dull blade before his head was finally severed. Thereupon and at Tsuji's orders, Parker's body was dismembered and the flesh taken for cooking and eating.

Signed: Arthur D. Pettigrew (Major)
British War Crimes Section
Meiji Building, Tokyo.

On the bottom of the original document was a hand-written notation from Major Pettigrew to Captain Godwin. It read:

If you come across this monster, Jim, please let me know. Hanging will be too good for him.

❊   ❊   ❊   ❊

Index

Australian War Crimes Section
(1); 11, 55-56, 58-59, 61, 65, 68,
70-72, 75, 88, 109, 143-144, 147,
151, 157, 160, 167, 241,
Australian War Crimes Section
(2); 76, 97, 104, 110, 114-115,
122-123, 139, 148, 226, 257-258

B

Bakri; 37, 118, 125, 174, 181,
203, 205, 206-208, 219, 273
Bailey, Professor Kenneth H.,
Solicitor General; 146, 241-242,
244, 245-248, 250-251, 253, 256
Bataan Death March; 82
Batavia; 113
Batu Pahat; 125, 140
Bismarck Sea; 12, 34,
Blakeney, Ben Bruce; 228-229,
234
Blenheim; 113
Brennan, Justice Francis Gerard;
146
Brennan, Justice F. T.; 145
British Commonwealth
Occupation Force (BCOF); 99-
100
Bryant-Smith, Stan; 38, 40
Burma; 54, 171, 259

C

Canterbury; 113
Carpenter, Colonel Alva C.; 97
Central Army Records Office
(CARO); 258
Changi Jail; 37-41, 61, 64-65, 74,
78, 84, 87-88, 154, 165, 271, 274

Chambers, Cyril, Army Minister;
103-104
Chapman, Lt. Commander
Arthur; 11, 13, 23, 25-26, 29,
33-34
Chifley, Prime Minister
Benjamin; 91-92, 100-101, 103
Clarke, Major W. E.; 163, 225,
253-254
Cocos Islands, 113
Colombo; 113
Curlewis, Captain Adrian
"Curly"; 39-41

D

Dark Evening; 217
Darwin; 90, 157
Denniston, Major; 61-62
Dick, Major H. F.; 111-112
Director Legal Services (DLS);
222, 234
Duncan, Brigadier H. C.; 207
Dutch West New Guinea; 33
Dutch East Indies; 54, 159

E

Eastern Command
Headquarters; 65-66, 75

F

Far Eastern War Crimes Section
(UK); 79
F-Force; 40-41
February 26 Incident; 51
Flannagan, Lt. Colonel John W.;
94-95, 98-99, 102, 147-148,

Francis, Josiah, Army Minister; 109, 145, 241, 251, 253, 255,
Fukuoka prefecture; 50, 267
Fujita, Lt. Seizaburo; 103, 116-123, 149, 155, 159, 161, 163, 175-176, 186-187, 194, 218-220, 233, 238, 248-249, 255

G

Gerling, Major E. J.; 163, 253-254
Gilchrist, Lt. Colonel R.; 256
Gilroy, Norman Cardinal; 249, 268
Godwin, Captain James Gowing; 113-115, 117, 120-24, 129-137, 139, 141-144, 164-165, 167, 169-170, 173-174, 187-190, 192-193, 196, 229, 232-234, 236-238, 246, 248, 258, 268
Goodwood Park Hotel; 55, 58, 61-63, 70, 73
Goslett, Lt. Colonel D. Beresford; 97, 111, 123, 128
Gotanda Tank Company; 206, 216
Ground Self Defence Force (Japan); 84

H

Habeas corpus; 98-99, 159
Hackney, Lt. Ben Charles; 22, 38-39, 40-41, 44, 47-49, 56-58, 60, 62, 64,-66, 70-72, 75, 112, 115, 118, 122-123, 125, 140, 142, 148-149, 164-170, 172, 177, 180, 187, 198, 201, 217-218, 234-236, 238, 245, 249

Ham, Major Maxwell R.; 235-238, 240, 244-245
Hayes, Major H. F.; 163, 253-254
Hirohito, Emperor; 21, 52, 108, 264
Hiroshima; 264
Hinokuma, Fukashi; 125-127, 140-142, 165, 177, 185, 187, 190, 193, 195, 231-232, 234, 238, 242, 244, 268, 270.
HMS Illustrious; 113
HMAS Tarangau; 33, 225
Hong Kong; 66, 68, 75, 90-92, 144, 153, 158, 163, 173, 224

I

Ikegami-Hommonji; 274
Imai, Colonel Kamejiro; 127-199, 240, 248
Imamura, General Hitoshi; 159
Inagaki, Tadahiro; 125-126, 165, 176, 185, 187, 191, 193, 231, 232-234, 238, 242, 248, 270
Indian Army (5th Divison); 41
Indian Army, 45th Brigade; 206, 207
Indo-China; 260
International Military Tribunal for the Far East (IMTFE); 66, 79, 89, 163
Inukai, Prime Minister Takeshi; 51
Itsui, Hiroshi; 270
Iwakuro, Colonel Takeo; 72, 112, 248-249

J

Java; 171
Johore; 20, 38, 61, 202
Johore Bahru Prison; 72
Judge Advocate General (JAG)
223, 227, 237, 239-240, 242, 256
Julius, Major W. W.; 207

K

Kai-Tak Airport; 68
Kamakura era; 274
Kawamura, Lt. General Saburo;
80-81, 84-85, 87
Keenan, Joseph B.; 130
Kempeitai; 80, 84, 87
Kent-Hughes; Lt. Colonel
Wilfred; 39
Kobayashi, Major General
Takashi; 71
Kojima, Yoshinori; 219
Kokura City; 50, 261, 264
Konoye Imperial Guards
Division; 21, 45, 48-49, 52, 54,
57, 59, 71-72, 115-116, 154-155,
188, 217, 250, 273
Konoye Imperial Guards 5th
Regiment; 197
Kuala Lumpur; 38, 87
Kyushu; 50

L

Labuan; 90, 157
Land Headquarters (LHQ); 63
Liberal Party (Australia); 107
Liberal Country Party Coalition
government; 157
Liberal Democratic Party (LDP);
82

Lombrum Point War Criminals'
Compound; 11-12, 15, 19, 23,
25, 36, 155-157, 176, 221, 251
Los Negros Island; 11-12, 14-17,
22-23, 31, 35, 77, 143, 146-147,
150-152, 155-157, 159-160, 166,
171, 192, 197, 199, 202, 216-
221, 224, 227, 239, 245, 250-
251, 253-256, 260, 268, 273

M

MacArthur, General Douglas;
21, 44, 91, 95-97, 99-100, 101-
104, 108, 129-130, 135, 143, 158
Machida; 259, 266, 273
Madura, 54, 65
Malayan Campaign; 52, 59, 65,
70, 125, 127, 191, 202, 220
Manchester Guardian; 158
Manchuria; 52, 129
Manila; 44, 82, 97
Mansfield, Justice; 56
Manus executions; 36
Manus Island; 16, 99, 104, 109,
111, 144-145, 147, 152-153, 155,
157, 159, 172-173, 224, 231,
255, 258, 264
Manus Trials (Manus Island
Trials); 23, 141, 143, 146, 148-
50, 221, 226, 229, 236-237, 241,
251, 256
Matsui, Lt. General Takuro; 45,
47, 59-60
Mayamoto, Ipachi; 255
McLeod, Major N.; 163
Meiji Building; 97, 113, 116-117,
136-137, 139, 142, 248
Meiji restoration; 50

W

War Ministry, Tokyo; 66, 77
Waltzing Matilda; 208
Warden, Charles; 204-205, 208, 212, 213
Webb, Sir William; 89
Wellington; 113
Wewak; 90, 157
Wigmore, Lionel; 203-204
Wigram Airbase; 113
Wild, Celia; 55, 68
Wild, Major/Colonel Cyril H. D. ; 41, 43-47, 50, 55-56, 58-61, 66, 68, 77, 79-80, 89, 123, 168
Willoughby, General Charles; 130, 135
Wollstonecraft; 142
Woodborne Airport; 113
Works and Housing Department; 14, 17, 109

Y

Yakuza; 129,
Yamashita, Lt. General Tomoyuki; 21-22, 41, 44-47, 49, 51-52, 56, 77-78, 81, 87, 97, 155, 174, 202, 223, 260,
Yokohama; 153
Yong Peng; 45, 202-203, 206-207, 216

*Lombrum Point War Criminals' Compound as recalled
by former Prison Commandant Arthur Chapman.*

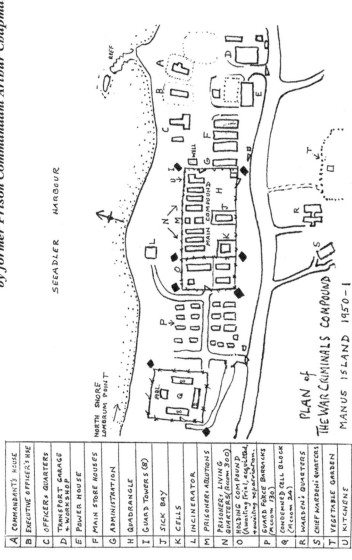

SEEADLER   HARBOUR

NORTH SHORE
LOMBRUM POINT

A	COMMANDANT'S HOUSE
B	EXECUTIVE OFFICER'S HSE
C	OFFICER'S QUARTERS
D	TRANSPORT GARAGE + WORKSHOP
E	POWER HOUSE
F	MAIN STORE HOUSES
G	ADMINISTRATION
H	QUADRANGLE
I	GUARD TOWERS (8)
J	SICK BAY
K	CELLS
L	INCINERATOR
M	PRISONERS ABLUTIONS
N	PRISONERS LIVING QUARTERS (Accom 300)
O	HOLDING COMPOUND (Awaiting Trial, acquitted + awaiting repatriation.)
P	GUARD FORCE BARRACKS (Accom 130)
Q	CONDEMNED CELL BLOCK (Accom 24)
R	WARDEN'S QUARTERS
S	CHIEF WARDEN'S QUARTERS
T	VEGETABLE GARDEN
U	KITCHENS

PLAN of
THE WAR CRIMINALS COMPOUND
MANUS ISLAND 1950-1